Dynamics of Group Action

By

D. M. HALL
Assistant Professor
of
Agricultural Extension
University of Illinois

Published by

THE INTERSTATE
Printers and Publishers, Inc.
Danville, Illinois

119543

Copyright 1957

THE INTERSTATE

Printers and Publishers, Inc.
Danville, Illinois

Printed in the U. S. A.

Preface

Dear Reader:

You and I are caught in a typical action-situation. We are trying to react with each other. You no doubt have selected this book because you expect to gain something from it. I must guess your expectations and do something to meet up with them within the next few moments, otherwise, you will lay the book aside. Unfortunately, our communication will have to be a one-way affair, so let me tell you what I have done.

In this book I have dealt with both the theory and practice of those many situations in which people try to work out their problems together. These situations contain almost everything we do. Anyone who thinks he can go it alone is doomed to disappointment for not even those things we imagine as problems are of our own making. Society has woven us into a web of socio-economic interdependence from which we can never escape. It has tied the life and welfare of all of us into an ever expanding spiral of common interests. Nature, other persons, and the community all lay claims upon us and much of our growing up consists of reacting to these demands. Some of us submit, some adjust, some rebel. Our behavior is our attempt to strike some sort of a balance between the prospects for gratification and deprivation.

In the pages which follow I report many facts uncovered during the last 10 years by students of the dynamics of group behavior. In some cases I try to tie these facts into hypotheses and then attempt to draw some conclusions.

If you are president of a service club or of a woman's club which has broad objectives you will be interested in the problems of establishing ideals, goals, and objectives. If you are chairman of a committee of the P.T.A., League of Women Voters, Chamber of Commerce, Business and Professional Women's Clubs, Anti-Defamation League, Community Council, Medical Association, Farm Bureau, a Cooperative Society, or a Labor Union, you will be especially interested in the distinction between membership and reference groups, and in the leadership patterns of each. If you are a member of the program committee for an annual meeting or a convention, you'll want to understand how to involve delegates and get participation. If you are a teacher or leader you will want to become skillful in problem-solving and in developing leadership skills. If you are an adult educator, an extension specialist, or a trainer of leaders, you will want a great deal of both the theory and practice of group work. If you are a group member not satisfied with the way parts of your community are functioning you will want to understand the principles of change and how to initiate changes.

I like to think of this as a handbook to which leadership teams may refer for answers to the many "how," "what," and "why" questions which will arise. If the "how" questions seem most important to you, I suggest you read the first 20 pages then skip to Section III, "How Groups Tackle Problems." If you are interested in the "why" questions, you will find some answers in Section II and IV. In sections II and III I have devoted considerable space to the consideration of goals and philosophies. This may seem strange because we so seldom talk about our motives. They are like undergarments, sort of unmentionables, which, when we do talk about them, we disguise with strange names, such as briefs, shorts, panties, or drawers. But motives are important and it seems to me better to bring them out into the open and try to decide where we want to go before we set out upon our journey.

In Section III I have considered the skills needed by groups in solving their problems. There are certain steps which must be taken if we ever get to a solution. We *must* decide, otherwise we become frustrated—but how can we decide wisely?

In Section IV I've taken up the problems of group growth and maturity. Democracy was not born full grown, neither did it mature in a day. In fact, it had a difficult birth in 1776, and almost died in its youth. The hopes of its fathers have not yet been fully realized. Today we find some people even denying its legitimacy by declaring it to be a republic with themselves as our representatives. We are once again engaged in the struggle between freedom and force. We see Communism as a threat to freedom and fellowship, jeopardizing the existence of every independent nation. This threat within our country has occasioned the rise of a sixth column which is fighting the fifth and much of the fourth and third column. In the double struggle many a liberal, many an outspoken critic, is intentionally injured by witch hunters whose goals and methods are no more worthy than those of the Communists. They expect by fear to force conformity to the wishes of the first column. Our duty to the world is to demonstrate that free government is desirable and workable. To do this we must stand for certain principles, and understand how groups grow and develop.

The first principle is: we must make democracy work at home before we can expect to convert others. Freedom to take part in government or in the economic benefits resulting from social organizations is not the special right of a few no matter how highly they are regarded. There are many good reasons for believing in man—all men; and rather than ignoring the processes through which man and society matures we should diligently seek to understand them and then increase our skills needed for making democracy work. We must deny to Communists certain places in our society, but we must not label every outspoken critic of the government "a fellow traveler." To coerce by fear is anti-democratic.

I have devoted much time to the analysis of action-systems and their sources of authority. My hope in doing this is that you will carry on, helping to extend our knowledge and skill in democratic control, because only through an informed citizenry will we be able to keep our house in order. We need to do this soon for our time is running out.

I have tried to present an interesting, and readable handbook, but you should be warned that some of the topics may be strange and perhaps difficult. Should I omit them in order to make the book easy reading or include them and suffer the consequences? If I include topics familiar to you, things you agree with, you probably will pronounce the book, *good!* because you agree. But then I would have presented nothing new and that would be bad. New and strange ideas will be difficult (familiar things are always easy) and consequently, many pronounce the new, *bad!* It seems then that books with which you agree and pronounce good are really bad and that those with strange new ideas generally pronounced bad are really good because they offer something new to learn.

It is difficult to advise you where to begin reading. Some may argue that you should know what to do before you start. Others will say that you learn by doing. Both statements seem correct to me. I can't complain because "you lack experience." Who doesn't? Who has had any experience in solving a new problem? I think your problem resembles a wheel. You may start at any point and if you keep at it, you may get all the way around. To help here, I have added many forward and backward connections as page references. I have cross indexed ideas marked with an asterisk. These terms you should look up in the index. I've included a number of things to do in the appendixes.

The facts and conclusions presented have been gleaned from many authors. I have attempted to credit them but I fear my acknowledgements are incomplete. So many of one's impressions are the results of ideas gathered here and there and absorbed into one's consciousness that it is indeed difficult to identify their origins.

D. M. HALL

July, 1957

Table of Contents

SECTION I

*Group Action*_____

It is not what we know but what we do that counts. Living is doing, and seldom do we act merely for the sake of acting and never with the expectation of failing. We may do what appears to be "contrary to our best judgment" merely to prove that "it shouldn't be done that way." Even emotional behavior is purposeful as is demonstrated by the motorist who, maddened by the bright lights of an approaching car, swerved into its path saying, "I'll teach him to dim," thus killing all but one in both cars. Behind most acts is a need, a problem, a wish or a purpose.

This is particularily true of group life. Groups never come into being without a purpose, and they never form expecting to fail. But many of them do. They fail because their organization is not suited to their purposes. They fail because they have not become skillful in solving their problems. They fail because they have not learned to regulate their group life. And they fail because they were not composed of the right combination of persons. Groups fail not because they want to, but because they do not know how to succeed.

The success of any group will depend upon individual abilities but it will also depend upon how skillful it becomes in solving its problems and in regulating, strengthening, and perpetuating group interactions. Success depends upon understanding these problems and acting upon them accordingly. We succeed only if we do the right thing at the right time. This is not impossible; it's not really very difficult, so let's not become discouraged. Let's study the job, then call another meeting or appoint another committee—only the next time let's do better.

Chapter 1._____

WHY GROUPS FAIL

Not so long ago a business executive appointed a committee. As he finished the job, he leaned back and heaved a sigh of relief. He was sure he had selected an able group of workers. Each was a specialist in his field; each had strong ideas and would not compromise his professional integrity by yielding any one of them.

Several months later this committee issued its report. To everyone's dismay, it was found to be watered down; it showed evidence of deals and "horse-trading" and attempts on the part of individual members to carry off the honors. The whole thing was pretty generally labeled a failure.

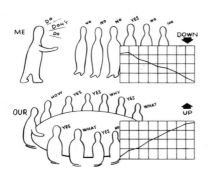

About the same time another committee, unwilling to chance a failure, began its work by listing the reasons why committees fail. Then it took stock of each member's abilities and experiences. During the course of this inventory, each member found it necessary to examine his own personal motives. As he became aware of them, he also became aware of the motives of others. In this way he began to see the role he could play in the work of the committee.

From time to time this committee stopped its work to check its progress and procedures. Largely because of these appraisals the members began to think and work as a unit. Every now and then, the report said, the discussion would break down just because someone found it difficult to do group thinking or because someone took on the role of prosecutor or defendant. But in time the group matured and wrote a report so clear-cut and decisive that it became the basis for the entire Atomic Energy Commission.

Committee work can be highly productive, provided we make it so instead of letting it run its course by chance.

Usually it is not hard to get a crowd together. People congregate easily and naturally. But merely bringing people together does not insure group productivity. When a crowd first gathers, it is a collection of individuals held together merely by an immediate interest. If these individuals remain together and are able to discover ways of solving their problems, the bonds between them will grow stronger and broader and finally they will develop into a group that cannot easily be destroyed.

We live in groups, we belong in groups and our group life can be made successful, if we increase our understanding of group organization and group processes.

Why did the atomic committee succeed and the other committee fail? Was it because the atomic group had better organization, better skills, and better attitudes? Or was it because the other group failed to "grow up"?

Most failures are due to one or more of the following reasons:

1. The "atmosphere" inhibits group action.
2. The group is not composed of the right combination of persons.
3. The members lack skill in playing their respective group roles.
4. The organization is not suitable for accomplishing the desired purposes.

The value we place on each of these four causes will determine largely how we think of ourselves as group workers. Many teachers, leaders, and public relations men think of themselves as working *on* groups; consequently they place organization first. Persons who think of working *for* groups often place "right combination" first. Those who work *with*, or *within* groups, generally place atmosphere or roles first.

Usually the autocrat works *on* groups, the laissez faire
leader works *for* groups; and the democratic leader thinks of
himself as working *with* and *within* groups. The democratic
leader thinks of atmosphere and persons before he thinks of
organizational structure.

WRONG ATMOSPHERE

We are what we are, not because of our inheritance alone,
but also because of the effect other people have on us. We start
life in a family group; soon we enter a play or school group; and

eventually we become part of a
work group. In each of these
groups we seek out those who
respond to us, and we avoid
those who do not.

Thus we operate in a field of
social space, acting and being
acted upon by other persons, in-
fluencing and being influenced
as we circulate in our various
groupings. In this way we are
like a constellation of stars.
Each has gravity and is influenced by gravity, and the little
clusters (memberships groups) close together exert a stronger
influence on each other than the more scattered bodies.

It seems clear, then, that the atmosphere that group members find or make will in large measure determine the success
of the group.

Three different atmospheres have been described and tested[1]
in a school room:

1. *Laissez faire*—in which the teacher was passive and
   every pupil was free to do as he pleased.
2. *Autocratic*—in which the teacher determined all policies
   and details. Directions were given piece-meal, rewards
   and punishments were bestowed arbitrarily, without reason or explanation, and future activities were never
   made known beforehand.
3. *Democratic*—in which all policies and details were discussed, criticisms were invited and the group made the
   decisions. The teacher gave alternative procedures and
   suggested the consequences which might be expected.
   When rewards were granted they were objectively given.

[1]Lewin, Kurt and Lippett, Ronald, "An Experimental Approach to the Study of
Autocracy and Democracy, *Sociometry* 1:292, 1938.

What were the results when ten- and eleven-year-old boys and girls were inducted into these atmospheres? The study showed that both autocratic and democratic teachers were really leading.[2] The autocratic teacher was 118 per cent and the democratic teacher 42 per cent more active than the average member.

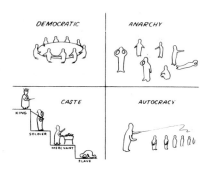

Hostility was thirty times higher in the autocratic than in the democratic group. There were more demands for attention, more criticism and more tensions. The autocratic group was largely "I" centered, whereas "We" statements occurred twice as often in the democratic group. In the autocratic group every child became the potential enemy of every other.

In general, the laissez faire group resembled the autocratic except that aggressive behavior was even higher.

When the democratic leadership was changed to either autocratic or laissez faire the once friendly, cooperative, energetic, democratic group became, within half an hour, rather pathetic looking and discouraged. Then it became aggressive. The former autocratic group gradually became friendly and cooperative under democratic leadership. The passive group under laissez faire leadership changed to democratic or autocratic depending upon the change in leadership.

This experiment leads us to believe that it is impossible for us to live alone. And those who extol "rugged* individualism" really believe in a form of autocracy.

Autocracy has a long history and measured by its tenure it has been a success. It is self-centered and perpetuates itself by skillful leadership alone. Under its system the skilless masses are made both economically and emotionally dependent upon the leader.

---

[2]Maier, Norman R. F., *Principles of Human Relations,* Wiley and Sons, N. Y., 1952, (Maier diagramed three types of leadership which correspond with the three atmospheres above and he showed intermediate types), page 21.
*Note. Asterisks indicate cross references in this text. Look up the word so marked * in the index for other page references which apply to the topic.

Most of us have been reared in autocratic atmospheres. We
have been dominated at home, at school, at church, and on the
job. We have been coerced, disciplined, regimented, and often-
times terrorized by parents, teachers, and bosses. About the only
roles we have had any chance to learn are those associated with
domination and submission. Is it any wonder, then, that we
expect to dominate or submit, as the situation may require?

Unfortunately, autocracy works. It works in business, where
we expect to be dominated. There, workers often become irritated
when called together to discuss the problems of the business.
They say, "Let's stop the chatter. Tell us what you want done
and let us get on with the job."

Autocracy worked in Germany because the people expected
to dominate. Regardless of how much we may hope to the contrary, the German people did support the Nazi culture. The ideals
of a self-centered, ruthless power had been taught and had
thoroughly penetrated all levels of German life. Nazi culture was
centered about power as a supreme value. Competition was
taught as the means of building a superior race. The killings
were the natural rights of the victor over the vanquished. Weak-
ness was inexcusable; the strong, no matter how they got that
way, were considered free to do as they pleased.[3]

Domination also works in our political life. The bosses
dominated Jersey City and Memphis until their physical energies
failed them. They used aggressive methods to work themselves
ahead, and the citizens did not know how to stop them.

Domination works in the sales field. Salesmen try to force
us to buy in spite of ourselves and they succeed. A story in "Business Week"[4] described an aggressive sales campaign full of flash,
dash, color, and some kind of psychology designed to force everyone to buy a Chevrolet. It started at the top; regional sales managers were sent to tell area managers, who in turn were to train
18,000 local salesmen how to get everyone to go along with General Motors in capturing the small car sales leadership. This was
considered the approved way to sell cars.

Domination by knowledge or skill works too. Recently our
neighbor took her baby to the doctor for a whooping cough shot.
The doctor went out, got the needle, slipped in, "shot" the baby,
disappeared and then returned through another door and said,

---

[3]Lewin, Kurt, *Resolving Social Conflicts,* Harper and Brothers, New York, 1948.
[4]"Chevrolets' Battle Plan," *Business Week,* July 10, 1948, page 64.

"What are they doing to the little fellow?" Little Kenny was completely dominated and didn't know who did it.

Because rulers rule and salesmen sell, we find teachers wanting to copy their tactics. We find them urging each other to sell their ideas more aggressively. Some of them probably wish that they too might use a big hypodermic filled with their kind of facts. Then, after having shot us, they would hold their thumbs over the needle mark so that the stuff couldn't run out.

LET US SPREAD INFORMATION OUT RATHER THAN DOWN....

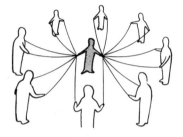

But ideas are not sold like automobiles. When you get a signature on the dotted line, when you receive payment, have you sold an idea? Have you made delivery? Have you given clear title? Has the buyer got something in his head or only "on his hands."

Lewin[5] found lecturing, requesting, pleading, and demanding—all dominative procedures to be of little value in changing food habits. He organized the experiment in two student co-operative houses. In one case the experts came in to tell the values of the new foods and to urge the students to eat them. In the other case they gave the facts, but in addition suggested that people generally resist change. The group then discussed how food likes develop and the various ways of changing habits. The students finally voted to try the new kinds of foods. This group ate much more of the so-called variety meats than did the lectured group.

ANY FURTHER DISCUSSION?

Even though autocracy works, the autocrat must forever hold down the lid. For whenever a leader, teacher or a parent exhibits dominative behavior, he provokes the same behavior on the part of his followers, and he sets off a whole vicious cycle of

[5]Lewin, Kurt, "Group Decision and Social Change," *Readings in Social Psychology,* p. 330, Theodore M. Newcomb and Eugene L. Hartley, Editors. Henry Holt Co., 1947.

aggression and hostility.[6] And such oppressive conditions are not conducive to good work; most of us do better under a democratic atmosphere. Roethlisberger[7] found that production and efficiency increased when a democratic atmosphere was introduced into a factory. On the other hand, Bakke[8] found that teamwork and morale were destroyed:

1. When the system failed to make clear what kind of performance resulted in what kind of rewards and punishment.
2. When the rewards and punishments were dispensed arbitrarily and by whim rather than by plan.
3. When discrepancies in performance and responsibilities existed among those receiving the same pay.
4. When rewards and punishments were geared solely to individual performance, rather than to cooperative endeavor. This sets man against man instead of building them into teams.
5. When social respect, freedom, capacity performance, self-respect and other personal values were ignored and all emphasis was placed upon economic rewards and deprivations.
6. When rewards and punishments did not conform to what the people concerned consider to be rewarding or punishing. This he considered the most important short-coming.

Democracy does not mean no power and no authority—that  is anarchy — and one of the gravest mistakes we make in democratic control is to give responsibilities without authority. Autocracy is founded on fear, but within a democratic atmosphere there is no fear—no fear of being misunderstood, no fear of losing status, no fear of telling about our problems and difficulties, no fear of admitting our errors, and no fear of expressing differences.

We want differences; that's the reason for forming a group. We want our conclusions sound; therefore we ask for different viewpoints, and we criticize each idea regardless of who contributed it. The British people organize "His Majesty's loyal opposition," but the Germans fail to comprehend this notion. To

[6]Anderson, H. H., "Studies of Teacher's Classroom Behavior," *Applied Psychology Mono. 6 and 8,* Stanford University Press, Palo Alto, California, 1945.
[7]Roethlisberger, Fritz J., *Management and Morale,* Harvard Univ. Press, Cambridge, Massachusetts, 1943.
[8]Bakke, E. Wight, "Teamwork in Industry," *Scientific Monthly* 66:213, 1948.

them loyalty means obedience; they have never been permitted to criticize their bosses.

By the very nature of the atmospheres in which we have lived, we have had but little experience in democratic activities.

Consequently it may take much practice and patience before we are able to create a truly democratic* atmosphere.

WRONG PEOPLE

A second reason for group failure lies in the combination of persons who attempt to form a group.

Experience shows that successful groups cannot be formed from just any combination of persons. We must carefully select each member. And to do a good job of selection, we need to understand why people are what they are, why they do what they do, why certain ones want to be together, and why some can cooperate and others can't.

Man is what he is because of his nature and his nurture. His productivity, both physically and mentally increases to its peak at about 25 years of age. The decline thereafter is more rapid than it should be because his will to remain at peak performance does not persist. Reluctance is the major reason for his failure to continue to grow.

Man does what he believes. If he chooses wrong he does so thinking he is right. He does not purposely deceive himself, nevertheless he is in danger of mistaking the lesser for the greater, the immediate for the remote or of acting habitually rather than deliberately. Right or wrong, whatever he does appears at the time to be the most desirable.

To understand a person's beliefs we must understand his needs.

In the scheme below there are three kinds of needs: (Later we will present a different classification.)

1. Survival needs—air, food, sleep, drink, and body comfort.
2. Personal needs above the survival level—
   a. Pleasures associated with clothing, shelter, health, etc.
   b. Ownership of tools, equipment, and property
   c. Recognition for activity, achievement, and self-expression
   d. Security, freedom from fear and danger
   e. Integrity, the feeling of consistency in principles and acts, in understanding nature and the universe, in knowing one's place in the universe, in understanding one's own nature and conduct.

3. Social needs—companionship, friends, and love. An understanding of one's relation to his group, his rights, obligations, and interests.

Wants have been described as the things we desire that are outside the area of our needs. This distinction is not clear. There is considerable overlap between what some people may want and what others may need. Wide differences in wants create tensions between group members.

All of us focus upon certain objects which appear of practical importance to us. If we succeed we generally set up a higher goal, if we fail our aspirations go down. Since our development is greatly influenced by the balance between our successes and failures, we should plan our group activities so that each member has a reasonable chance of succeeding. We must not make group tasks so easy they fail to stimulate nor so difficult that they depress. For man to learn he must do; all educational programs are action programs.

It seems that we have followed a circle in our explanation. Man *does* because of what he *is* and *is* because of what he *does,* and he chooses what to do because of his likes and dislikes. In much the same way he finds his associates by chance and bases his final selections on his likes and dislikes. All of us generally like those who agree with us and dislike those who don't.

But groups formed only from those who think alike have little chance to succeed. Progress is built upon differences. Of course we need a certain similarity in interests and attitudes, but we also need distinct differences in skills and abilities. Unless we cultivate these differences, as well as the attitude to question, to examine, to criticize, and discourage loyalty identified with obedience, we will have no democracy.

PEOPLE ARE DIFFERENT

People have many sides, many goals, and many affiliations. They may want to affiliate with one group for one reason and with another group for a quite different reason. Here are some of the most important reasons persons give for joining groups:[9]

[9]Redl, Fritz, "Group Emotion and Leadership," *Psychiatry* 5:573, 1942.

1. Because they seek an outlet for aggressive drives.
2. Because they want to escape responsibility for decision and action.
3. Because they seek protection against temptation.
4. Because of fear.
5. Because of admiration and desire to imitate.
6. Because of respect or awe for certain members.
7. Because it permits them to do something they could not do alone.

They do not always admit their real reasons, and their expressed desires do not always indicate their real expectations.

The most opportune time to discover the best combination of persons for a group is when they begin to select their problems. At that time the group selection* blanks should be used.

Life in a small group is always a person-to-person activity. Unless these face-to-face relationships are mutually stimulating, a real group can never develop. Of course, unsatisfactory combinations of persons do exist in armed neutrality, carrying on a sort of cold war, but they will never develop any feeling of "groupiness."

WRONG ROLES

The third reason for group failures lies in our lack of knowledge and our lack of skill in playing group roles. We all play roles and the role we select for a particular occasion depends upon how we view ourselves within that situation. We were not born to these roles; we learned them first from the teachings of our parents and then from our successes and failures in dealing with our playmates and teachers.

Roughly roles may be classed as (1) group building, (2) group destroying, or (3) group dependent.

Group-building roles: A group builder is generally a frank, friendly, expansive individual with warmth of feeling and a firmness of purpose. He has the ability to dissociate his own interests from that of the group and to cooperate with others in group activities.

Group-destroying roles: An immature, aggressive person who feels and acts in terms of his own interests is a group-destroyer. Lewin[10] describes one such person as:

... a clever fellow (who) quickly learned the amenities of the American style and made his way by showing a friendly,

---

[10]Lewin, K., *Resolving Social Conflicts*, Harper and Brothers, New York, 1948.

smooth surface. He was usually considered a likeable fellow and
well adjusted.

Having a fine sense for relations of status and power, he
could learn almost immediately where lay the strengths and
weaknesses of everyone. Thus he could quickly determine with
whom to make friends or enemies. He extolled the "Great" in
order to ride in their reflected glory. He complimented those he
considered inferior, thus obligating them to return the favor. He
became a master of tact and diplomacy. He entered competition
only when he could win, figuring how to block those he couldn't
outrun and how to destroy those who got in his way. He was
smooth, sweet, and treacherous. The more clever he became the
more dangerous he was, because he was so hard to identify.

Group-dependent roles: Lacking the physical force to dominate, the aggressive person may assert his status by submission.
A secure place is granted to those who permit others to climb
over them. This sacrifice is not remarkable, because if one is
permitted to dominate, others must submit, and the order is
maintained all down the line.

The immature, dependent person needs continuous reassur-
ing friendship. He will lean upon or be carried by the group and
tend to capitalize upon his helplessness. If he fails to receive support, he may drift away, becoming indifferent and detached.

If we expect groups to succeed we must discourage the playing of group-destroying and group-dependent roles and encourage the playing of group-building roles. The first five roles below
fall into the group-building category.

O.[11] *Orientor.** The orientor seeks to guide a group through
the various problem-solving steps in order that it may reach a
satisfactory solution. He realizes that a group should determine

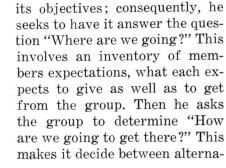

its objectives; consequently, he
seeks to have it answer the question "Where are we going?" This
involves an inventory of members expectations, what each expects to give as well as to get
from the group. Then he asks
the group to determine "How
are we going to get there?" This
makes it decide between alterna-

[11]The first letter is used as a code symbol.

tive ways and forces it to place the problems on a priority* list.
The third question the orientor asks is, "Who is to help?" In
answering this he forces the group to inventory members' skills
and abilities. From the inventories of expectations and skills he
uncovers certain differences. Realizing that differences are desirable and that unless group members are different no new ideas
will be produced, he encourages each to express his differences,
to "stick his neck out." Having differences a group can grow,
provided these differences are integrated. Consequently he attempts to hold the group together even if it means disciplining
the recalcitrant member. He tries to prevent filibustering, repetition, babbling and blarney for these tend to disrupt. Whenever
certain members drift he asks that they return to the matter at
hand. To him problem-solving is a cooperative venture, and, in
asking the questions he does, he forces the group to outline its
goals, specify its activities and determine its rate of progress.
He realizes that a certain amount of tension is necessary to keep
a group "on the track."

  F. Facilitator. The facilitator has been called a fact-giver,
a specialist, an expediter, a summarizer and a resource person.

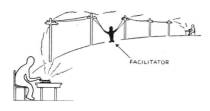

He serves a group in keeping
communication channels open.
He asks for and gives facts, beliefs, experiences, definitions, interpretations and clarifications.
He looks ahead trying to determine obstacles and then gathers
facts and materials to overcome
them. When serving as a resource leader he is careful not to
talk more than one-fifth of the time or to insist too strongly
that his viewpoint is the only one. He tries to liberate the best
in everyone rather than to display the best in himself. He seeks
the best methods and thus asks that facts be evaluated and organized into outline form. At times he summarizes by pulling the
ideas together in order that relationships might be more clearly
seen. He asks the group to set up standards for evaluating the
competencies of authorities and for measuring progress. He
provides the facilities and performs the services which promote
the efficiency of the group.

  E. Encourager-harmonizer. The warm friendly spontaneous
person who gives sympathetic response to individual needs, who

accepts rewards and reaffirms dominant values plays the encourager's role. He feels that group work should be a cooperative venture instead of a battle, and that all members should be bound together in harmony. He dislikes conflict and offers to give ground, to yield status or compromise issues to avoid it. He senses the rhythm of the group and knows when to de-tensify it with humor or understanding. He understands that aggressive persons may use humor to attack or demoralize, to defend themselves, to

avoid criticism, and to evade responsibility. His genuine humor reduces tensions when conflicts exist between the demands of the group and the needs of individuals. There are persons who avoid becoming involved in any task function because this is a threat to their being liked.* They seldom take any stand for fear it will make an enemy. These are unproductive roles so far as problem-solving is concerned but they may be productive of "good will."

*R. Recorder.** The recorder keeps the minutes and other official records of the group and reports the happenings to the group and to outside persons. Adequate records materially assist a group in making decisions.

*Ob. Observer.** Groups that take time to ask themselves "How are we doing?" are on the road to maturity. No time will be more valuable than that spent in analyzing activities. If objectively done it can show the group whether it is growing in maturity or is disintegrating.

A. Aggressor-dominator.[12] This person attempts to rule by fear, threatening or attacking the well-being, knowledge, skill, acts, feeling, or value-attitudes of others. Or he may attempt to manipulate others or to put something over on the group by flattery, by conditional promises, by alliances or, by pitting person against person or group against group. He tries to direct attention toward himself by boasting, by claiming long experience or great accomplishments, by asking questions, or by approving the acts of others in such a way as to show his own

[12]See also Adorno, T. W. and others, *The Authoritarian Personality,* Harper, N. Y., 1950.

superiority. He cleverly uses jokes to attack others or to defend himself.

C. Censor-blocker. This individual resists change because he fears his loss of status. He opposes beyond reason, obstructs, discourages, or blocks any action the group desires to take. He ignores statements of others, censors or withholds information, and delays action by needless talking. He attempts to maintain social barriers. He may ask the group to surrender its rights to his control.

B. Blamer-dodger. This person displays his lack of involvement in the group by cynicism, horseplay, or lack of interest. He fails to do his part and blames others for his shortcomings. He prides himself upon his tact in being able to "get by" by voting a job upon another.

S. Submisser. When any person submits because of fear, he may show his nervousness by flushing, gulping, doodling, giggling, and speech pressures. The submisser may permit others to climb over him or let himself become the scapegoat in the hope of securing status. Thus he plays for sympathy and capitalizes on his helplessness. He seeks compromises and curries favors.

I. Isolate. The isolate is socially apathetic, indifferent, and detached. He claims no need for others because he has built himself a barrier of indifference. He expresses himself as, "I don't bother, care, mix, go out, or like people." Much of this is due to lack of skill in playing group-building* roles.

D. Dependent. This individual is a helpless individual who needs constant reassurance. He frequently wanders off the subject and indulges in visiting, or random disturbances. His difficulty may be due to low ability, to lack of skill in problem solving or to personality defects.

You will note that we have avoided the terms leader and follower in describing roles. We consider it a fallacy to divide people into these two classes. Each of us exerts some influence at some level and in some field, and that influence, however little, is a measure of our leadership. Leadership does not reside in a person; it resides in the situation. Groups do not act because they have leaders. They select leaders to help them act.

LETS SPEAK OF PERSONS
WORKING WITH US RATHER
THAN UNDER US

The most effective help a leader can give a group is to help it help itself.

When a situation calls for a certain kind of action, those persons able to mobilize that action become the leaders. For instance, a group lost in the woods will follow the person who can lead them out. A group seeking social expression will follow the persons having skills for generating fellowship. A group that wants to discuss issues will seek the tolerant, critical, informed, and permissive discussion leader.

Skills of many kinds are needed and when they are not present, it seems appropriate to organize skill-training courses. Murphy[13] makes three suggestions for leader* training activities.

1. Training should be organized about the tasks a group sets up for itself. If it is a social group, it needs social skills. If a discussion group, it needs discussion skills.

2. Those persons given training in handling the materials and tools needed in their job show increased confidence in their ability.

3. In situations in which an individual's skills count, his shyness disappears and his participation increases. This would make it seem desirable to train all group members in playing the roles needed in group activities.

We should not expect to see good behavior substituted for bad by adopting a "Hands Off" policy. Neither can we train a group in democratic procedures by autocratic methods. Nevertheless, a democratic leader must be given the authority to rule out influences that hinder the growth of democracy. These ideas may seem contradictory, and they will be unless the leader relinquishes his power as the group gains in democratic procedures.

---

[13]Murphy, Albert J., "A Study of Leadership Process," *Am. Soc. Rev.,* 6:674, 1941.

WRONG ORGANIZATION

Groups organize for different purposes and their organizational pattern should be varied as their purposes vary. No group can long exist unless it serves its members and its members serve it. Interaction is a two-way proposition, but this fact is often overlooked. Courtis[14] suggested 12 group functions, some of which serve the members, others of which serve the organization.

If a group is failing, it is well that its behavior be examined in relation to these functions. Some function may have been omitted and others may have been wrongly used. The coach of a losing team, if he is wise, attempts to seek out and strengthen the weak spots. He does not hesitate to make changes for he realizes that no one can be any better than he is unless he does change.

Planning. Every group must lay plans. To do this it must come to an agreement upon values; consequently, its first discussions should be aimed at developing a group philosophy* and a set of working policies. Unfortunately, too few groups spend enough time in determining where they want to go.

Legislation. Every group must devise ways and means for carrying out its objectives.* In a small group it is not difficult to formulate rules, but in the larger group, legislation often becomes a matter of compromise. When representatives come together expecting to impose their special views it is too late for truth to

prevail. Supporters seldom point out the weaknesses of a measure even though they see them. To gain some special privileges they compromise the truth and, if they win, all the rest of us lose.

Compromise* is fundamentally anti-democratic. It depends upon the balancing rather than the blending of thought, skill and power. We can have no good legislation without the frankest and fullest recognition of our differences. We are different, and, with different ideas we can either compete or cooperate. If we join together we may enact broad comprehensive legislation, but

---

[14]These functions were suggested by Dr. S. A. Courtis, formerly of Wayne University, Detroit, Michigan.

if the effort of working out agreements becomes too strenuous, we may fight it out without solving any problems.

Education. Decisions are no better than the facts supporting them. Whenever the members do not possess the facts, it becomes necessary to call upon the so-called resource* person to supply them. When we need to assemble all the facts, it may be necessary to ask many persons, and that often involves taking a survey. Fact-finding* activities are important; and once the facts are obtained, they should be made available and widely discussed. If the program involves many persons, then smaller groups should be assembled in order that each person may have an opportunity to discuss the facts, isolate the most important ones, and then arrange them in order of importance. These meetings besides being important means of communicating knowledge, are also important in skill training. Educating a group is a task often assigned to a special committee.

Decision. A group needs to follow procedures that will permit it to make decisions. Parliamentary rules provide formal

procedures for accepting or rejecting a proposition that has already been formulated. These rules would be more effective in helping a group make a decision if the discussion was permitted before the statement of the proposition.[15] In fact, if a motion

to discuss[16] were given a priority in parliamentary procedures it would make decision* easier. Various members should be urged to offer alternative solutions. Then, after several such proposals have been presented and the most probable outcomes of each discussed, comes the most opportune time for formal motions.

Action.* A group must carry out its plans. After the jobs have been assigned, the activities must be coordinated so that all parts of the attack may go forward at the proper time. It is important that a time-table be established and that frequent progress reports be made.

Representation.* A group must delegate someone to receive incoming requests, to speak its general opinion in promoting or defending its program, and to negotiate with other groups.

[15]Knowles, Malcolm S., "Move Over Mr. Roberts," *Adult Leadership,* 1:2 June 1952.
[16]Robert, Frank L., "Using Discussion Techniques Under Parliamentary Procedure," *Journal of Communications,* 5:149 1955.

Delegation. A group must have the right to delegate certain responsibilities to certain persons for specified periods. In general, only those functions described as action, representation, expedition, and membership should be delegated. All other functions should be reserved for the group as a whole, and never delegated.

Expedition.* A group must have records, reports, materials, and facilities that will expedite its activities.

Recruitment.* The members of a group must be identified, initiated, and instructed in their rights and responsibilities.

Control. The members of a group must be controlled, harmony must be maintained, and the common good held above individual interests. This is a matter of establishing authority.

Evaluation.* The group's programs and processes must be evaluated in order that a choice may be made between the good and the bad.

Organization. A group* organization must be perfected that will permit the above functions to be performed.

Persons gather together in groups for any number of reasons. They succeed if they set up an organization which permits them to accomplish their purposes. There are two types of groups, a knowledge of which may enable us to decide which type of an organization we should perfect for various stated objectives.

The first type is membership groups. They are primary groups, always small in number and always characterized by intimate face-to-face interaction. Within these groups there is a high degree of "we-ness" which is spontaneous, personal, sentimental and inclusive. In these closely knit groups we find the

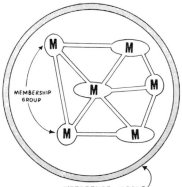

MEMBERSHIP GROUP

REFERENCE GROUP

answers to our more personal problems and the satisfaction of our urges. They support us in times of despair and restrain us in times of rejoicing. They are the major controls of society. In fact, it is in membership groups that we acquire our behavior and value patterns.

Examples of membership groups are families, gangs, clubs, work groups, play groups, social groups, and discussion groups. They are small because it is impossible to interact closely with any large number of persons.

The second class is reference groups. Reference groups are those larger associations we join more or less passively, accepting their ideas and going along with their action with some degree of feeling but without much participation. Examples of this type are farm organizations, political parties, scientific societies, trade associations, labor unions, Ford owners, country clubs, and similar groups.

Reference groups usually are formally organized with constitutions, by-laws and specific objectives. Objectives are usually stated in terms of economic, religious, recreational, relief, welfare, civic, health, educational and community goals. The number of reference groups is increasing due to changes in our social structure and public policies, and due to improved transportation and communication systems. Where once we thought that friends and neighbors were all-important, we now see our increasing dependence upon folks more remote, more impersonal.

Our contacts with reference groups are through their representatives and the relationship is semi-bureaucratic. This tends to promote an agency type of program usually dominated by a membership group at the center of the reference group. The number of members is no criterion of the number involved in a particular issue nor does it represent the number of those who support the officers. When the central group operates in a dominative manner, sooner or later there will arise complaints about lack of democratic control and lack of membership participation. These problems deserve careful attention.

Reference groups are formed by persons who find themselves unable to solve some problem alone. They are task-centered groups and their existence depends almost entirely upon their ability to solve problems* with dispatch. This means that members need skill in building an action* type of organization.

Other types of groupings we need only mention. Crowds are temporary, unorganized masses of people in physical nearness. Audiences are persons mutually stimulated by some activity but not very actively participating. Casuals are persons sharing common facilities, for example travelers or clerk-customer.

Our organizations for control, that is community, state or national governments are a part of the larger social group known as culture. More will be said about these and the institutions arising in them in the next chapter.

Let us pause a moment and reflect, then look forward.

Society has woven us into a web of inter-dependence from which we cannot escape. Nature, other persons, and the whole community lay claims upon us. And much of our growing up consists of learning how to react to these claims. Some of us submit, some adjust, some rebel, but none can escape. We live in and belong in groups, but our group life hasn't always been successful. Most of our failures have been due to lack of skill, because we did not do the right thing at the right time. More specifically groups fail in matters of organization, leadership roles, and atmosphere. These are very practical problems, and since what we do about them will depend upon what we believe, what we know and how we feel, it seems appropriate that we devote some time to integrating our beliefs into a consistent theory and to developing our skills through correct practices.

LETS NOT BE TOO SURE IT WONT WORK RATHER SAY I CAN'T WORK IT

Both theory and practice are necessary. Therefore you may either continue with Section II and read the theory or jump to Chapter 9 for practices or go to the appendix for some specific materials. Your immediate interest should determine your procedure. You will want both the theoretical and the practical. The practical facts will be easier and permit you to get along with the group work, but the theoretical parts may be the more important. To understand theory is to gain insight into the problems, to become skillful in practice is to reap satisfactions in doing. Knowing both "how to do" and "why to do it" is important. No matter where you start you probably will want to read the theoretical parts more than once.

SECTION II

*What Holds Us Together?*_____

In this section we intend to discuss action as a system and include in the act both actors and objects.

Actors are biological organisms but they are also members of groups. Both organisms and groups grow, but they can't grow unless the various parts are held together.

Growth means the process through which an immature organism reaches maturity. There are physical, mental, emotional and social aspects to growth, and growth forces may be roughly classed as nature and nurture.

By Nature we mean the quality factors of inheritance. For individuals these are sex, health, aptitude, memory, energy, etc. Nurture factors are those of food, exercise, sleep, instruction, associates, emotional stresses, etc. These are potency factors of environment. Maturity factors are those associated with the complexity of the task toward which maturation tends.

Knowing the quality factors of the organism or the group, knowing the potency of the environment and the complexity of the task, we may then predict its growth.

A complete understanding of these factors of growth is an achievement of the future. Nevertheless we undertake to discuss such parts as are known and hypothesized, for it is these factors which bind us together.

In Chapter 2 a general theory of action is discussed. Chapter 3 shows how social integration has produced four major social systems. These are described in Chapters 4, 5, 6, and 7. Then in Chapter 8 I've attempted to show how the communications processes play a part in any action system in holding the group together.

Chapter 2 _____

A THEORY OF ACTION

An action system, like any system, has both parts and boundaries. Having parts it has problems of allocating its energy among its parts and then it has the problem of integrating the parts into an acting whole. Having boundaries, it has problems of maintaining them and of adjusting to forces both within and without. Since it is self-maintaining, it has problems of optimizing its gratifica-tions. Action systems must be considered in time and space relations, and they should be considered broadly enough to include organisms, individuals, groups and cultures. Let us diagram the action-situation as simply as possible.†

ACTION, REACTION, INTERACTION, OR TRANSACTION?

The center of an action system is what happens and it has at various times been called action, reaction, interaction and transaction. Dewey and Bentley[1] present arguments favoring the term transaction. They show the various levels of action are:

Re-action————where things are viewed as acting under their own powers.

Inter-action————where thing is balanced against thing in cause-effect relationships.

Trans-action————where all phases of action are dealt with as a unit. This viewpoint treats actors as knowing men and objects as things known and it

---

†Western civilization has been deeply influenced by the philosophies of the Mediterranean countries as interpreted and added to by Aristotle, St. Augustine, Locke, Hume, Kant, Mills, James and Dewey. I, too, have felt the influence but want to give special credit to the following publications, since they are the basis for the material in this section.
 Hilliard, A. L., *The Forms of Value.*
 Parsons, Talcott, and Shils, Edward A. (Eds.), *Toward a General Theory of Actions.*
 Dewey, John, and Bentley, Arthur F., *Knowing and the Known.*
 Bentley, Arthur F., *An Inquiry into Inquiries.*
 [1]Dewey, John and Bentley, Arthur F., *Knowing and the Known,* The Beacon Press, Boston, 1949.

does not permit them to be separated in the
transaction. It holds that knowing is an
integral part of communication, that it is
not fixed but flexible and is related to time
and place. It treats knowledge as a means
and not an end in itself.

In Western society the individual and his personality system has long received the major emphasis. This was the re-action
viewpoint. More recently the emphasis was shifted to the small
group and an inter-action viewpoint. Cooley[2] pointed out the importance of the small group by saying that the fusion of individuals into small groups gives rise to a sort of common life
with common purposes. This gives the individual occasion to become identified with something outside himself.

Mead[3] also used the term interaction, and said that at first
individuals respond to each other by taking part in a common
activity without attaching any particular meaning to their own
response. But gradually they observed and then imitated the
attitudes of others, and in so doing they called-up in themselves
the same response they called-up in others. This makes it possible
for an actor to anticipate his effect upon another and to control
his own behavior so as to maximize his rewards and to minimize
his punishments.

Dewey and Bentley urge us to keep all the parts integrated,
making the action situation include all the knowings and knowns,
all the actors and objects. They maintain that actors direct
action toward objects with the expectation that the transaction
will produce gratification. Actors seek and choose those alternatives which are most pleasant regardless of whether the action is
motivated by whim or deliberation.

This fact of human behavior is the basis of the egoistic
psychological hedonism set forth by Hilliard.[4] Nature, he said,
is entirely indifferent to whatever happens. The stone "cares"
not whether it is crushed or cut and polished and placed in a
building. Neither does the ocean "care" that ships burden its
waves. Inorganic things are "feelingless"; only living things
enjoy pleasantness.

[2]Cooley, James Horton, *Social Organization*, Charles Scribner's Sons, N. Y., 1912.
[3]Mead, George H., *Mind, Self and Society*, University of Chicago Press, Chicago, 1938.
[4]Hilliard, A. L., *The Forms of Value*, Columbia University Press, N. Y., 1950.
   Those anxious to follow a discussion of the criticisms of this theory are advised to
   read this book. The several varieties of hedonism are discussed and irrelevant criticisms are pointed out.

Organic things enter into stimulus-response relations and thereby occasion positive or negative affectivity or no affectivity at all. Hilliard maintains that pleasantness is the sole end pursued and the only way an organism can act. In order to better understand his hypothesis let us examine the postulates he sets up. There are six.

1. "There are two types of behavior, those determined by stimuli which operate through the nervous system and those which operate outside it" (e.g., a blast of wind). We are concerned with the first. Four definitions are needed at this point.
   a. An organism is a relatively stable, coherent set of events which respond to environment.
   b. Response is a unit of organic behavior determined by a stimulus.
   c. Stimulus is any change in environment capable of determining behavior.
   d. Environment is the universe less the organism. The line dividing the universe from the organism is very indistinct.

2. "Of all the alternatives presented to an organism, that response which occurs is at the moment associated with the greatest pleasantness." Four definitions are needed here too.
   a. "At the moment" means that the organism can be directly influenced only by present affectivity.
   b. Affectivity is a class of which the sole members are pleasantness, indifference or unpleasantness.
   c. Pleasantness means positive affectivity, in other words, "being for"; unpleasantness means "being against"; indifference means "being neutral."
   d. Alternative responses are present when there intervenes between stimulus and response any integrative pause at the level of the higher nerve centers. This is intended to demarcate simple reflex behavior.

3. "Where no alternative responses are present, the sole response has been conditioned so that it is associated with the greatest pleasantness were alternatives present." For example if my hand touches a hot stove I have no alternative but to snatch it away. Further comment is important here. Postulates two and three serve to reduce all choices to a class of reactions associated with most pleasantness. Affectivity is a datum about which it is impossible to be mistaken. Error is applicable only to inferences.

4. "The affectivity associated with alternative responses is determined by past experiences." For example, being

hungry and being offered both meat and a stone, I choose
the meat because in past similar situations meat has
been satisfying.

5. "If a certain stimulus is accompanied by unpleasantness,
   pleasantness will be associated with responses which
   remove it. If a certain stimulus is accompanied by
   pleasantness, pleasantness will be associated with responses which continue it."

6. "In so-called deliberate behavior the pleasantness and
   unpleasantness which determines choice are those en-
   gendered by the symbolic performance of those responses." Symbolic performances may be sub-vocal ma-
   nipulations of verbal symbols, assumption of alternative
   muscular sets, imagination (manipulation of visual symbols), memory of past experiences, etc. Two definitions
   are important herewith:

   a. A *last means* is an object which when reacted to
      determines a stimulus-response situation containing
      affectivity.

   b. An *intermediate means* is an object, related to an-
      other object, such that reaction to it is a condition to
      the actualization of a particular last means. Thus
      filling a glass with water may be the intermediate
      means, and drinking it the last means, which pro-
      duces pleasantness. The drink is not the end, it is
      the last means, pleasantness is the end. We cannot
      teach ends but we may influence a person to attempt
      means to the experience of pleasantness.

These statements seem sufficient for our purposes. Hilliard
has assembled much evidence to prove that the basic end in an
action system is affectivity, either pleasantness, unpleasantness
or indifference in feeling. Let us now turn to the object pole of
the action situation.

Objects. An *object* includes any set of events which it is convenient to consider as a whole, either permanent or transient,
and it is convenient to group them into three classes:

1. A *social object* is another person or group of persons
   towards whom an actor is orienting himself. If a social
   object responds, two-way communication is established.

2. A *physical object* is an entity which does not react with
   the actor. Then only one-way communication exists,
   which may be esthetic or empathic.

3. A *cultural object* is a symbol of cultural traditions. It is
   a belief, expressive symbol or value-standard which has
   not been "internalized" as a part of the personality of
   the actor.

Our concern with any of these classes of objects is that they have value for us. That is the reason they stimulate us and that we respond to them.

Values or value-standards. Values are basic to every educational program, and understanding them is of highest importance to every teacher or leader. Value is affectivity occurring in a situation determined by the response of an organism to a stimulus object. Objects are not values, they have value in that they are means to ends, the end being affectivity.

Value according to Hilliard is a generic term which may be qualified by nine adjectives, divided into four sets. Any value which occurs must therefore be qualified by one adjective from each set and only one. The sets are as follows:

direct	terminal	actual	positive
			indifferent
indirect	instrumental	potential	negative

The terms *positive, indifferent,* and *negative* are correlative respectively with the affectivity terms, pleasantness, neutralness, and unpleasantness. Indifference is postulated only for purposes of analysis, it might as well be omitted for indifference means no response.

Direct value is that determined by the direct, unmediated reaction of an organism to an object—the object being present. *Indirect* value is that determined by the indirect, mediated reaction of an organism to an object. It implies the presence of connectives, usually symbolic, between the organism and the object. It is the reaction to an object through some other object. In direct values the structures of both organism and object make possible a reaction without intermediate objects.

Actual value is determined when the object is present in the relational situation. Actual value exists only when affectivity is occurring by the direct or indirect reaction of an organism to an object. For example should you look through the window at a thermometer registering zero degrees and feel unpleasantness, the cold weather has actual indirect negative value for you. Actual direct positive terminal value is enjoyed by a hungry cat eating meat. *Potential* value is the potentiality for actual value. Potentiality implies probability. If an actor is enjoying an object, he may enjoy it at some future time provided he does not change. If he isn't enjoying an object he may enjoy it, provided

he does change. If the object changes it should be considered as
a new object. In both cases the object and actor must enter the
action situation. These qualifications have probabilities of happening. Actual means taking place, potential means capable of
taking place.

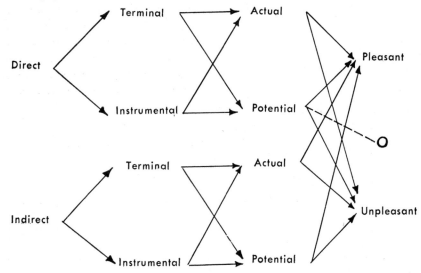

The dashed line from "potential" to the circle on the diagram above
indicates the probability of an indifference value should center action or
object change in the future.

Terminal values arise in situations wherein the affectivity is
determined by a reaction to an object "for its own sake," in
other words, when the object is the last means to the end of
affectivity.

Instrumental value arises when the affectivity is determined
by the reaction to an object "for the sake of some other object."
For example, we take pride in ourselves because of some object
we have created. The satisfaction inherent in pride is an example of instrumental value.

Since these descriptive terms are independent it follows that
there are twenty-four propositions asserting the existence of
values. The six propositions expressing actual direct values offer
us no difficulty. They are either terminal or instrumental and
positive, indifferent or negative patterns. They are expressions of
last or intermediate means and of pleasant, neutral or unpleasant
feelings. These are the values that everyone, regardless of age,
understands.

The six actual indirect propositions express values derived from symbols of objects rather than from the objects themselves.

The twelve potential value propositions have a time reference which implies not the present nature of the organism or the object but its nature at the time in question. Judgments of potential values are more important to us than judgments of actual value. This is because of their future reference and because they are intimately concerned with purposive behavior. Purposive behavior is that directed toward the alternative of greatest pleasantness. In general we will choose that means, either last or intermediate, which we believe will lead to the actualization of the greater potential positive value.

It is the educator's business to make forward connections between the six actual, direct values and the 12 potential value propositions and to show that actual values may be enjoyed through indirect means.

A final word of far reaching consequences is that no proposition asserting value is more than probable. This means that no moral rules, no ethical standards, no maxims of jurisprudence, no legal statutes in so far as they are propositions asserting value can be more than probably true in a greater or lesser degree. These in so far as they represent values widely distributed in space and time may be called *cultural values*.

Potentially all objects have value but natural and social objects have value only within the particular action system. Cultural objects are different in that they have values transmissible from one action system to another. Cultural objects are symbols. When these are objectified in writing or in graphic or plastic arts they may then be separated from the action system in which they occurred and be preserved intact. Any creation which arouses responses in the minds of others may become a cultural object. Sometimes these are adopted by the community because they arouse so strong an echo in the masses that they feel as if they themselves had created the objects.

Any reality which has been given meaning by one member can be shared by other members of the community and thus it becomes the property of all. This was called objectification by Romero[5] and he said it was the common root of the community and culture.

[5]Northrup, F. S. C. (Ed.), *Ideological Differences and World Order,* Yale University Press, New Haven, 1949.

Cultural objects are particularily important because they serve group needs and regulate conduct.

Written laws, agreements, contracts and the like are regulatory cultural objects. They provide control. Control over people is political power. It is the power to tax and to imprison. Control over things is economic power. But because control over things means control over the lives of the persons engaged in production and consumption of things, it often becomes necessary to establish limits beyond which persons holding power over things may not go.

Kinship relations are examples of cultural institutions which serve biological and psychological needs. A child needs a family. Being dependent upon his family he develops deep rooted attachments to those who serve him. This makes it easy for him to learn to want those things that his kinsfolk want for him.

Occupations are cultural institutions which have developed from the division of labor. Persons possessing the higher skill are given the better tools, the higher wages and the greater social prestige. But pay and prestige are not sufficient for all needs. Emotional security, love and response are not satisfied by one's occupational role, and for this reason we find kinship and occupational relations supplementing each other. Attempts to abandon family life for industrial workers have failed.

Before discussing the actor in the action situation let us summarize the preceding sections.

That pleasantness will occur under certain circumstances is based upon experience, as are all matters of fact. The experience may be past or present. If personal experiences are lacking, then we may observe the behavior of others under similar circumstances and from these infer pleasantness or unpleasantness. Lacking this we may still react to the symbol of the object or we may arrive at a judgment of feeling by analogy. These are the procedures used in matters of fact. In matters of values we should keep three things in mind, namely:

1. We must not mistake means for so-called "ends."
2. We should realize that symbols serve for actual objects.
3. We should understand the importance of potential values in the formation of purposive behavior.

Actors. The third component in an action system is an actor. An actor is an organism in the broadest sense. We have defined an organism to include any living thing from the simple one-celled creature up to the State or Society.[6] Not only does man seek pleasantness as an individual but he seeks it as a group. Cattell[7] defined a group as an aggregate of organisms in which the existence of all is utilized for the satisfaction of some needs of each.

Actor orientation. Actors strive to establish relations with objects in three ways. Actors *"cathect"* objects, that is they desire (with feeling) to obtain or avoid them. Actors *cognize* objects, that is they discriminate between objects and assess their respective qualities. Actors *evaluate* objects, that is they choose between objects on the merits of present or future expectation of gratification.

When cognitive orientation receives the emphasis, gratification results from coming to know. What we know falls into two categories (1) empirical beliefs which are open to scientific manipulation, and (2) non-empirical beliefs which are at present beyond the reach of scientific method. The limits between these two classes are not fixed, for what once were non-provable beliefs often become empirical beliefs due to advances in investigational methods.

Cognitive meanings may be wrong but they nevertheless will be meaningful, and the process is almost immediate. We say we jump to a conclusion, and it is a natural process. Meanings tend to persist until the actor is blocked in reaching some goal. Then he attempts to think his way out and in so doing he effects a cognitive reorganization. If, however, he attempts to reduce his tension in an aggressive or regressive manner, disorganization may follow.

We should understand that there are no impartial facts. Even though cognitive orientation is receiving the emphasis, it is still influenced by cathectic modes and value standards.

When the cathectic mode receives the emphasis, action is directed toward the last means for immediate gratification. This kind of behavior is known as expressive behavior. However when the artist or propagandist sets out to influence people by expressive behavior or symbols he does have a purpose, and then his orientation is cognitive. Emotion rarely stands alone, expressive behavior is usually influenced by meanings and values.

The evaluative mode becomes paramount whenever an actor is presented with two or more gratifications only one of which

[6]Lundberg, G. A., *Foundation of Sociology*, Macmillan Co., N. Y., 1939. Lundberg is credited with pointing out this broad classification.
[7]Cattell, Raymond B., Saunders, David R., and Stice, Glen F., "The Dimensions of Syntality in Small Groups," *Human Relations* 6:331 1953.

can be attained. Then he must take into account the consequences of alternative means and choose between them with the expectation of maximizing his gratifications or minimizing his deprivations. His interest will reach forward in acts of listening, looking, and searching, or backward to confirming experiences.

Despite the primacy of one or another of the three modes, on any particular occasion, that mode is never free from the influence of the other modes. This relationship is shown in the diagram below in which A or B is represented as being influenced

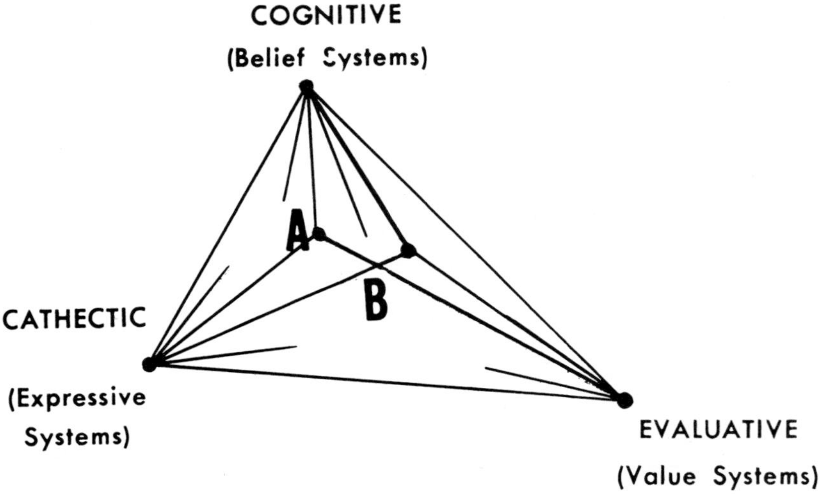

in a manner that is inversely proportional to the distance from each apex.

Having discussed objects and actors and having pointed out that affectivity is the last means or goal in any transaction let us diagram the action system in greater detail and then discuss the variables and the decisions an actor must make as he selects appropriate means to reach pleasantness.

THE ACTION SYSTEM

Responding actors	Modes of orientation	Integrating transaction	Stimulating objects
Individuals →	Cathectic } →	Five decisions which must be made in	← Physical
	Cognitive }	order to give the action some	← Social
Collectives →	Evaluative →	meaning	← Cultural

We must not make the mistake that many persons do who, when analysing, fail to recombine the parts separated. Although we have separated the modes of orientation for purposes of analysis we must not keep them distinct. Every person has feelings and holds values and can discriminate in some degree.

Once an object has aroused interest and been cognized, the actor must choose between immediate gratification, that is actual direct terminal affectivity, and the expectation of greater satisfactions later, that is its potential value either direct or indirect, terminal or instrumental. He must decide whether his energy is to flow over the most direct pathway or be inhibited and disciplined by an evaluation of the consequences.

Should he accept the lesser pleasantness now, he must then decide who shall be the beneficiary of his action. He has two alternatives, self and the group. The culture is of some help in answering the question, "Would it be better to seek future self-gratifications or should I be concerned with the welfare of the group?" because it has designated certain areas as "private" and other areas for "shared action." In "private" areas one is free to seek self-gratifications but in "shared" areas actors are obliged

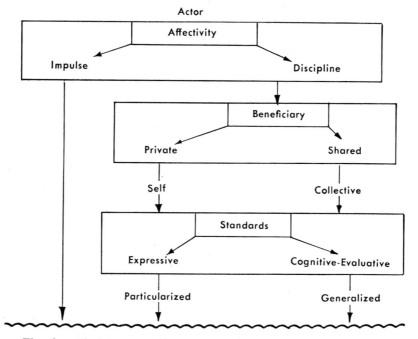

The three decisions are diagrammed with arrows pointing away from the actor and toward the object, to indicate that the actor responds to the objects.

to consider the welfare of others. This division of territory seems reasonable because no individual can subsist without gratifications, neither can culture exist without discipline. To choose the group as the beneficiary is to give primacy to moral value-standards over other standards or over no standards (impulse). Moral standards have been defined as those which give priority to the system whether it be society or a sub-group or even a

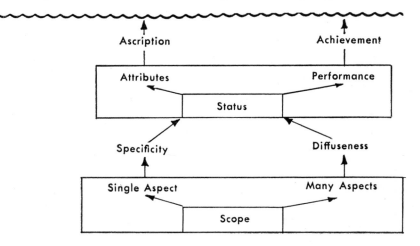

Object

    These two decisions are attached to the object side, they are diagrammed with the arrows pointing up or toward the actor, to indicate that objects stimulate actors. This diagram may be joined to the one on page 41 by matching the wavy lines.

deviant sub-culture. In a sense this second decision duplicates the first one but upon a different level.

    The third decision facing the actor is how he shall relate himself to the object. "Shall he respond to it in general or particular terms?" Generalization transcends the particular and reaches out to broader applications. Particularism gives priority to choices which relate to the actor's self. Thus we follow the relationship through the disciplined, collectively oriented and generalized poles. Likewise we see the relationship between impulse and self.

    When confronted with an object, an actor must decide whether he shall consider it in the light of what it *is* or what it *does*. This is a decision between attributes and performances.

Social objects have qualities such as age, sex, intelligence and physical characteristics. If these or other attributes of the object take priority the orientation is known as *ascriptive*. If however the object is considered in terms of its *performances* the actor is said to be *achievement* oriented.

The transaction is summarized in the flow chart which follows. The decisions to be made are numbered according to the outline which follows. The intervening variables are shown in their positions between the actor and the object.

There remains a fifth decision; and that is the breadth of significance the object takes for the actor. The scope may be either broad and diffused or narrow and specific. If the actor allows himself no restrictions and considers the object in many different ways his orientation is said to be *diffused*. But if he restricts himself to a single specific response, excluding all other responses his orientation pattern is said to be *specific*.

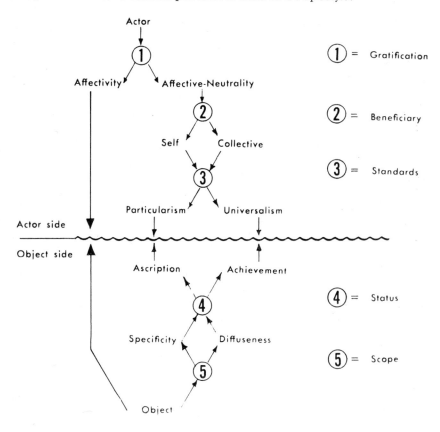

We have discussed five decisions an actor makes in valuing an object. These decisions involve 5 paired variables or alternatives. They form what Parsons and Shils call "pattern variables." Below we have outlined the problems, the alternatives and the variables:

Problem	Alternatives	Variables
1. How shall I allocate my energy?	(Impulse (Discipline	Affectivity Affective "Neutrality"
2. Who shall be my beneficiary?	(Private (Shared	Self Collective
3. What shall be my value orientation?	(Expressive (Cognitive-Evaluative	Particularism Generalism
4. What sort of status shall I grant the object?	(Attributes (Performances	Ascription Achievement
5. How broadly significant shall I consider the object?	(Single aspect (Many aspects	Specificity Diffuseness

These five paired variables vary in importance between persons. It is in the resolution of the problems of dominance that unique behavior patterns emerge.

The first pair merely presents the problem of impulse or discipline. If impulse prevails the actor needs not decide between self vs. group nor between particular vs. general value standards. If however the more or less neutral side of affectivity dominates (neutral is not quite the right word, non-impulsive might be better) then one must decide between self vs. group interests. The next decision is between expressive vs. cognitive-evaluative standards. If the pathway is through an expressive standard to particularism then some particular relationship to self prevails. If the pathway is through the cognitive-evaluative standard then the object is judged in some more generalized frame of reference. Thus only three pathways can be derived from the dominance of the modes of the actor. The upper half of the Transaction System diagram shows this rather clearly. On the other hand only two pathways are available for choices with regard to objects. These are shown in the lower half of the Transaction System diagram.

In this rather brief description of an action system certain propositions stand out. Let us summarize them as follows:

1. Men are both alike and different. This results from their inheritance and their experiences.

2. Actors are motivated by cognition, cathexes and evaluation. Pleasantness of feeling is the goal of action. Cognition and evaluation may be either intermediate or last means. Objects are intermediate and last means also.

3. Actors place values upon objects, individuals, groups and the community. The relative dominance of these value patterns are the basis for action systems which will be described in the next section.

4. Every action system must be relatively stable and this stability produces a pattern of authority.

5. Every action system must maintain an equilibrium between the expectations of its members and the members needs and gratifications. For example a group must provide opportunities for a person to both become an individual and to loss his individuality. It must render service to the individuals and it must expect individuals to render services to it. Festinger's study[8] on de-individuation supports this statement.

[8]Festinger, Leon, Pepitone, A., and Newcomb, Theodore M., "Some Consequences of De-Individuation in a Group," *Journal of Abnormal and Social Psychology,* 47:382, 1952.

Chapter 3.

ACTION SYSTEMS

To exist and persist, every system must be stable and cohesive, yet at the same time it must be flexible and adjustable. These conditions it does not find. It produces them as it seeks to solve its problems of allocation and integration and its problems of maintaining and adjusting its boundaries to its external and internal pressures.

Because biological and social systems are alike in certain respects, we may learn things from each by analogy. In biological systems genes are highly stable and provide the continuity from generation to generation. The units in a social system are stable in both inheritance and in learning. Nevertheless in both systems the organisms make adjustments to the circumstances under which they live. This gives them both stability and variability.

It is enlightening to draw the comparisons in greater detail as in the outline below:

Natural Evolution	Social Evolution

1. Genetic variability
    mutations
    sexual recombinations
	1. Social variability
	    new discoveries
	    conceptual rearrangements

2. Reproductive isolation
    perpetuates a gene pattern
    gives separate species
	2. Cultural isolation
	    produces a social pattern
	    gives cultural groups

3. Natural selection
    eliminates the unfit
    permits successful
    adaptations
	3. Social selection
	    eliminates inefficient practices
	    permits social integration

So far as anyone knows nature has no feelings regardless of what happens. The competition for space, food, light and moisture eliminates those less able to stand the rigors of the environment. There is some of this competition in social systems too, but there is also an element of cooperation. Cooperation tends to increase the well-being and efficiency of the individual and thus permits the selective processes to operate in his behalf.

46

Through cooperation a group becomes powerful, but power does not lead to survival unless the power is used to augment the long-term well-being of the entire group.

How big the "entire group" should be is a moral issue. The decision rests upon our understanding of the four questions below. Frank[1] found man everywhere trying to discover:

1. The nature of the universe: how it arose, how it operates, who or what makes things happen and why.
2. His place in the universe: his origin, his nature, his destiny, and his relation to others while he is here.
3. His relation to his group: his individual rights, titles, obligations, and interests, and who must be sacrificed for whom.
4. His nature and conduct: his image of himself, his motives, what he wants and should have, how he should get these things, and how he should be trained and socialized.

When he finds satisfactory answers to these problems he will be able to integrate his activities and beliefs at different levels of organization. There are five levels extending from individual to world-wide integration.

INDIVIDUAL INTEGRATION

At the personal level, integration is on the basis of pleasantness, and the experience of pleasantness is a private matter. It is an error to think of duty as the forced choice of an unpleasant alternative. Every man has the choice of obeying duty or not, and if he obeys it is because that course of action promises greater cumulative positive pleasantness. If the duty structures of society were not potentially pleasure-productive they could not possibly be maintained for long. The binding forces of all moral, ethical and social obligations is the prospect of negative values following non-conformity.[2]

SEXUAL INTEGRATION

How man relates himself to the same or a different sex is an important ethical problem. Sex differences are basic to social differentiation and division of labor. The sex pair must be integrated as a biological entity and likewise as a social entity. Any behavior which disrupts this integration is unethical.

---

[1]Frank, Lawrence K., *Society the Patient*, Rutgers University Press, New Brunswick, N. J., 1948.
[2]Hilliard, A. L., *The Forms of Value*, Columbia University Press, N. Y. 1950. Hilliard's explanation of these points is well worth reading.

FAMILY INTEGRATION

The family unit is a socially integrated group. It controls shelter, food, defense, and training of offspring. Much of family behavior is learned and transmitted through symbols. Behavior which leads to family well-being is ethical. But there comes a time when the same behavior is unethical, for example, parental control over mature offspring which interferes with the establishment of new families is unethical.

SOCIAL INTEGRATION

Races are partial genetic segregates. Although competition occurs between individuals, it is more severe between groups and between races. Individual exploitation of other members is harmful to the whole group and will be negatively selected. Cooperation, division of labor and integration usually result in increased well-being for all concerned and will be positively selected.

Brotherhood of mankind rests upon a firm biological basis. Good ethics would be that which integrates the various races. Racial exploitation, slavery both political and economic are bad. So is international conflict and war. Division of labor and specialization between cultural groups is compatible with biological principles. That each group should contribute its unique values to the common social welfare, is good. Any other plan which advocates discrimination, domination, prejudice and bias with unfair advantage-taking is bad.

Any thoughtful observer of present labor-management relations is struck with the inefficiency of the antagonistic viewpoint. Labor and management could combine to the benefit of all, or they could combine to exploit the rest of society. Communism based upon the theory of antagonistic social classes is doomed in time as is all selfish exploitation of society. What is termed good business competitively, may be found ethically bad, particularily when the selfish profit motive runs counter to the beneficial services to society.

INTERSPECIES INTEGRATION

Populations avoid severe competition when they integrate their activities. The limits of man's integration with his own and other species is no less than world-wide, and it extends into the past and into the future.

Our present concern is with social integration and the establishment of controls (authority) which stabilize, allocate, integrate and provide for adjustments within the various cultures.

Benne[3] saw authority arising as the relationship between a bearer and a receiver in a problem situation. He called this educational authority which we identify as the relationship between the actor, a social object and an educational task. To these Grace[4] added a fourth factor, the community and then he diagramed the authority constellation on the coordinates of independence and responsibility as follows:

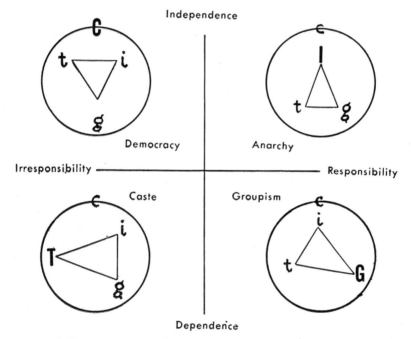

c = community; g = group; i = individual; t = task. When any one of these is dominate the symbol is capitalized.

This diagram shows four different action systems each determined by the factor receiving the major emphasis. For example in democratic societies the emphasis has been placed upon social responsibility and independence. As a consequence the authority rests in the community. Even though the community

[3]Benne, Kenneth D., "A Conception of Authority," *Contribution to Education*, No. 895, Teachers' College, Columbia University, New York, 1943.

[4]Grace, Harry A., From his class lectures in psychology at the University of Illinois, 1952.

(C) is the base, due regard is given to the individual (i), the group (g) and the job to be done (task = t).

Some persons confuse democracy and anarchy but this diagram makes clear the idea that anarchy is characterized by independence and irresponsibility and considers each individual an authority into himself, whereas democracy places major emphasis upon the community.

A task centered society is a typical caste society and finds its authority in the tasks which each person is destined to perform.

A group centered society places the group members above all others. Within such a society we find high dependence and high irresponsibility. It is a typical totalitarian organization.

Some philosophers think it possible to trace the evolution of society from a task-centered to a democratic form. We might follow them in a review of the great visions which have guided western civilization since the early days of the Christian era.[5]

During the dark medieval period man's hopes were centered in Heaven, his fears in hell. He believed in a Kingdom on Earth and a Kingdom in Heaven, and his major problem was to perform his duties here so as to merit a place in the hereafter. Each person had his position prescribed according to the duties he was destined to perform. The major emphasis was upon the **task**.

During the Reformation a new vision appeared. It was a vision founded upon personal freedom. Millions of weary, frustrated souls whose lives were held in static molds revolted and demanded freedom to enjoy the Kingdom on Earth. This vision placed emphasis upon the free **individual**.

The third vision was born of the disillusionment of the millions whose dream of freedom had been betrayed. They wanted freedom replaced by security underwritten by the group or the state for the well-being of a classless society. The proponents of this philosophy charge that individualism undermines the concept that wealth is essentially social and therefore subject to a control in the interests of the group. Herein emphasis is placed upon the **group**.

A fourth vision has appeared which combines individual freedom with social responsibilty. Every individual alone and in his various groupings and with the various tasks needed for

[5]Moore, Charles A. (Ed.), "The Second East-West Philosophers' Conference: A Preliminary Report." *Occasional Paper No. 52*, University of Hawaii, 1949.

the advancement of the community—all these are valued in the democratic vision. Herein the emphasis is placed upon the **community**. Furthermore, the individuals of the commonwealth are granted freedom to shape their own future, but charged with responsibility to the rest of the community.

These visions are not as clearcut as historians describe them. Within a single society groupism might dominate the business and political areas; individualism, the homes; and democracy, the cooperative organizations.

In the next sections we discuss the characteristics of action systems when the major emphasis is placed upon the individual, the task, the group or the community. It seems important that we understand these distinctions for some of our present day difficulties have arisen because some of us have confused democracy with anarchy, or free enterprise with groupism, or have placed too much emphasis upon the task. Then, too, we seem unable to control the organizations we have built.

Whenever an organization becomes relatively stable we say that we have established a pattern of authority to control it. There are four patterns, characterized by independence—dependence and responsibility—irresponsibility. Although we discuss these as pure systems, this is hardly true. Each has elements of the other system but this should not confuse us in our analysis.

Chapter 4.

THE ACTION SYSTEM — WHEN EMPHASIS IS PLACED UPON THE TASK

We will always have work to do so long as humans need food, clothing and shelter, and so long as they fail to find the world as they want it. Most societies declare work is necessary but some think of it as a means while others consider it an end.

In the typical caste system[1] work is considered an end in itself. Each man is born into a predetermined position largely on the basis of his family's standing. The system is inflexible with the family at the center and its elders in control. All func-

tions were prescribed. The family dominated the selection of marriage mates, the training of its children, and the behavior of its adults. Mothers were assigned the task of child bearing and children were taught to trust and obey.

Since the masses had no control over their future they made no plans, but lived from day to day. Life was static. Scarcity existed because the people produced just enough to get from one season to the next. Roads were not built because no one expected to go anywhere. As a consequence standards were low, and the responsibility for the conditions of life was shifted to the supernatural.

This sort of a system as it developed in India began with a series of successive invasions, each of which subjugated the former inhabitants. The first invaders placed themselves over the Aborigines, and this gave rise to the soldier-slave caste. Later the Aryan invasion imposed a culture which held in contempt the trivial things of life, and from it arose the priestly caste. Gradually the system expanded into a stratification of

[1]Sanders, Irwin T., "Characteristics of Peasant Societies," *Farmers of the World*, Bruner, Edmund, D.S. (Ed.), Columbia Univ. Press, N. Y., 1945.

society based upon hereditary occupations. Furthermore, it specialized morality with function thus making each person's job his end, his moral responsibility.

At present four castes are identified; namely, priests, merchants, soldiers, and slaves. Each caste has its particular tasks prescribed; each operates within its own sphere; each follows the special laws of its position. Once the system is established future generations follow the pattern of their parents.[2]

During the Middle Ages, society was cast in a system somewhat similar, except that its beliefs traced back to Plato and Aristotle. Plato taught that the two worlds, physical and spiritual, were unrelated, and that the spiritual was the superior world. Aristotle thought physical and mental matters were related but graded into a system of descending excellence.

The early Church expressed these ideas in terms of the Kingdom of Heaven and the Kingdom on Earth. Earthly values were placed in the lower brackets. And, since only God could know the perfect state of man in the Kingdom of Heaven, the Church taught that man must accept His rules, which were authoritatively outlined by His interpreters. St. Thomas Aquinas applied Aristotle's ideas by teaching that all beings—"from acorns to archbishops, from polyps to Popes"—could be categorized in a chain of ascending excellence. In such a heirarchy, each existing thing had a special purpose and each person, a moral responsibility. Each man had a special station or vocation in life and the world ran smoothly so long as each fulfilled his purposes. Some were born to rule by the Divine Right of kings, others by their lowly ancestry were relegated to performing the menial tasks of serfdom. True, a great many social inequalities existed, and, as compensation for these, each man was promised his just reward in heaven.

St. Thomas Aquinas poured Aristotle into a cast-iron mold which rigidly shaped the thinking of the medieval Church. Gradually, with the introduction of new inventions, a new natural philosophy came into being. The scientific postulates of St. Thomas's system were upset by Copernicus whose studies of the movement of the stars contradicted the idea that the earth was the center of the universe. Then, about 100 years later, Newton formulated a single universal law of gravity which became the basis for all science until the twentieth century. New-

[2]From "Indian Question" and "Caste" in *Encyclopedia of the Social Sciences.*

ton said that the universe was a great constellation of free moving bodies, each held in its place and all operating under the unseen forces of gravity.

Attempts were made to apply the new natural theory to man. It was argued that "if all atoms are alike then man's body is controlled by the natural forces which control atoms." But this explanation was not acceptable to John Locke. Locke concluded that the human being contained a special "mental substance" which gave men the capacity to reason and this made him free to determine his own way of life.

Thus Locke helped open the way for a new emphasis upon the individual. Science, technology, and invention provided new materials for new tasks. The pattern of authority based upon the task broke down and disorder followed until a new pattern was established. Pope Leo XIII writing much later expressed it as: "That fatal and deplorable passion for innovation which was aroused in the sixteenth century first threw the Christian world into confusion, then passed on to society and thence pervaded all ranks of society."

Today we consider tasks to be important, but not all important; we think of them as means rather than as ends. If they are necessary, they must be done, and it may be as important to clean the sewer as to point the way to salvation. One of our greatest social problems is to provide suitable incentives for work and satisfactory outlets for the fruits of work. The solution depends in large part upon where we place the emphasis.

The main features of the system when emphasis is placed upon the task are summarized as follows:

Task centered—closed society—caste system

1. High dependence—high responsibility
2. Leadership—paternalistic
3. Individual behavior patterns—stable, secure, non-changing, "believe and obey"
4. Emotional attachment to symbols of station or position
5. Group behavior—emphasis upon duties and privileges of class
6. Education—apprenticeship types, skill, discipline
7. Changes introduced because new technologies and the recognition of individual differences broke up the system

Chapter 5.

THE ACTION SYSTEM — WHEN EMPHASIS IS PLACED UPON THE INDIVIDUAL

Individualism is used here to describe a society in which people claim to "think for themselves," regard themselves as free agents and as best able "to judge their own interests." They pay little respect to tradition and tribal responsibilities.

Even though the term is often used to characterize modern Anglo-American society it had its beginning in Greece. The fifth century was marked by a disintegration of the authority of tradition which came about partly by the scientific discoveries of Greek free thinkers who proposed various theories to explain the relation of the individual to the state.

Zeno was the first to propose the ideal free society. He placed emphasis upon the individual who he said should be free from all external controls and guided only by his own conscience. His plan called for each member of society to be so considerate of every other member that government would be unnecessary.

His system which he called anarchy hasn't worked except in a very limited way or under experimental conditions, where a passive type of leadership was provided. Even then aggressive behavior was higher than in any other atmosphere.[1]

The more modern ideas of individual freedom may be traced to patterns outlined by Locke, Mills and Hume. Locke first systematized the consequences of science and showed its implications for religion and politics. He conceived of nature as being made up of "material" and "mental" substances and that all experience was the product of the interaction between these two. He argued that objects had color only because color was perceived by persons. Likewise sounds and odors were only sensed substances. These arguments supported the theory that man had both mind and body. Furthermore, he argued that the mind

---

[1] Lewin, Kurt, and Lippett, Ronald, "An Experimental Approach to the Study of Autocracy and Democracy," *Sociometry* 1:292, 1938.

would be unaffected by the dissolution of the body in death. The philosophy of a mortal body and an immortal soul are corollaries of Lockean theory.

Locke was not the only interpreter of the happenings of the times. The task-centered authority of former ages was breaking down. Science as always the first great disturber, had upset the older philosophies. Economic changes, the second great disturber of authority patterns, was upsetting the business world. Explanations seemed to be in order and many persons tried their hands.

Adam Smith in writing the "Wealth of Nations" attempted to explain economic forces as free and independent. Smith applied Newton's concepts to economic laws. He proposed an end to economic controls. He argued that business should be free and permitted to stand or fall upon its own merits. He said that, like gravity, economic forces would hold things in balance, and his argument seemed reasonable to those who saw in the roar, smoke and bustle of the Industrial Revolution unprecedented opportunities to get themselves ahead.

Free land with abundant resources, new machines, great volumes of tools, shoes, food and other goods, provided the "materials" for the development of a laissez-faire theory of economics. The theory developed in England, which saw not only the first mills, and the first millionaires but also the first economic philosophers. Jevons explained that the goal of this new economics was "To satisfy our wants to the utmost with the least effort—in other words to maximize pleasures."

Darwin's doctrine of evolution was presented as an argument in support of Locke's idea of "mental substances." By free competition we could develop the "mental man" most fit to survive.

It does not take much stretching of the imagination to go from this idea to the notion that the most valuable man is the one who most forcefully expresses his will in acquiring property. Thus the triumph of the individualist, the victory of the strong became the basic motive for business and the reward for initiative was the pleasure given by wealth. But this argument confuses means with ends. For example: a bank in Chicago advertised "One good investment is worth a lifetime of work."

Many economists accepted the competitive idea and argued that social order and human betterment would follow, if we would only permit the "natural forces" to operate, as free men sought to satisfy their wants. Some gave a great deal of attention to the description of man's wants and needs, especially the wants of the upper classes and the needs of the lower. Then they turned their attention to motives and explained man's struggles as arising from a central motive of greed. They led us to classify man as an economic being and his behavior as economic behavior. But in so doing we overlooked the fact that men like to love and fight and think and play because of the pleasure these provide.

Theologians accepted the idea of independent "mental substances." They took Locke's statement, "The care of every man's soul belongs unto himself and is to be left unto himself," to mean that the source of all good and evil was located in the individual. And they attributed social evils to the individual and not to political or social circumstances.

Locke's philosophy prepared men, after giving expression to their own opinions, to accept the verdict of the majority and to tolerate certain attitudes of others. It was only natural that this idea should be added to an individualistic philosophy although it seems contradictory. Men cannot live alone and they cannot live in groups without some toleration. Those who had gained economic freedom were not too secure in its enjoyment. Being full of fears they sought out and joined with others in forming governments to protect their lives and property.

Many, even today, confuse freedom with democracy. It is true that individuals deserve emphasis, but certainly not all the emphasis. Individualism seldom produces a democratic atmosphere. It is more likely that chaos then autocratic domination will follow. We see this clearly in our schools when teachers of so-called progressive education have mistaken anarchy for democracy. When children have tasks to learn, there are places for teachers and parents with influence. And parents who rear their children without controls generally raise little tyrants.

Individualism is fruitful only so long as individuality is something to be achieved and realized, but when it becomes something to be defended against attack it becomes indistinguishable from egotism, that passionate love of self.

Britain's long history has shown unfortunate consequences when individualism and Non-Conformist Protestants have been in power. The intolerance set off by the Duke of Somerset, the Poor Law revolt when Lockean democrats were in power, the disgust following Cromwell's Protectorate are examples. Individualism reached its final condemnation in England in the slums of Birmingham in the nineteenth century, and in America in the 1930's.[2] "It seems," said Northrup "that if we act upon the basis of traditional Protestant individualism and traditional laissez-faire economics and politics we fail to solve or even to face the inescapable social, national, and international problems and dangers of our times."

Following Locke there arose the philosophy of Bishop Butler who emphasized duty and social responsibility. Lindsay said, "Being let alone is an antiquated idea of freedom." Unless "freedom from" is replaced by "freedom to" he thinks we will be forced to choose between laissez faire and totalitarianism.

At present it is difficult to identify any philosophy or major interest which suggests the way the Western World may go. If democracy is to function it must build a program which has majority support, and this demands both a philosophy and a set of practices. If either is lacking, the system breaks down and the people break up into many competing groups.

Whether Anglo-American culture turns to democracy or statism is still a question. Unfortunately the outlook favors statism because the totalitarian philosophy seems to be more explicitly stated and its practices more definitely outlined. No doubt this came about because its leaders have most entirely and completely given up the philosophy of individualism.

Anarchy was a defense against the inflexibility of the caste system. Anarchy proposed to achieve individual freedom and it achieved this only in limited areas of endeavor in western cultures.

Our problem is different today. Rather than concentrating authority in individuals it is to find the kind of an atmosphere which will permit the widest distribution of individual authority. This is a major problem of democracy.*

In summarizing the main features of a system of authority based upon individualism let us not confuse anarchy with democracy.

Individualism—Anarchy—Laissez faire

    1. High independence, — low responsibility
    2. Leadership—passive

---

[2]Northrup, F. S. C., *The Meeting of East and West*, Macmillan Co., New York, 1946.

3. Individual behavior patterns—rooted deeply in selfishness, aggressive, competitive, "everyone for himself," fear of being outdone, cunning, crafty, secretive.
4. Emotional attachment to material goods
5. Politics—free will, equality. "Everything will come out all right if we don't interfere."
6. Group behavior—none—and this makes the whole system impossible.
7. Education—child centered school—no discipline
8. Science—Newtonian mechanics, simple play of forces, inquiry stressed the importance of units and elements and their interaction, space was a thing, it expressed a relation.

Chapter 6.

THE ACTION SYSTEM — WHEN EMPHASIS IS PLACED UPON THE GROUP

The concept of individual freedom which had been growing during the seventeenth and eighteenth centuries found expression in our culture in 1776. In that year the colonists declared their political independence from the *crown princes*. In the same year Adam Smith made a declaration of economic independence from the *merchant princes*. These were protest movements based upon the concept of individual freedom.

But an individualistic society cannot exist, for as soon as persons form a society they form a group. Even a self-regulating political state built upon Newton's concepts of free natural forces is a fallacy. Social forces are man-made and it is not safe to evoke a physical science concept to explain social behavior. Nevertheless, efforts to achieve individuality may be fruitful. But once individual freedom has been achieved, efforts to defend it are indistinguishable from selfish egoism. To do as one pleases often means a disregard for the pleasures of others.

In the turmoil of the 18th century political theorists were not forgetful of the need for social order and political control. Even though the pioneers brought to America strong feelings regarding man's individual liberties they also brought the idea of political order. Out of this dualism they built a nation with emphasis divided between the individual and the group. They wanted to be free but they realized they needed to organize to solve their problems. How to have both freedom and control was their major problem.

Many in the Constitutional Convention were fearful about general freedom. John Marshall thought "mankind is incapable of governing himself." Gerry claimed, "All the evils we experience flow from the excesses of democracy." Hamilton placed people in two classes: "The first are the rich and well-born, and the others are the masses of people who seldom judge or determine right." Madison argued, "You must first enable the government to control the governed." The Constitution when signed did not guarantee the rights of the people. Benjamin Rush said, "I consider it an honor to the late convention that this system has not been disgraced by a bill of rights."

Freedom lost to group control at the Constitutional Convention. The federal government was christened a Republic. The Chief Executive was not elected by the people. The Senate was selected by the state legislatures. The judiciary was appointed for life. Only the members of the lower house were elected. The checks and balances were intended to prevent the people from controlling the government. The Constitution itself was not submitted to popular vote and only about five per cent of the population had a chance to vote on its adoption.[1]

But people demanded their "Bill of Rights" and ten amendments were added. The western states and the slave question brought up the problem of majority rule. (Earlier only property owners were permitted to vote.) Finally Lincoln stated the hopes of a government "of the people, by the people and for the people."

The government of the United States was built upon a philosophy which divided the emphasis between the individual and the group. Out of this dualism we evolved a motto "United we stand, divided we fall." The symbol often used was the Roman fasces, a bundle of sticks tightly bound together with a battle axe protruding. Individuals were thus shown bound into a group because in a group there is strength. We held out for freedom to organize and saw no contradiction in our arguments.

But out of this philosophy a bitter struggle for control was generated. We freed our economic activities and permitted the giants to slug it out regardless of what happened to the noncombatants. Of course this resulted in larger and larger organizations and finally in government by "pressure groups."

Thus the nineteenth century sociologists saw society as large scale group organizations. They saw workers being obliged to organize into large unions.[2] They saw the masses being solidified by propaganda designed to influence according to some predetermined ends. They found individuals being held together by law and social pressure even when they lived in constant con-

---

[1]Gettell, Raymond G., *History of American Political Thought,* Century Co., New York, 1928.
[2]Mayo, Elton and Lombard, G. F. F., *Teamwork and Labor Turnover in the Aircraft Industry of Southern California,* Harvard Univ. Press, Boston, 1944.

flict. They saw the state as a highly impersonal and closely co-ordinated rational-legal authority. This idea was expressed by Calhoun when he said that government was necessary in order to control man. Control was a major issue.

Control of crowds is largely a matter of manipulation. The technique implies a mindless mass, and a leader possessing some unique and mysterious powers which can only be ascribed—not described. Hitler expected to control the mass of lower classes whose class consciousness had not been awakened. He gained control of most sources of communication and then said, "It is the object of propaganda to force a lesson upon the whole nation."[3]

Long ago Le Bon[4] from his study of the psychology of crowds predicted, "the advent of the crowd will perhaps mark one of the last stages of Western civilization—a return to the confusion and anarchy which preceded the emergence of the new society." He saw crowds as being dominated, becoming submissive and possessing "unbounded credulity," "lack of foresight" and "incapacity to be moved by reason."

But crowd control was not sufficient to control Germany. Hitler placed great emphasis upon building and controlling groups. He formed The Party and made membership in it a privilege. Identification was by a badge, a flag and a uniform. The Party was soon made the State and this then became the New Order. He first adopted a military order which he applied to every possible grouping—to youth groups—to industrial groups—to labor groups. He disciplined his followers by methods designed to create fear. He made each person dependent upon a group—then he controlled the group. The method according to Mannheim[5] was "to perpetuate the psychological attitudes of adolescence in these groups. Just as it is possible to direct family influence toward the retarding of maturity and the establishment of a juvenile mentality so is it possible to spread an adolescent dependence upon the group throughout society at large."

He attempted to consolidate various groups, first by setting up a common enemy, then by using terms like "Fatherland," "brotherhood" and "our cause." He promised each social stratum the realization of its own aspirations if the people would only

[3]Pick, F. W., *The Art of Dr. Goebbles,* Robert Hale, Ltd., London, 1942.
[4]Le Bon, Gustave, *The Crowd, a Study of the Popular Mind,* English edition, Fisher Unwin, London, 1900.
[5]Mannheim, Karl, *Diagnosis of Our Times,* Kegan, Paul French, Tubner and Co., Ltd., London, 1943.

follow him. He used slogans, "All for all," "All belongs to one" and "To each that which is his."

Whenever undue emphasis is placed upon the group we expect to see special interests in conflict and each attempting to maneuver its group into the privileged position. We expect aggression, compromises and rebalancing of power. Some say that this is the natural law of the jungle. They condemn war, but condone individual and group conflicts. They consider these small-scale aggressive actions as safety valves against the consequences of frustration. They claim competitive athletics is character building,[6] especially when the team is losing.

Emphasis upon a group generally implies a leader—follower relationship. By hundreds of stunts Hitler built a picture of the popular beloved leader as the hope of millions of suppressed Germans. For example, he carried packets of cigarettes having placed in each a one- or two-mark piece. Suddenly the black car carrying Germany's would-be Fuehrer would stop along the road and after a few words of nationalistic teachings he would give one of his cigarette packs to a surprised workman.

The great man theory of leadership which has caught the fancy of many Americans too, places a distinctive stamp upon  those whom it claims are predestined to lead, because of their possession of unusual traits and powers. Great men are pictured as power holders who have learned to use their personal characteristics, t h e i r face-to-face associations and their grasp of political, economic, and social resources to increase their position. Generally they do not wait to be chosen by their followers, but present themselves pre-chosen on the basis of a mysterious inner call or unusual ability. Evil men never come to us as evil, they always disguise themselves as good.

The rank and file in complex societies apparently find a need for power-seekers, and appear to accept the authority flowing from these dominant characters. The first modern exponent, Napoleon, possessed a flair for self dramatization. He was not only a master at manipulation of himself but of other people as well. He was a rationalist of the highest order who utilized all the various mass persuasion techniques known to his age.

[6]Lewin, Kurt, *Resolving Social Conflicts,* Harper and Brothers, New York, 1948.

Many autocrats have followed Napoleon. Their pattern of leadership was much the same[7] whether it was developed in Italy,[8] Germany,[8] Russia[9] or America[10] or whether it be in government, in business or in our homes.

CAPTIVE AUDIENCE

When leaders conceive of themselves as working upon a group, they strive to make the followers dependent both economically and emotionally. Domination seems natural in homes because of the immaturity of the children. In other situations dependence is artifically maintained by various systems of controls. And because the whole system of group domination is charged with hostility, the leader must forever be on his guard. Consequently the inner-circle will build up a bogeyman for the group to fear and hate. And if the leaders are successful in causing the followers to project their troubles upon this outside enemy, the group may live gloriously while caught up in the movement.

Everything within the direct dominative atmosphere depends upon the leader. He carefully selects and emotionally colors what is taught and disproves everything except the prescribed patterns. Dominative leaders realize that fear is a strong integrating force and that it moves us to action. They realize too that fear is destructive, defensive, deadening and disconcerting, so they try to direct it outwardly. They realize that a group dominated by fears and hates provides a golden opportunity for another aggressive leader through whom its pent-up hostilities may be expressed. They know too that hostility may be cleverly disguised in order to avoid retaliation.

Dominative leaders claim to be saviors and promise relief from the tensions they helped create, if the followers will only surrender as willing instruments. And what they demand we surrender seems wholly reasonable since it satisfies our cravings for status in the dominative arena.

Domination does work. Our political history shows how com-

[7]Weber, Max, *The Theory of Social and Economic Organization*, Oxford University Press, New York, 1947.

[8]Gouldner, Alvin W., *Studies in Leadership*, Harper and Brothers, New York, 1950.

[9]Mead, Margaret, *Soviet Attitudes Toward Authority*, McGraw-Hill, New York, 1951.

[10]Dollard, John and others, *Frustration and Aggression*, Yale University Press, New Haven, Conn., 1939.

pletely bosses and kings controlled their domains throughout their lives.

The most successful tyrants realize that the limits to their authority lie in what the group is willing to surrender. Consequently rulers have always had great concern about the ideas held by their followers. What do they think, how do they feel, what will they tolerate are ever recurring problems. Regimentation of thought satisfies the dictator. Some thoughts are encouraged, others are forbidden. The program is largely one of propaganda by reiteration and imposition. Where propaganda ends, censorship begins. Early churchmen used the excuse of blasphemy to throttle thinking. Then they called it heresy and Kings replaced heresy with the crimes of sedition. Today we have "witch-hunting" and character assassins. The individual loses again and we are told that it is for the good of the group.

In Germany the group emphasis reached its zenith. The German philosophy followed the lead of Kant, Fitche and Hegel. Fitche and Hegel assumed that social instructions evolved like the market place and that which existed was good, because it existed. Thus the Germans developed a culture in which the individual was swallowed up in the state. They developed the chain reaction —will—force—conflict—victory—right, and paid heavily for this error.

Nehru pointed this out in a speech in Chicago. "Somehow in the last thirty or forty years because of two world wars, our minds seem to run on terms of force even more than they used to. I know that as the world goes today it is a little difficult to do without force. Nevertheless it is a major error to suppose that the problems of the world are solved by force. Even past history does not support such an error."

To set one class against another can never bring happiness. To attempt to set up a classless society by force will fail. To deprive men of their right to think for themselves is stifling. To determine what each man should do will result in dissatisfaction and low production. These are based on the wrong concepts of the nature of man.

The main features of the system when authority is placed in the group are:

Groupism—Statism—Totalitarianism
1. High dependence, low responsibility
2. Leadership—dominative, autocratic, administrative fiat

3. Individual—Expendable, emphasis upon citizenship duties
4. Habitual behavior pattern—insecurity, conformity, submissive-aggressive, low production, lip service
5. Inter-group behavior—competition, cliques, segregation, "loyalty pays off"—"chosen people"
6. Education—group centered school, core values, one-way communication, discipline, goose-step.
7. Science—directed toward aims of party
8. Politics—divine right, aristrocracy, racism
9. Religious—predestination, chosen people
10. Social planning—taken over by "inner circle," individual merely a part of the plan. Economic power in relatively few hands. Government influences newspapers, broadcasters, and universities.

Chapter 7._____

THE ACTION SYSTEM — WHEN EMPHASIS
IS PLACED UPON THE COMMUNITY

A commonwealth consists of persons, both alike and different, of tasks, both large and small and of groups of many interests, all integrated into a more or less stable system which operates in the interests of general welfare. This roughly defines a community too. Sociologists[1] described a community in more specific terms as:

1. A population aggregrate.
2. Inhabiting a definite contiguous area.
3. Sharing an historical heritage.
4. Participating in a common mode of life.
5. Possessing a set of basic service institutions.
6. Conscious of its unity.
7. Able to act in a corporate way.

This last, said Cook[1], is the most distinguishing mark of a community. Its organization for action gives a community its authority. How it distributes its emphasis between tasks, individuals, groups and the community determines whether or not it can rightly be called a commonwealth. General welfare is a relative term, but unless the major emphasis is upon "general" the community cannot qualify as a commonwealth. We call the system which places its major emphasis upon the general welfare a democracy.

Democracy is both old and young. Individuals have cooperated in family life since the human race began. Groups have cooperated in conducting their common business and in regulating group behavior since tribal life began, but as a political experiment, democracy is of recent origin.

Political democracy developed out of the turmoil of the seventeenth and eighteenth centuries. The authority of the task-centered culture was breaking down under the assaults of in-

---
[1]Cook, Lloyd A., and Cook, Elaine F., *A Sociological Approach to Education*, McGraw-Hill, New York, 1950.

dividualism. The common man wanting to be free to work out his own salvation, declared his political independence from the "crown princes" and his economic* independence from the "merchant princes," in the same year. Both were protest movements and had their basis in the happenings of the day.

Political theorists searching for something secure upon which to rationalize the conflicts of the times laid hold of the 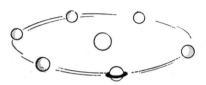 concepts of celestial mechanics developed by Newton. Newton had proposed a system which demonstrated how the forces of gravity held all natural things in place. The earth, the sun, the moon, all the heavenly bodies and everything upon them were held as it were by an unseen hand. This idea became the basis for building a self-regulating political state. The builders thought that they only needed to devise a set of checks and balances which would serve as forces of gravity to control the natural tendencies of man.

A little later economic theorists took up the task of rationalizing our economic life. They, too, were swayed by the great achievements of celestial mechanics. So they began the search for "economic forces" which operating like gravity would determine what should and could happen. Adam Smith denounced the older pattern of control by merchant princes as interfering with economic progress and invoked the guidance of an "unseen hand," because he was convinced that there existed an economic order which would automatically regulate economic activities and bring social benefits out of selfish strivings.

In the same tradition sociologists accepted the Newtonian concept and explained social order as a natural system too. Then they justified things which existed, whether good or bad as natural and inevitable and beyond man's reach. They fostered the idea that social life is something fixed—something to be endured but certainly not to be tampered with. Some went so far as to say "What is" is "What ought to be."

All this began to look like nonsense, especially to those whose lives were being blighted by the accumulated misery of the mines and the mills. The tragic irony is that the doctrine of man's inability to control social and economic order has been used throughout the centuries to cause us to submit to the control of the princes whether they be crown or merchant princes. We see now that the idea might have been abandoned long ago, but for the discovery of America and Darwin's doctrine of evolution.

Darwin's concept that the struggle for existence produce the most fit to survive, served to reinforce the belief in the efficacy of free unrestrained competition. America's rich resources provided the competitive materials, so we took another spin on the economic wheel of chance.[2] And America prospered, largely because of free land, abundant resources, human enterprise and optimism.

We think of America as being the present seat of democracy. But America has a type of democracy peculiar to the special circumstances under which it developed.

The first circumstance was the wilderness. Although the pioneer wanted to be free both politically and economically he found that his individual enterprise was limited by a wilderness filled with savages. Consequently he banded with others to gain freedom from danger but found that he had assumed responsibilities to his group.

The second circumstance was the rich resources of the country. Whenever a situation is favorable to all, everyone wants to be free. This was the case in the settlement of America and in the "run" in Oklahoma. But this free competition for resources leads to lawlessness which is soon followed by a demand for order. Then we form an organization to take control. Soon some of these groups developed into blocs dominated by the idea that America was a land in which life should be freer for me regardless. These blocs used the "united we stand" idea to obtain rights for particular individuals. Unfortunately pressure blocs think of government as an agency through which particular individuals obtain special favors. They want to put the government out of business and put their business into government.

Out of our circumstances we build our philosophies and then use these philosophies to either shape or rationalize our behavior. Social order is not something given, but something sought. It is man-made.

Pioneer circumstances favored the development of a pioneer philosophy. The frontier is now gone but some of its attitudes linger on and direct us into trails which no longer exist. It is

---

[2]Kallen, Horace M., *The Rise and Decline of the Consumer,* D. Appleton Century Co., New York, 1936.

wise that we examine some of the circumstances and the attitudes resulting therefrom in order to determine which attitudes
we want to save or abandon. Those most easily identified are:

1. Free land and resources made for economic equality.
2. Competition for these resources made for individualism.
3. Advantages gained from knowledge made for free schooling.
4. Common enemies made for cooperativeness, but it was
   cooperation "against" rather than "for."
5. Isolation made for hospitality.
6. Racial differences made either for tolerance or prejudice.
7. Scarcity of labor made for social equality.
8. Scarcity of goods made for a saving economy.
9. Success made for optimism.

The philosophy which evolved from these circumstances
placed emphasis upon independence, freedom and liberty, upon
the individual and his right to organize into groups to obtain his
wishes. It has resulted in a bitter struggle for control. We now
have government by tug-o-war. The present trend has been described as follows: "Balanced discussion of public issues has
given way to propaganda directed by government and party
officials. Extreme executive concentration has largely replaced
executive-judicial balance. . . . With the upsweep of regimentation in both government and business the balance between private and public zones of living has been lost. Today the balanced
skill-state has given way to the monopolist-state, the propaganda-
state or the party-state and if militarization continues we will
soon find ouselves living in a garrison-state."[3, 4]

Somewhere along the line a mistake was made; no doubt by
our policy-makers. They permitted democracy to lose, first to
anarchy, then to statism, and many of us cannot understand why
they could have let it happen. Perhaps it was because they had
an incomplete idea of authority. Perhaps they had their own
axes to grind. Perhaps they did not know how to generate an
atmosphere favorable to general participation. Perhaps it was
because they evoked a physical science concept to explain social
behavior.

We would stress the first reason and suggest that our policy-
makers permitted the emphasis to be shifted from responsibility
to irresponsibility or from independence to dependence.

---

[3]Lasswell, H. D., *The Analysis of Political Behavior,* Routledge and Kegan Paul Ltd.,
London, 1948.
[4]Webb, Walter Prescott, *The Great Frontier,* Houghton Mifflin Co., Boston, 1952. An
enlightening review of the circumstances which favored the development of American democratic institutions, and a prediction of the adjustments which can be expected as a result of
the disappearance of the frontier.

But Le Comte du Nouy,[5] the French philosopher, emphasized the last reason as he pointed out the fallacy of transferring concepts across gaps between unrelated fields. He said there is no scientific truth in an absolute sense. Scientific laws are dependent upon the reaction of many individuals to the same external stimuli. And it is our scale of observation which creates the phenomenon. For instance we know that the atom is made up of protons, electrons and neutrons, but between electrons and atoms there is a broad chasm. The scale for observing electrons is of no use in observing atoms. The analytical method, he said, has led us to believe that all matter is granular. Molecules are composed of atoms and beyond atoms lie electrons and protons but these are grains of electricity and no longer matter. Here there is a gap between matter and electricity, and the same laws do not apply when we pass from one to the other.

When we extend the scale of observation and examine living matter we cross another gap. We must bridge still another gap when we cross into the area of human personality. Personality emerged from the moment speech developed. Man's intelligence, his hands capable of shaping tools, his larynx capable of emitting sounds enabled him more and more to control his fate. He has choice, and thus can decide between what is good and what is not so good. Here evolution reaches the psychological plane, and we must not confuse our arguments because we change our scale of observation.

The concepts of celestial mechanics cannot be translated freely and fully onto the plane of psychological evolution. Our social and economic forces are under the control of man and it is man's duty to control them. To expect man's affairs to be controlled by an unseen force or by the laws of chance is an easy way out, but a wholly unsatisfactory solution.

Democracy still is a hazy concept. It developed in an era of conflicting beliefs and reflects conflicts in conduct. The Pilgrim fathers came to America to enjoy freedom but proved themselves to be intolerant to other seekers of freedom. They sought freedom to worship as they

[5] du Nouy, Le Comte, *Human Destiny*, Longman's Green Co., New York, 1947.

pleased, but demanded conformity to their tenets and creeds. They fell upon their knees and upon the Indians and Quakers at the same time.

The pioneer's individualistic dream succeeded so long as there was plenty of room. Free enterprise brought comfort to many people, it brought power and it brought privation. Individualism fostered special interests upon which monopolies have thrived, and monopolies have denied freedom to other persons.

Today certain far-sighted men are trying to think themselves out of the confusion. White[6] describes three ultimate and six near ultimate democratic values. The ultimate values are (1) individual welfare, (2) group responsibility and achievement, and (3) freedom. These may attain if six conditions prevail. They are:

1. We must be receptive to other viewpoints, that is, be tolerant.
2. We must be active, responsible contributors.
3. We must be free from class and status mindedness.
4. We must be oriented toward reality, that is, actively seeking the facts.
5. We must maintain a friendly atmosphere.
6. We must make possible the group's decisions.

Counts[7] outlines six principles of democracy as follows:

1. The human being is of surpassing worth.
2. The human mind can be educated and should be free.
3. Men can and should rule themselves.
4. Minority groups and interests should be respected.
5. Both natural and cultural resources belong to all men.
6. Peaceful methods are superior to war.

Democracy is man's most recent social invention, and its articles of faith have not yet been codified. They are found in the words of the prophets and seers, in the occasional writings of the ordinary man and in the lamentation of the oppressed. Gradually they are being worked into the customs and institutions, into systems of law and court procedures, into the bills of rights and the codes of ethics. At this point in the evolution of democracy three principles stand out:

1. The fundamental worth of human life and personality.

There is no real aristocracy above that of ability to produce. Therefore it is society's responsibility to see to it that every

---

[6]White, Ralph K., "Ultimate and Near Ultimate Democratic Values," *Progressive Educ.*, 27:165, 1950.
[7]Counts, George S., *The Education of Free Men in an American Democracy*, Educ. Policy Comm., Washington, D. C., 1941.

person develops his personality up to the limits of his capabilities, and has a right to enjoy the full fruits of his labors.

2. Free associations of people should be permitted to govern themselves.

On the whole, man is capable of solving his own problems and he should be permitted to organize to do so. But he will need the help of extended research and education in both the physical and psychological areas. More progress has been made by peaceful methods than by warfare and the cost is much less. There is more to government than the consent of the governed, it encompasses the involvement of the governed.

3. Natural and cultural resources belong to all mankind.

Resources should be used for the benefit of all, this includes both present and future generations. There is no such thing as being socially liberal and economically conservative, for human welfare includes physical and economic goods. You cannot separate man into body and spirit and treat his spirit freely and his body frugally and generally those who talk that way have not been denied access to the flesh pots.

Those of us who have experienced some democracy think it is a most desirable form of authority. And we are aware that democracy is not all commonwealth; it includes individuals, tasks, and groups too—each receiving its proper emphasis. It seems that all of us in each generation should reevaluate the following factors essential to a democracy in order to convince ourselves of its ultimate values.

DEMOCRACY

Democracy—when emphasis is placed upon the community.
1. High independence, high responsibility
2. Leadership—positive and widely distributed
3. Individual behavior—genuine interest in welfare of all
4. Group behavior—cooperative sharing of various group functions
5. Freedom—freedom *to*, everyone working, everyone progressing
6. Education—community centered school, broad educational program for all ages, two-way communication system
7. Politics—representative, accountability, fraternity, protector, referee, coordinator
8. Science—heredity and environment. Time and space brought into the system along with the facts of nature.

Relativity. Gravitation explained instead of being viewed as a force behind the scenes.

Note: In the next four sections we point out the importance of the task, individual, group and community in a democracy. This amounts to a setting up of values, an identification of best means or a determination of "oughts" for democracy. No doubt many will disagree with us. Democracy is not a stable concept; it is evolving and is expected to continue to change.

The Importance of the Task in a Democracy

Although man does not live by bread alone, he does live by bread and so long as his primary physical needs are for food, clothing and shelter there will be work to do. The problem is what kind of work shall carry prestige?

America grew great because nearly everyone worked. We have been a busy nation, we saw jobs to do and we had the energy to tackle them. We divided our labors and specialized our skills and thus converted more resources into economic goods during the last 80 years than in all former times. Our particular success has been due to our inventiveness, our energy, our organization and the abundant resources at hand. This is often used as an argument for individualism, and it is a convincing one to those who see work as something distasteful—something to be endured only until they can accumulate enought to retire. Unfortunately those who work only "for what there is in it for me" and who expect to "get by on their wits" hold a faulty concept of the fruits of labor. They think of themselves as privileged idlers, willing to live off the rest of us. They are unmindful of the fact that the world exists on goods and services produced by work, and advances as one generation produces more than it consumes. Neither do they think of the social loss when one generation puts its energy into destruction.

These unfortunate attitudes have brought us dangerously close to a system of castes. Industrialization and division of labor has tended to establish a hierarchy of workers, with a laborer class, a management class and an owner class. The class boundaries are becoming harder to cross and controls over others are becoming tighter. Goble[8] states the problem in these terms "Ownership of industrial property means more than control of physical property, it means control over people too." The management in a large measure controls the hours of work, the pay, and the

[8]Goble, George W., *The Design of Democracy*, University of Oklahoma Press, Norman, Okla., 1946.

conditions of the environment in which the worker lives. The worker, being dependent upon his job, is but little freer to move from it than he is to move from his government. And yet he has little voice in the rules and policies under which he lives and works."

Those of us who want democracy to survive have great re-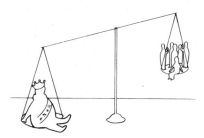sponsibilities to formulate plans which will dignify work and discourage idleness and special privileges. We need to train workers to high levels of efficiency, we need to plan industrial organizations which serve all the people, and we need to develop l a b o r organizations which reward the industrious worker. Survival means interdependence. Final victory is not won by stronger muscles, sharper claws and greater bulk, but by mutual helpfulness and responsibility for all one's fellows.

Wherever we find the over-privileged we also find the under-privileged.

Unfortunately we have largely ignored our responsibility to plan for our future growth. We have developed but few plans and are advised by some against any planning. We have spent hardly any time in speculation over our own character and the sort of a civilization we want to create. Yet "until a master idea is manifest to *all* there is no guiding star nor compass to the ship of state."[9]

To expect desirable results without careful planning is hazardous. "Failure to plan," said Compton,[10] "is one of the dangers of a democracy; since the pressure is so great to secure immediate benefits we tend to pay too little attention to the laying of proper foundations for our future welfare and that of our descendents." Our first problem is to determine what is good; what ought to be done.

Farmers and businessmen generally acknowledge the desirability of planning.[11] First in their individual business, next with their neighbors, and finally with the state. They plan their businesses with the view of lowering the costs. They extend

[9]A. E. (George W. Russell), *The National Being*, Macmillan Co., New York, 1930.
[10]Compton, Karl T., *Patterns in Our Ways of Thinking*, School and Society, 42:209, 1935.
[11]Duddy, Edward A., *Authority and Responsibility of Business Measure*, 1:26, 1950.

their plans to include their neighbors in cooperative organizations, in order to obtain certain goods and services. And they realize that their only h o p e s of obtaining roads, schools, and protection at reasonable costs lie in community planning. They plan on the individual, the neighborhood, and the national levels, and see no reason why one is any better than the other. They see all three as needed and able to exist together. They see individual ownership, cooperative ownership, corporate ownership, and governmental ownership existing side by side. Their major problem as they see it is to decide which economic enterprises can best be operated by individuals, which by cooperatives, which by corporations, and which by the state.

It is the state's responsibility to protect the future generations from being exploited by the present. Consequently it is good that our soil, water, mineral, lumber and oil resources be used in such a manner that they will furnish us a high level of living, yet so conserved that future generations may maintain adequate standards, too.

Democracy can flourish only if we accept the responsibility to plan the tasks which need to be undertaken. There are jobs to do and so long as they are needed, who can say which is the most worthy, which demands the most from the performer and who deserves the greater reward?

The Importance of the Individual in a Democracy

Tasks become tasks only when individuals decide to apply energy to some human or natural resource to change it into a more acceptable form. The nature of the decision depends upon the nature of the individual making it. Tasks are important but so are the people who make them tasks. A task-centered society makes individuals non-important while a individualistic society attempts to make individuals all-important. There is a middle way which seems better than either, and while we are discussing the importance of the individual in a democracy, let us not lose sight of the task or the rest of the group.

Our first problem is to understand something of the nature of the individual, something of his feelings and especially his

values and intentions. Our cathectic*orientations, that is our
sensations and feelings, are part of our private knowledge. No
one can ever see, taste, hear or feel for us. These cannot be
shared but must be self-experienced to be known. Likewise, we
cannot understand anothers' plans, intentions, opinions or experiences except as these are revealed through expressive behavior.

These things are often declared to be intangible. But goals
are real, and humans do have intentions toward acquiring and
using means toward attaining them. Proof of this is found in
recent investigations[12] which show that certain biological organisms respond to symbols as if they were valuable enough to
be repeated.[13] These experiments are a bit difficult to explain but
they are too important to omit, for they show how a person
acquires notions of valued objects which guide him in determining
what are the right means to take.

There are two kinds of value-objects,[14] one is concerned with
serving man's wants, the other is concerned with determining
what his wants should be. The process in both cases is outlined
by McCullough and Pitts. At first a theory is set up. This takes
place in the nervous system by means of regenerative loops. Consider first the simple case of a nerve signal firing a motor neuron
and then perishing. This is a response to a mere particular. Consider now five neurons in a circle in such a way that the impulse
travels the circuit and returns to the first neuron. This signal
will not perish and memory will be set up. The impulse will be
transmitted continously so long as the necessary energy is re-
stored to the cells. This regenerative loop in addition to carrying
impulses in a circle may be so related that it can fire a motor
neuron and thus produce an overt act. Thus a constant "universal" becomes manifest in a specific behavior. With many regenerative loops in the nervous system joined together, many
"universals" may be related and thereby the postulates of natural and social theories are constructed.

In the case of a natural theory, facts coming through the
sense organs either do or do not correspond to the theory. If
they do not, the information fed back forces the scientist to con-
struct a new theory. But in the case of a social theory (what

[12]McCullough, Warren S., and Pitts, Walter, *The Perception of Auditory and Visual
Forms*, Bul. Math. Biophysics, 9:127, 1947.
[13]McCullough, Warren S., and Pitts, Walter, *The Logical Calculus of the Ideas Immanent
in Nervous Activity*, Bul. Math. Bio-physics, 5:115, 1943.
[14]In speaking of values, we use the term as intermediate or last means in the same way
that Hilliard does. We are forced on occasion to use the word "goal" but we use it to mean
intermediate or last means to affectivity.

ought to be) the feed-back comes from the theory (regenerative loop) instead of the sense organs and it serves to change behavior rather than the goal. Should a serious contradiction become apparent a new social theory could be constructed to replace the former one. This process explains why it is correct to say that one's ideas as well as one's environment determines a person's behavior.[15]

Broadly speaking behavior means any change in an actor. The classification of behavior adopted by Rosenblueth, Wiener, and Bigelow[16] helps clarify the matter of the development of values. They first identify active vs. passive behavior and find in active behavior that the motor neuron itself is the source of energy released in the firing. Active behavior falls into two classes.

1. Non-purposeful—random behavior.
2. Purposeful behavior—behavior directed toward some value-object in time or space.

Purposeful behavior was further divided into:

    a. Non-feed-back—that is, once the course of behavior has begun no signals from the object are received to modify the action.
    An example is—swatting a fly.
    b. Feed-back—that is, signals are received from the object which modify action.
    An example is—a cat chasing a mouse.

A feed-back is a circuit within a closed system which returns some of the output energy as input. When the returned input restricts the output so that the behavior does not overshoot the goal-object the circuit is known as negative feed-back.

All this makes it seem clear that the process of deriving one's values is much like that of deriving any natural principle. We attempt to repeat those experiences with objects which satisfy biological needs. Likewise we seek to repeat what our parents and teachers have told us was "good." This we do so long as we accept them as authorities and desire to react with them. Our own experiences, or the accumulated experiences of others or the frequency with which the same outcome follows a specific action are our best criteria for "truth." Consequently we see no reason for separating moral and natural "truths." Kant made this distinction and Western civilization accepted his ideas, but

---

[15]Northrup, F. S. C., *Ideological Man in His Relations to Scientifically Known Natural Man in Ideological Difference and World Order*, F. S. C. Northrup (Ed), Yale Univ. Press, New Haven, Connecticut, 1949.
[16]Rosenblueth, Arturo; Wiener, Norbert, and Bigelow, Julian, *Behavior Purpose and Teleology*, Philo. of Science 10:18, 1943.

the investigations reported above show how natural theories and moral values are derived by the same processes.

Values* have been variously classified as needs, wants, objectives, motives, goals, ends, and means. In an action system, actors are oriented toward or away from objects because the objects promise pleasant or unpleasant consequences. When we relate Hilliards' hypothesis that the end of all behavior is affectivity, with McCullough and Pitts' explanation of regenerative loops, we are forced to abandon all terms except "means" and "ends." Hilliards'* qualifying adjectives, "indirect," "potential," and "instrumental" broaden and make more explicit the term "means."

Biological growth depends upon an organism's obtaining certain elements from air, water, food, and light. These are external factors which the organism takes in. In higher animals growth is aided by activity. Activity may appear to be generated internally, but in most cases we are active in relation to some thing and this stimulus-object may well be the reason for our activity. Higher animals do not or need not be continuously stimulated. Intermittent stimulation is enough for cells to recover and rebuild themselves.

Let us now attempt a classification of values keeping in mind the external-internal and the stimulation-recovery distinctions. We set up only two ends pleasantness *vs.* unpleasantness. These fuse at the middle of the continuum, as indifference. Indifference is postulated merely to complete the scheme, it actually is lack of stimulation.

A means-end classification of values (needs*).

	Means to ends of:	
	Pleasantness	Unpleasantness
In the area of physical affectivity.	Food	Lack of food-hunger
	Drink	Lack of drink-thirst
	Air	Lack of air-suffocation
	Body comfort	Discomfort
	Exercise	Its lack
In the area of physical and/or psychological affectivity.	Rest	Tiredness
	Sleep	Lack of sleep
	Activity	Boredom
	Expressive-ascriptive response	
	Sociability	
In the area of psychological affectivity	Friendship	
	Love	
	Cognitive-evaluative response	
	Ability	
	Performance	

The introduction of the physical-psychological classification tends to emphasize a transition in value terms from direct-actual-terminal, to indirect-potential-instrumental values. As one reads down the columns, the terms change from actual objects to symbolic objects and from last to intermediate means. In nearly every category there is a "too little" or "too much" factor, both leading to unpleasantness.

Many terms have been proposed as value terms and it may help clarify our ends-means classification if we consider some of the most common ones, for example wealth, well-being, skill, knowledge, rectitude, respect, and power.

The terms *"wealth"* and *"economic value"* are frequently used as if they were objectives. To no one except a miser is money an end. We want money because it is a means for acquiring other objects or states which are last means to enjoying pleasant or avoiding unpleasant feelings. The good in wealth is that it permits a person to buy housing, clothing, respect, and certain amounts of health and power.

Taylor[17] maintained that a political economy is needed which encourages a balanced abundance of wealth and he demanded parity income for comparable services. Parity consists of both profit and progress sharing. A few instances of profit sharing have been reported but only one of progress sharing. Progress sharing[18] provides not only parity income but it provides that purchasing power shall increase as industrial efficiency increases.

Dollars are not income, they are merely a media of exchange. It is not difficult to determine the number of dollars needed to make exchange satisfactory for the majority of people. Dollars should expand as wealth expands, but the fabrication of dollars is obscured by the technical operations involved. It is the Government's business to make dollars. The Constitution states that Congress shall "coin money and regulate the value thereof." On the other hand it seems that the bank's business is to loan money. At present the process is almost reversed.[19]

It is important in a democracy that the citizens hold ownerships to economic goods or wealth not as an end in itself but as a means, but practically all the powers of advertising have con-

[17]Taylor, H. C., *Immediate Backgrounds of Present Agricultural Policies and Programs,* University of Illinois, Agricultural Extension Service, Mimeo. E. S. 1111, Urbana, Illinois, 1938.
[18]Wilson, Charles E., "Progress Sharing Can Mean Industrial Peace," *Readers Digest,* Sept., 1952.
[19]Voorhis, Jerry, *Out of Debt, Out of Danger,* Devin-Adair Company, New York, 1943.

centrated upon persuading us to take our satisfactions in "monetized" forms. People have been taught that money is the key to all their satisfactions so when they find something wrong they naturally demand more money. But a demand for more money merely means that something is wrong, it does not tell us what. And unless we more carefully investigate we may never learn the real trouble. We know that people do not recognize their needs for food—it even takes laboratory tests to indicate some vitamin deficiencies, so why should they unaided understand their psychological needs? As a matter of fact, in two investigations of worker motives, money was placed sixth and seventh in a list of reasons why people work.[20]

There is practically no literature in the United States which stipulates how income should be distributed in order that production may be expanded, new wealth created and democratic processes preserved.[21]

Skill is a term often used as an end in itself. Actually skill is a means for acquiring earnings or for gaining prestige. Both of these are means to pleasant responses which the skillful receives from his associates. Those who have skill are known as authorities and about the only test we have regarding the dependability of an authority is his possession of the appropriate diplomas, certificates, and licenses or his membership in professional associations. These are symbols only and should not be taken as proof. Democracy must depend upon skillful authorities. We need them and must be mindful to them, but we want them to be mindful of us too.

Neither is *knowledge* an end in itself. Knowledge is a means to other ends, and it is especially important that every individual in a democracy be learned in whatever facts are necessary to the perpetuation of democracy. This is the reason we have placed such high value on teachers. Teachers owe their authority to the office which the community has granted them. In their office they are expected "to teach the culture to the cultured," and to teach the cultured something new. This grants them certain liberties but imposes certain responsibilities.

Teachers in America have for the most part been free to select the facts they consider useful and worthwhile, and this is "good." Free flow and full access to facts, to channels, to news,

[20]Taylor, Gordon R., *Are Workers Human?* Houghton Mifflin Co., Boston, Mass., 1952.
[21]Lasswell, H. D., *Analysis of Political Behavior,* Routledge and Kegan, Paul, Ltd., London, 1948.

are essential to democracy. Concealment and secrecy are dangerous.[22] Both teachers and students should have certain liberties. Liberty in education means consent by persuasion without compulsion. But in this there is a danger, for we could be free not to learn as well as we could be free to differ. It is important that the individual have both quantity and quality, in his learnings. Not only should society uncover old facts, it has responsibilities to discover new facts. Consequently we should make certain individuals responsible for discovery. Research workers must be free but they must be careful, so that we can depend upon them. No one can discover all the facts, neither can he verify all the facts he is taught. He has to depend upon the experts, not only for new knowledge but for debunking old knowledge as rapidly as new knowledge is discovered. Thus it seems important that we provide research personnel to legislative, administrative, and judicial bodies, and help industry, agriculture and labor uncover facts regarding health, production, and the civic, social and recreational aspects of living. Otherwise democracy can perish by default.

Health, fitness and *safety* are means to individual and to social enjoyments. Doctors and nurses are the intermediate means to health.

Our analysis of health shows it to consist of four parts, and these could easily be mistaken for objectives. In each of the categories there are things to do which if done will lead to ultimate physical pleasantness.

The four categories are:

1. A sturdy physique—a body well developed for its age and properly proportioned in bone, muscle, and fat.
2. Organic fitness—a strong heart, efficient lungs, a good digestive system, normal sensory organs and freedom from disease and bodily defects.
3. Motor fitness—passable skills involving balance, agility, flexibility, endurance, strength and coordination.
4. Body protection—the ability to protect the body from dangers. This means knowledge and skill in sanitation, disease prevention, safe practices, first aid and ability to swim.

It is good that all persons enjoy the pleasures of good health and the outline above may indicate some means for reaching that end.

---

[22]Wilson, Richard, and Mollenhoff, Clark, "What Really Corrupts Washington:—Secrecy," *Look,* May 20, 1952.

Rectitude has been defined as goodness and virtue, but we have the problem of making more explicit what we mean by "good." Usually any conduct which conforms to reason and is approved by the respected members of a community is considered "good." Many characteristics could be named but we will mention only four that most of us will agree are "good." Let us state them as qualities of a citizen of a democracy.

1. **A good citizen is dependable.** He does not fail to do what he agrees to do when he agrees to do it. He is accurate and trustworthy, he accepts responsibilities and discharges his obligations. He is fundamentally honest.

2. **A good citizen is determined,** because he has goals. But merely having goals is not enough, the goals must be personally useful and socially acceptable and the expectations of attaining them must be good.

3. **A good citizen is socially effective.** He is understanding and considerate of the convictions of others and thus is able to participate in the activities of a group without becoming a dissenter or a tyrant. He is fair, he believes in fair prices, fair costs, fair play and a fair deal for everyone. He is willing to carry his full share of the cooperative activities of the community and the nation and he plans his activities to profit *with* rather than *from* the social group.

4. **A good citizen is progressive.** He realizes that during the past 80 years scientists have practically remade the world. He knows that in reconstructing a world, just as in reconstructing a building many odds and ends are cast into the discard. Discarding old ideas and practices leaves some persons painfully confused. In order to avoid confusion, one must seek to remain flexible and accept an attitude which permits him to make adjustments as the world moves on.

Any person whose behavior is described by one or more of these four terms will enjoy the response he receives from his associates. Then, too, his associates will enjoy pleasant feelings because his behavior advances the group's program. In this case all share in the satisfactions which come from accepting and being accepted. We have classified rectitude as an expressive-ascriptive interaction and included therein friendship and love. Acts reflecting affection are or are close to being last means.

Respect in our classification is a cognitive—evaluative response to some achievement. We respect persons for what they do but love them for what they are. Certain accomplishments are more valued than others and this is the basis for our occupational hierarchy with its differences in rewards.

Power is perhaps the most fundamental concept in the whole political process. Power is participation in decisions which affect the behavior of others. In power relations there is a giver, a receiver, a task, and an arena. Both A and B may have power over C but with regard to different tasks and in different situations under which the encounter takes place.

Not everyone can have an equal amount of power. In all organizations from the nation to the community club, decision-making is placed in the hands of a small proportion of the membership. The major problem is not equality of power, rather it is to see that the opportunity to exercise power is equally distributed. This means that the recruitment of power holders should be such as to provide an equal opportunity for power acquisition. Recruitment on the basis of skill is not in itself equal unless there is an equal opportunity to acquire skill.[23] And this is an important problem for a democracy, for democracy means wide sharing in decision making.[24] Those who want power generally act to acquire and maintain it. They often claim that they are more competent and should hold the favored positions on decision making bodies. How should we deal with power seekers? How should we extend and expand the skill to make good decisions?

Society continously alters its demands upon our conduct. Aggressiveness was considered a desirable trait in the pioneer  days, but aggressiveness and intelligence can give us a great statesman or a blood-thirsty tyrant. Tact and diplomacy have been extolled but it can be argued that by these means some persons try to dodge their responsibilities. At any specific time we hold in high esteem any pattern considered "good," and because it is rewarded we try to possess it.

Democracy is composed of people and for that reason the individual is important. Moreover it is important that the individual hold certain values.

[23]Bryce, J., *American Commonwealth*, MacMillan Co., New York, 1893.
[24]Lasswell, Harold D., and Kaplan, Abraham, *Power and Society*, Yale University Press., New Haven, Conn., 1950.

In this last section we have attempted to show how persons develop values and what values they ought to develop as citizens of a democracy.

The Importance of the Group in a Democracy. We hope the emphasis we have placed upon the individual has not caused anyone to take full credit (or blame) for what he is. Usually the "self made" man credits himself for what he is, but blames others for what he isn't. It is true that we inherit certain capacities but we develop them only in the interplay between members of a group.

In the group the individual finds security and satisfying experiences. In a group he has advantages in his search for food and shelter. In a group he can divide his labor and thus increase his skill and his supply of goods. This permits him to solve those big problems which demand a variety of viewpoints, skills and abilities. In a group he finds or formulates his behavior patterns,[25] and ways of regulating conduct.[26] In fact it is useless to attempt to "save" a youngster unless there is a like attempt to save his gang.[27] For these reasons groups are important to a democracy.[28]

No matter what brings a group together,[29] it cannot long survive unless it learns how to solve its external problems and how to control its internal processes. Both these are topics for future chapters.

Groups in a democracy have shown their effectiveness in production and morale[30], in arbitration, in administration, in community planning and in breaking down discrimination. This is because groups have purposes, drives, moods, and memory and because they are capable of responding as a unit.

The degree of success achieved by any group will in a large measure depend upon the following principles:

The problems should be real.

The leadership should be a leadership team.

The membership should be based upon willingness to work.

The amount of participation will depend upon the gratifica-

[25]Tyron, Caroline, and Henry, William E., *How Children Learn Personal and Social Adjustment,* 49th Yrbk. Nat. Soc. for Study of Educ., Part 1:156, 1950.
[26]Thelen, Herbert A., and Tyler, Ralph W., *Implications for Improving Instructions in the High School,* 49th Yrbk. Nat. Soc. for Study of Educ., Part 1:304, 1950.
[27]Thrasher, Frederic M., *The Gang,* University of Chicago Press, Chicago, Ill., 1936.
[28]Gordon, Thomas, *What Is Gained by Group Participation,* Educ. Leadership, 7:220, 1950.
[29]Doddy, Harley H., *Informal Groups and the Community,* Bureau of Publications, Teacher's College, Columbia University, New York, 1952.
[30]Mayo, Elton, and Lombard, G. F. F., *Teamwork and Labor Turnover in the Aircraft Industry in Southern California,* Harvard University Press, Boston, 1944.

tions derived from accomplishments; consequently, something should be achieved.

The group should determine its own autonomy.

Group decisions should be subject to revision based upon the action taken.

Most of these principles will be enlarged upon in following chapters, so it may be sufficient at this point to conclude by saying that we see no substitute for groups in a democracy.

The Importance of the Community in a Democracy. Those of of us who have lived in both small and large places often miss the neighborliness and sense of security that comes from intimate face-to-face contact between nearly all of the community folks. As the communities grew we found it impossible to know all the people. This forced us to choose our associates, and generally we chose those with interests like our own. The result was that many interest groups supplanted the one community group. The divergent and often conflicting views of these groups tended to weaken the bonds which held the community together, so quite naturally community influence has melted away. It came about because there were too many people to know and too many things to do.

This made us feel that we were too busy, but the facts are that 50 percent of rural New Yorkers[31] belong to no more than one organization and only 10 percent belong to more than three and 31 percent of Urban Detroiters[32] belong to only one organization. When we say we are too busy we really mean that we are not interested.

We may not have realized it but it was these face-to-face contacts which made the small community about as important as the family and the church in controlling behavior. As the community was losing this influence over us we likewise were losing our influence over it. Various special interest groups captured certain segments of the community's organization. Although these groups urged us to participate, they only wanted us to participate in their pre-cut and assembled plans. The inner circle controlled the publications, planned the conventions, loaded the resolutions, selected the nominating committees and executed the orders, thus preventing us from running our own organizations. There was no use to speak up, because our voice couldn't

[31]Anderson, W. A., "The Membership of Farmers in New York Organizationns," Cornell University, *A. E. S. Bul. 695,* 1938.
[32]Freedman, Ronald, "Who Belongs to What in a Great Metropolis," *Adult Leadership,* 6:1, Nov., 1952.

be heard, so naturally we felt of little importance, overwhelmed and alone. We knew we couldn't enact democracy, neither could we operate it by proxy. Democracy is something we learn to do together and it doesn't come naturally.

How can we rebuild our interests in our community? How can we regain control of our captured organizations? Our first problem is to understand the nature of knowledge,* how it is produced and what it means to the community. It is true that knowledge is power even though that knowledge be false.

There are three classes of knowledge, two being public, the third being private. Technical knowledge gives us power over nature. The faculty of abstracting, analysing and giving meaning to an object, produces knowledge that can be shared by others. Thus scientific knowledge becomes public knowledge since it is collected into a sort of community inheritance.

Practical knowledge is the second class of public knowledge. It is the accumulation of centuries of practical wisdom. Such knowledge has been transmitted to the practical man by his predecessors and has for him either positive or negative significance. The law is the product of practical knowledge and as such it establishes and maintains order and control over behavior.

There is a third class which usually has been given great emphasis by Eastern cultures. It is peculiar to the individual and is called subjective knowledge because only the subject can feel his own emotions or think his own thoughts. It is intuitively derived knowledge. Principles so determined depend upon sensory data made up of colors, odors, sounds, flavors, pains and pleasures which must be experienced to be known. No amount of description can convey the sense of blue, or sour, or pain.

Northrup[33] described this as the aesthetic component of knowledge in contrast to the scientific and practical components. The creation of artistic products like music, paintings, statuary, is based upon the notion that something ought to be. If these creations arouse similar responses in the minds of others they serve their purposes by merely being present. Artistic creations are intentional products and they have their roots in our values, and values help or hinder a person's actions. The importance of these expressive symbols in our community life are not easily overemphasized.

[33]Northrup, F. S. C., *The Meeting of East and West*, Macmillan Co., New York, 1946.

We know considerable about the public knowledge of the task-centered, individual-centered and group-centered communities. We need to know more about what kinds of practical and aesthetic components of knowledge the democratic community should have.

Generally we think of a democracy in terms of equality of power but it is more than that. It involves responsibilities and benefits as well as authority, and it demands the making of rules which prescribe ways of operating.

In small face-to-face groups where information, goals, purposes, and feelings are easily communicated we have no difficulty in making rules. But in larger communities there arise many problems of sharing the responsibility and the authority. These have been solved by certain democratic organizations and their solutions are stated below:

Principles of Cooperative Organizations

1. Benefits shared in proportion to the use made of the organization. In a non-profit organization where patrons share the risks and responsibilities, their interest in a sale continues until the transaction is adjusted to a cost basis. Neither the proceeds from the sale nor the cost incurred belongs to the organization which serves merely as an agent and cannot realize a profit or incur a loss. In consideration of the advantages anticipated by the consolidation of individuals into a cooperative, each individual obligates himself to patronize the association. Thus members assume responsibility to each other and to the officials who are planning the business operations. This principle should guide us in assessing costs or paying for benefits in all public organizations.

2. Democratic control. This principle implies freedom and equality between members.

a. Freedom. If cooperation is good for one it is good for all, so no limitation is put upon membership because of race, creed, or politics. The only restriction is that members must join in good faith, not aiming to destroy the organization. Everyone is free to join. Everyone is free to speak. Elections are free, the press is free and communications go in both directions.

b. One member—one vote. This places a value upon human worth and provides for the distribution of power. Members control a cooperative not because they contribute capital but because they participate in its activities. When the member fails, the organization fails. There are no proxies. Nominations are open—several persons are nominated for each job. Officers are elected for specified terms and required to report annually. Rules provide for the rotation of elected officials.

c. Appointed officials and employees are given tenure and security but not organizational control. Their authority is limited and subject to review. They are given power of decision only on certain matters which demand immediate decision. These officials are required to keep adequate records; the books are open to all members and audited by an outside agency.

3. **Capital return is limited.** The capital fund for a democratic organization is a deposit against the costs of doing business and these costs are charged to the patrons as they use the facilities. Thus capital is paid a wage and nothing more.

4. **Membership information.** No democratic organization can long exist without informed members. Members need to be informed about the nature of their business. They need to know how to analyse the records and reports, they need to be able to tell falsehood from truth, to distinguish between reality and given "facts." No person whether he be a new member or an expert can possibly know it all, even the specialist lives about two-thirds of his time in general society and for that period he is a layman. Education is a continuous process for both old and young in every cooperative organization.

Although every generation thinks it lives in a critical period, there can be no doubt about the fact that we have permitted the loss of certain community influences without providing a substitute. Several factors have accelerated the trend.

The first is the almost incredible growth of material things in the western world. This has changed the ways of living and thinking during the last 200 years more than they have changed in the prior 6,000 years.

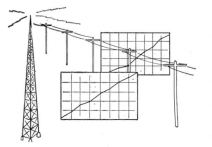

The second factor is the phenomenal growth in population. From 700 million in 1750, the population increased to 1100 million in 1850 and now stands at nearly 2.5 billion.

The third factor is the almost world-wide system of

communications. Most persons today know something about the rest of us.

These three factors combine to produce a critical, even dangerous, moment in human history. The good things have not been widely distributed and the peoples of the world know something about what they are missing. They are becoming impatient. They want the comforts and pleasures of life now, rather than in the hereafter. They are distressed when they see others free to enjoy what they are denied. They rebel when they hear the "enjoyers" boast that they are the most advanced and enlightened.

The situation is dangerous because so many persons lack the social skill needed to handle the responsibilities thrust upon  them. Those who enjoy advantages seem unable to understand the positions of the less fortunate. They even take pride in the differences and justify it by claiming that they have superior ability to enjoy. They maintain their position by the use of power, and now they have atomic power and threaten to use it. Those denied the advantages likewise are not adequately equipped to utilize the technological products wisely, but there is hope that they can soon learn these technical skills.

The real danger lies in the lag between technical and social skills. Rather than to attempt to slow down technical progress we propose to hasten social progress. This is the problem for our next section, but before we go on let's look at thirteen significant factors in the world today and speculate upon the problems they pose for democracy.

Significant factors in the world today:

1. The world has been revolutionized by technology. Old practices have disappeared and many new ones must be learned.
2. The productive capacity of the world is capable of producing abundance. We must adjust from an economy of scarcity to one of abundance.
3. Our economic and social organizations are interdependent and highly sensitive.

4. Both economic and political power is concentrated in relatively few hands.

5. Our most powerful mass communication media are privately owned.

6. The secondary groups controlling economic, political and communicative powers have large, perhaps too large, an influence.

7. The family, church, and local controls have lessened.

8. Almost complete anarchy reigns in international affairs.

9. Social mobility is limited.

10. There is increased time for leisure.

11. White supremacy is drawing to a close.

12. The natural resources are wearing thin.

13. Social skills have not kept pace with technical advancements.

If these statements fairly describe the situation today, they also point out the problems for our communities.

Chapter 8._____

COMMUNICATIONS SYSTEMS

The thing that holds each of the action systems together is understanding and understanding comes when persons are able to communicate their knowledges, beliefs and hopes to each other. A communication system is a necessary part of an action system. Its diagram resembles that of an action system in that it includes a sender, a message and a receiver and all these belong in the same community.

Sender———◄———| Message |———►———Receiver

We should understand our place in the communication system, our position and our responsibilities as senders and receivers.

Usually we think of communications as being the direct transmission of a factual statement from one person to another. This is too limited a view as we will soon see. Some senders of messages have intentions to influence receivers, but other senders merely want to express themselves. Thus messages may be either influential or therapeutic in function or they may be lost because no one received them. However, lost messages may be rediscovered and then become influential.

There is a noise aspect of communication which has been overlooked until recently. Even though messages carry no new information, their repetition, the noise, the chatter has been found to be important in building confidence.

American soldiers have been trained to be silent so as not to attract enemy fire. This was important to scouts in Indian warfare, but Marshall[1] questioned the practice in World War II. He reported the enemy was noisy and that noise generated confidence, By noise each man knew he was not alone and thus felt he had the support of his group. Likewise the chatter of a baseball team seems to build confidence. Grace[2] showed that pilot-ground communications were 99 per cent redundant and that these words were not wasted if they resulted in safe landings.

[1]Marshall, S. L. A., *Men Against Fire*, George J. McLeod, Ltd., Toronto, 1947.
[2]Grace, Harry A., "Confidence, Redundancy and the Purpose of Communications," *Journ. of Communications*, 1956.

Prestige places senders in positions of leadership. In agricultural circles we have thought of research workers, extension workers and community persons as a sort of leadership hierarchy. This gives rise to the assumption that opinion is formed by the elite and then percolates down through various strata. Leaders were considered as relay stations in the transmission of facts.

We recognize three classes of leaders. They are:

1. **The originators.** These are the great thinkers, the producers of ideas. They are few in number and seldom well known and their recognition usually comes after they are dead. Their communications are vertical.

2. **The disseminators.** These persons recognize the worth of a new idea. They use it, enlarge upon it and transmit it to others. Between disseminators transmission is horizontal but most of their communications are vertical relays from originators to opinion leaders. Disseminators are greater or lesser due to their access to mass media.

3. **The opinion leaders.** Opinion leaders are the influentials within their own face-to-face groups. They are the persons who have been reached by mass media because they look, listen and read and have developed some skill in searching out facts. Their communication is face-to-face and their transmission is along horizontal lines. They receive from disseminators and send to the great masses of intellectually inert.

The vertical channel is the major pattern for communication of fact. Fact travels from those who know to those who don't. But there is a large body of knowledge (unproven opinion) consisting of things we know but cannot prove. When we don't know, we take a vote, we depend upon the consensus of others. Without experiments we turn to experiences and the experiences we accept are those of persons in circumstances much like our own. There are a number of studies[3] which indicate that facts spread both vertically and horizontally but that the spread of opinion is mostly horizontal.

One other factor regarding the leader or the sender of messages should be considered—that is his plan for living, his purposes or his value-attitudes. Purposes of communicators were grouped into four categories by Grace.[4] These distinctions he said were clearer in theory than in practice.

1. Communication for self-expression. Herein the sender searches for a correct form of expression. He seeks the

[3]Katz, Elihu, and Lazersfeld, Paul F., *Personal Influence,* The Free Press, Glencoe, Illinois, 1955.
[4]Grace, Harry A., "Confidence, Redundancy and the Purpose of Communication," *Journ. of Communications,* 1956.

perfect blending of the symbols he uses into the background of eternity. In so doing he ignores himself and his potential receivers, he thinks only of the message. He may repaint or rewrite to obtain perfection but these repetitions have no effect upon the receiver.

2. Communications for immediate use. The sender's purpose is action. If he calls *Stop!* the success of his message is that people stop. Wanting action the sender individualizes his message, he uses sharp contrasts and startling patterns to attract attention. In this case there is no need for repetition, in fact it may reduce the effectiveness of the message. The boy who called *Wolf! Wolf!* learned that repetition was disastrous.

3. Communication for manipulation. These senders try to influence the receivers to conform. They use grandiose schemes and the group methods described in Chapter 6. They try to develop receptive attitudes without arousing suspicion. But their methods may boomerang. Having developed passive attitudes the group may not respond to action appeals or the audience may remain as it was conditioned before the shift in dogma was required.

4. Communication for integration. These senders hope that their messages will liberate men. Their purposes are democratic. They have respect for individual differences and human worth. They hope to develop confidence between the sender and receiver. They expect to change and to change their messages according to the effect of each message sent. Repetition is necessary so long as differences exist and changes occur. We have outlined in some detail the purposes of integrative actors in Chapter 7.

THE MESSAGE

The second part of the communication system is the message. Messages have two aspects, content and media. The content may be facts, or opinions or it may be emotional (cathectic).[5]

Media have been divided into mass and individual methods. Mass methods were devised to enable senders to broaden their influence. This objective has been both commended and condemned, on the basis of whether the sender's purpose was integrative or manipulative.

The first important mass medium involved the printing press. Messages were coded into words and sentences which the receiver was expected to decode and many times he didn't or

---

[5]Berelson, Bernard R., *Content Analysis in Communication Research,* The Free Press, Glencoe, Illinois, 1951. (Herein will be found the techniques for content analysis and the several uses to which it can be put.)

couldn't. Illustrations were added to help and the proverb "one picture is worth a thousand words" may be true in Chinese but false in English. Grace[6] explained this by declaring the "Chinese language is not very redundant" while English is. This enables English writers to develop rapport through redundancy. It's no wonder then that English speaking artists often accompany their paintings with 10,000 words.

We have some evidence from interviews with farmers that photographs are considered more valuable by persons classed as low-readers than by those classed as high-readers. The low-readers had read less than one-half the bulletin while high-readers had read three-fourths or all of it. Time was not a factor. Even so we think the pictures were over-rated. One leader who had taught a lesson based upon the bulletin had failed to see the photograph of his own farmstead until his wife pointed it out to him about four months afterwards.

Audio mass methods include the radio and transcriptions of various types. In many cases these carry emotional messages such as music and drama. These are one-way messages which usually do not demand the level of concentration needed to decode word messages.

Audio-visual methods as in lectures, dramas, movies and television are one-way systems utilizing two receptors. Two-way communications using audio-visual media are group discussion and its various adaptations. These media will be described in more detail in Chapter 13.

Mass media have certain technological, political and economic limitations. For example non-industrial countries may lack the electricity needed to operate telephones, radio and television. Totalitarian countries having control of the media may censor free communications. Then too, economic conditions may not permit poor people access to radio or television sets. There are two other limitations which mass media have, (1) the senders may not adequately code their messages and (2) the receivers may not decode them properly.

Individual methods include the telephone, the conference, the interview and the various small group activities which will be described in Section IV. The relationship between mass and individual methods in the flow of messages has been clearly shown

[6]Grace, Harry A., "Confidence, Redundancy and Purpose in Communication," *Journ. of Communications,* 1956.

in the report of the Decatur study. Herein Katz and Lazarsfeld[7] verify the hypothesis that ideas flow from press and radio to opinion leaders and from these to the less active sections of the population. Johnson[8] reported a successful program in the San Bernardino valley when mass methods and small groups were integrated.

RECEIVERS

Receivers are social objects with various dispositions to act or interact. These dispositions have been learned as the consequence of the individual's nature and nurture. Because of differences in the status and in the place in the life cycle different messages are received in different ways. Dispositions to react have been grouped together under the term motivations.

Certain aspects of motivation were described in Chapter 1 as needs and wants, but at that time very little was said about the relationship between motives and communications.

Motivation has long been a thorny problem. There have been many theories and most of them have certain defects. The biological theory explains motives as caused by the body's need for air, sleep, water, food, and comfort. But these survival needs have little significance unless they are understood and integrated by the organisms in which they exist. For example, there are reports that persons suffering oxygen starvation feel no craving for it; they simply lose their judgment and motor control and their movements become sluggish. Likewise persons dying of starvation feel no hunger after the first days. In cases of vitamin deficiency there is no craving for the vitamin. There is no evidence that sex behavior is determined by hormones. There is positive evidence that masculine and feminine roles are learned, that human sex adjustments are primarily symbolic and are learned through social experience in group situations.

The theory that instincts are the causes of motives has been virtually abandoned because for many of the so-called instincts no biological structures or physiological conditions have been found which explain them.

An admission of the importance of survival or the observation of activities which obtain food and drink does not explain the processes. It merely describes them and this is no justification for a "needs" psychology or a "needs" sociology.

---

[7]Katz, Elihu, and Lazarsfeld, Paul F., *Personal Influence*, The Free Press, Glencoe, Illinois, 1955.
[8]Johnson, Eugene I., "Groups with a Future," *Journ. of Communications*, 5:89, 1955.

Organic needs do not usually lead to anything but random restless behavior. Laskey[9] found that hunger did not motivate rats in running a maze until after they had learned to associate the maze with food. Organic needs become motives, only after the organism has learned to interpret them in certain ways and to associate them with certain objects or acts which satisfy the needs.

Individual wishes emphasized by Freudian theories of the unconscious are unsatisfactory because by definition the "unconscious" is virtually unknowable.

Marxist theories which place emphasis upon unconscious economic motives in contrast to Freudian unconsious sexual motives are unsatisfactory because of the definition of "unconscious" too.

The famous four wishes of Thomas and Znaniecki,[10] security, response, new experience and recognition do not explain behavior. The need is inferred from the act and then is used to explain it. This is a circular argument and explains nothing not included in a simple description of the behavior.

Rejecting the idea that motives are causes does not mean that purposes are unimportant. A person's motives are a part of the way he thinks and knowing how he thinks will enable us to anticipate how he will act. Persons living in similar status categories tend to think alike. There are three broad status conditions; namely, social, economic and educational status which deserve attention.

Social status is related to our membership in groups. Those belonging to many groups have many opportunities to receive messages. The messages received in face-to-face groups give anchorage points and meaning to life. The messages in family groups are usually accepted without proof and they give rise to similar feelings regarding religion, politics, and races. In-group communications have been underestimated in educational practices. They result in singleness of purpose, freedom from conflict and in the identification of the group's boundary lines.

Economic status divides persons on the basis of the kinds of messages sent and received. Both face-to-face and mass media are accepted differently by different economic groups.

---

[9]Laskey, K. S., "Experimental Analysis of Instructive Behavior," *Psychol. Rev.*, 45:445, 1938.

[10]Thomas, W. I. and Znaniecki, F., *The Polish Peasant in Europe and America*, Knopf, 1927.

Educational status places a limiting factor upon the kind and amount of information one can receive. This distinction is so clear that we easily note the vocabulary differences between persons of subject matter specialization.

In addition to status, life cycle position is important in motive analysis. As one moves through life, different media and different messages have different influences. At any one period similar influences tend to bring about similar motives. The most important variables which identify a particular place on the life cycle are age, sex, family and marital status.

Similar combinations of status and life cycle positions predisposes persons to react in similar fashions. These predispositions are learned. A person cannot express his motives in terms which he has not learned, neither will he be motivated by terms he does not comprehend. Furthermore, it is a mistake to explain another's behavior in terms of our own vocabulary of motives, particularily if status and life cycles are different.

Perhaps the most fundamental social influence upon human thought is exerted by the structure of language. Our thoughts in large measure are determined by our mother tongue and are controlled by our need to communicate them.[11]

Our needs to communicate are related to the structure and climate of our group situation. For example in an industrial organization Bach[12] found more messages went upward than downward or to peers. The lower status persons felt more needs to communicate upward than the higher status persons felt needs to communicate downward. Bales[13] found higher status persons tended to communicate facts and opinions while lower status persons asked more questions. Lippett[14] found that an autocratic atmosphere restricted the volume of communications, that a laissez faire atmosphere brought forth more requests for information from the leader and that in democratic atmospheres there were more requests for attention and more suggestions on procedure. Bach's study showed that communication about a particular matter spread between persons having similar views when the message was favorable rather than unfavorable to their

[11]Lindesmith, Alfred R. and Strauss, Anselm L., *Social Psychology*, Dryden Press, New York, 1956.

[12]Festenger, Leon, Schachter, Stanley and Bach, Kurt, *Social Pressures in Informal Groups*, Harper and Brothers, New York, 1950.

[13]Bales, Robert F., *Readings in Social Psychology*, Swanson, G. E., Newcomb, T. M., Hartley, E. L. (ed), Henry Holt Co., New York, 1952.

[14]Lippett, Ronald and White, Ralph K., "An Experimental Study of Leadership and Group Life," Newcomb, T. M. and Hartley, E. L. (eds), *Readings in Social Psychology*, Henry Holt, New York, 1947.

views. He also showed that those closely attached had more influence over each other than those loosely attached. Katz[15] discusses these matters in more detail.

The distinctive character of human mental activities is the development and use of language symbols. All mental activity is sign behavior. Goal activities involve responses to signs representing the future. Memory is response to signs representing the past. Perception is sign behavior representing the present. Skill in interpretation of signs and in response to signs is intelligence. Reason involves the use of symbols and is equivalent to conceptual thought. Perceiving, remembering and emoting are examples of complex sign behavior.

Language is a group product. It is a product of society and the means through which the culture is transmitted from generation to generation. Those who wish to understand group behavior will do well to study the natural and conventional signs which make up the communication system for the group.

---

[15]Katz, Elihu, and Lazarsfeld, Paul F., *Personal Influence,* The Free Press, Glencoe, Illinois, 1955.

SECTION III

How Groups Tackle Their Problems————

In this section we undertake the more practical phases of group work. A group gathers to solve a problem and the steps through which it must go are very practical. They mean either satisfactory or unsatisfactory solutions. Even though problem-solving is the major reason for the formation of a group, the problem can't be solved unless the group remains together.

This too is a very practical problem. How should a group go about servicing itself, satisfying its members and building its organization?

Although our special concern in this section will be with group problems, it must be understood that there are some problems which no group can solve. These are personal problems which an individual must work out for himself.

The steps are similar for both individual and group problems. The difference in emphasis will be seen by comparing the outlines on Problem Solving. The steps are divided into two parts. Herein we will discuss those steps which individuals and groups must take to get an answer.

In Section IV we will take up steps four, five and six, all of which are concerned with group growth and maturity. These are important because without a group there can be no group solution. The division of the steps into two parts is not a distinct separation for there are times when group building processes must function between the problem solving steps.

Chapter 9.

PROBLEM SOLVING STEPS

Whether or not an individual makes progress and arrives at a solution of his problems depends in large measure upon the steps he follows. Here are the natural steps in individual problem-solving:

1. **The individual becomes definitely aware of an existing difficulty.** It is doubtful whether any solution will be attempted until the problem is clearly understood. (The basis upon which things are identified as problems is found in a person's value-attitudes.*)

2. **Without delay he naturally attempts a solution.** It is natural for our minds to jump to a conclusion, but the cautious person checks his conclusions carefully before he states it. In this respect his first conclusion may be only tentative.

3. **Unless a person can readily recall enough facts to enable him to defend his conclusion, he at this point begins to search for data that will either prove or disprove the tentative conclusion he has drawn.**

4. **With each new fact he discovers and evaluates, he at once revises his tentative conclusion.** This process of revising continues until the burden of evidence is sufficient to convince him that his final conclusion can be substantiated.

5. **Finally, the scientific thinker subjects his revised conclusion to test.**

To show just how the mind works, we'll use an example suggested by John Dewey:

A midwesterner was a passenger on a ferry boat. As he stood at the rail, he noticed a long white pole projecting nearly horizontally from the upper deck. It was about twenty feet long and had a gilded ball at its tip.

"What is that pole used for?" his inquiring mind questioned.

"For a flag," flashed a reply. The color, shape, the gilded ball all confirmed this idea. But then he ran into a difficulty.

101

"The pole is horizontal, and that's an unusual position for a flag pole."

He looked around to check up. There were two vertical poles on the boat from which flags were flying. "No, it can't be for a flag, and besides now I see that there is neither a rope nor a pulley at the end. I'm sure it's not a flag pole."

"Possibly it's an ornament?"

"But look at that freight boat and those tug boats; they all have such poles too." He rejected this idea.

"Well, maybe it's for the radio?"

"No, ferry boats don't carry radios; they are always within sight of shore."

"Look! Each time the pilot faces forward, after he has turned to the rear, he seems to look at the pole and then adjust his wheel. To be sure, he's using the pole as a guide."

"That's right! The pole is below the pilot house so that he can always see it."

"When I come to think of it, that's the way I learned to steer a canoe last summer. I sighted over the bow tip toward the point on the shore I was trying to reach."

"The steersman, being at the front of the ferry boat, would need such a guide as this pole. Yes, certainly that's the reason for it."

The problem was solved, and a sense of satisfaction followed the achievement.

Even though a person can discover truth without any help, two heads are generally better than one and this is the main reason for forming a group. We want differences in skills, abilities, and viewpoints because they stimulate thinking and make it more critical.

HOW GROUPS SOLVE PROBLEMS

When people want group action, they talk to their friends, hold meetings, stir up old groups or form new ones. Whether or not they get group action depends upon whether the group accepts their problem as its problem and then takes the steps necessary to reach a solution. Group action revolves about problems, if there is no problem, there will be no action—in fact no group.

Problem solving is the process of arriving at an answer and begins when we become aware of an existing difficulty. Difficulties arise from situations in which (1) the issues are not clear, or (2) from issues for which a program is needed, or (3) from a program needing concerted action, or (4) when we must decide between alternative actions. Problem solving continues so long as we feel we are making progress toward a solution.

Whether the issues arose in the minds of the experts or came from the "grass roots," those persons who assemble do so hoping to find a solution. This is their primary objective and they may even hold it so high that they overlook the fact that they need to build a group. Group problems cannot be solved without a group. Consequently some of the steps in group problem solving are related to group building processes. In this respect the steps below differ from those just mentioned. These differences are important because not all our satisfactions in a group are derived from the solutions attained. Some of them come from the mere doing, from being present, and from being accepted as one of the group.

WHAT ARE THE STEPS IN PROBLEM SOLVING?

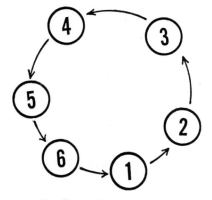

There is a cycle of events through which a group must pass in order to solve a problem. It seems possible to start at different points but generally all six steps outlined below must be taken.

1. Formulate and state a set of acceptable objectives or philosophies.
2. Define the more important problems and place them on a priority list.
3. Examine suggestions for all possible solutions and select the most probable of the several alternative solutions.
   a. Collect and classify the pertinent data.
   b. Critically evaluate each proposed solution.
   c. Decide upon a plan of action.

4. Integrate the activities of persons and agencies capable of working upon the solution.
5. Measure the results of the group's activities.
6. Extend the benefits to all persons concerned.

1. Formulating Acceptable Objectives

Too often values are ignored or inadequately explored. Too often we feel that time spent by our groups in planning is lost time. Too often we say, "Let's stop this chatter and get on with the work." But isn't it better that we decide where we want to go before we take to the road? Isn't it wiser to decide what we want to build before we set out to build it? Isn't it important that we set up the specifications for a good citizen before we start citizenship programs?

Behind what we think and do is our set of values, many of which we come by rather unconsciously. They are the products of our learnings and many of them are merely words. Words are not things, they are symbols, and symbols are not problems. Symbols may even block us in understanding problems just as they blocked the Senator who opposed any legislation to control syphilis on the grounds that the word caused a shudder in every decent man and woman. In discussing "goals" and means of reaching them we must go deeper than words.

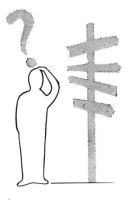

And this is very difficult to do in newly organized groups. Consequently, we are forced to make our own discoveries as to what things others value. We do this by observing what things frighten them, what things they work for, what things they choose, what things they like or dislike, what things they praise or ridicule, what things threaten their security[1] and what are their topics of gossip.

As the group matures it is easier and better to bring the matter of values out into the open. Intentional and purposeful stocktaking will draw to the surface both worthy and questionable values and enable us to come to agreement on things accept-

[1]Maier, Norman R. F., *Principles of Human Relations,* Wiley & Sons, New York, 1952. (See Maier's risk technique* method)

able to the whole group. There is an approved method for doing this and it consists of five steps.

1. Decide whether pleasantness should be widely shared or limited to certain persons and classes. If you decide it should be limited then determine whether you are to be given or denied it.
2. Next project as best you can what values or valued-objects are desired by various group members.
3. Then trace the consequences of each projection taking into account the competing facts and values.
4. Then weigh the consequences as to which will produce a maximum of pleasantness and/or minimum of unpleasantness.
5. Draft a program of action to attain these ends.

Although action is necessary it is not the most difficult step. Becoming aware of the need to search for values is generally considered the most difficult step, and it has far reaching consequences on the behavior of the group. During the search for and evaluation of various values each member comes to realize that he is in effect a "change-agent" responsible for changing his own attitudes as he attempts to change others. Any conscious effort to change values becomes an ethical question. We need not fear such a discussion for generally the areas of agreement are wider than those of disagreement.

An Educational Planning Committee's report which shows how one group came to agreement on a statement of fundamental objectives[2] is reproduced below:

Our Democratic Philosophy

National goals, like individual goals evolve out of experiences. The pioneer came to America because he wanted freedom but the moment he joined a family or other group he assumed responsibilities to it. These two factors; social responsibility and freedom to develop one's individuality seem to be the basis for our present philosophy.

Social Responsibility. We sanction the formation of groups through which individuals may obtain goods and services, but we maintain that these groups are justified only if they strive for efficiency, oppose unfair monopoly, and work for the welfare of all. A great deal of power is often delegated to the officials of

---

[2]Throughout this report the terms "objectives," "goals," and "aims" express the common usage. In our terminology they would be interpreted as intermediate or last means.

these groups. Power over things means power over people and power may reduce freedom unless those holding it discharge the greater social responsibility which it entails. For instance the resources controlled by the present generation do not belong exclusively to it. Future generations have some stake in them too. An unborn generation has the following rights:

1. The right to inherit healthy, well nourished bodies.
2. The right to earn one's way through efficient vocational endeavor.
3. The right to live in comfortable homes.

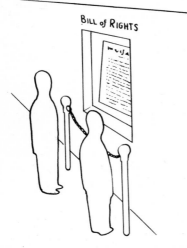

BILL of RIGHTS

4. The right to share in the natural resources.
5. The right to be free from irresponsible monopolistic control over resources and locations.
6. The right to be free from excessive debt.
7. The right to shape society in accordance with its own ideals of democracy.

The extent to which we make it possible for all generations to enjoy these rights is an indication of how we accept our social responsibility.

Individual Freedom. We uphold the right of every individual to develop his individuality up to the limits of his capabilities. This means that we first must discover his abilities, then provide facilities for his education. The process includes not only knowledge about how facts can be used but also how they should be used. And this cannot be done without absolute freedom of inquiry, of speech and of choice.

What Are Our Working Objectives? Educational objectives are concerned with desirable changes in people. We do not know what changes to attempt until we first write the specifications for a good citizen.

Educational facilities are the soils, the resources, the buildings, the equipment, the machines and the supplies needed in the development of a good citizen.

Educational tools are facts, interests, and skills.

Our problem is to become skillful in using these facilities and tools to help our groups reach desirable ends. We find most of our specific objectives can be placed under one or another of four broad categories. They are:

1. Every citizen should be socially acceptable and civically responsible.
2. Every person should be healthy.
3. Every person should be an efficient worker in some useful vocation.
4. Every person should have some recreational interests.

Good citizenship has generally been considered an intangible matter. We think this need not be so and therefore have named four traits which seem important enough to deserve a program for their attainment. (See page 83.) They are dependability, determination, social effectiveness, and progressiveness.

Children have a right to inherit healthy bodies and all of us have a right to grow up strong and vigorous. Since each is expected to be able to carry his own load, each must learn what is good and bad for his health; each must possess health knowledge, health skills, health habits, and health attitudes.

Work has built, written, spoken—in fact, it has produced all the good things in life. We need more of it. Our national economic goal should be to produce all the things people really need at prices low enough for them to be able to buy; and to so distribute incomes that no one will be shut off from consumption except those who refuse to work. Economic independence is an important goal in any realistic educational program. This depends upon a full functioning and efficient economy; which in turn depends upon well-trained workers and an expanding industrial development.

Trained workers does not necessarily mean more schooling but it does mean better schooling—schooling which prepares a worker to enter employment at an early age and which provides continuous study opportunities for all ages. A well adjusted

worker is a happy and efficient worker, but workers cannot do all the adjusting—part, in fact the major part is the responsibility of management. Most important in employer-employee relationships is the feeling of each worker that he is appreciated and has a real share in determining the policies that effect his life. A job is a man's life—he spent years training for it, and he expects to spend his future at it. The business is the employee's business too and many employees have a much longer time to spend in it than the employer. The War Manpower Commission stated the following four foundations for good relationships.

1. Let the worker know how he is getting along.
2. Give credit where credit is due.
3. Tell people in advance about changes that will affect them.
4. Make the best use of each person's abilities.

Industrial expansion depends upon a certain flexibility of mind on the part of both business managers and workers. The past is filled with restrictive agreements and stabilization accords which tend to freeze organizations, procedures, job duties, prices, resources, services, and policies into a traditional pattern. This is regimentation, whether it be business, labor or governmental institutions. If we are wise and flexible, we should plan to regulate big institutions to the lives of the people instead of allowing them to control our lives.

There are many reasons why we need more planning of a broader type than any business can undertake alone. Together business, labor, agriculture, and government could solve some of the problems confronting us. The facility with which the problems of the atomic bomb were solved leads us to believe that we need only mobilize our resources in order to solve any problem—and we have the resources. America has:

1. Skilled manpower
2. The largest industrial plant capacity in the world
3. Great resources, both natural and technological inventions and scientific procedures
4. The most scientific farm plant in the world
5. An enormous backlog of demand for housing, transportation, education, health, and communication needs
6. The greatest accumulation of savings any nation has ever known.

Conditions are ripe for the greatest era of advancement or the greatest depression we have ever known. Only resolute and courageous planning can save us from skyrocketing to our disaster. We must think forward, not backward.

The soundest basis for new decisions is facts. Facts are discovered through research. Both technological and socio-economic and educational research laboratories should be legislatively supported. These laboratories should be available to small business and small governmental and educational institutions on a fee basis or, in some cases, free.

An economic survey of each major industry should be made by qualified research workers who are given complete freedom in publishing results. These studies will provide facts to allay the fears of businessmen regarding the future.

Fear is the major reason underlying unemployment, business stagnation, and job dissatisfaction; and fear is generated by lack of facts. Management fearful of the profits of business because it does not have all the facts regarding the supply of materials, labor and power or regarding the demand for the finished product, hesitates to expand or change operations. Labor fearful of its returns, demands security in seniority rulings, work limitations, frozen job duties, job insurance and social security legislation. The remedy for fear is facts.

In an expanding and balanced productive economy, society must continuously redistribute the resources and the workers between different enterprises according to the needs of each. To facilitate the movement of materials and labor, such restraints as tariff barriers, differential transportation costs, patent office prohibitions and certain commercial, professional and labor association restrictions which permit one group to take advantage of others should be removed.

When there are people with wants in a country rich in resources, it seems unreasonable that the productive machine should become stalled—especially when there are workers willing to convert the resources into goods which could satisfy their wants. The answer is facts plus the right attitudes.

It is good for everyone to have leisure but it is better if he has earned it. The world's work must be done even if it is difficult and routine. Only after we have produced more than our daily consumption are we free to enjoy leisure. Some people would have us believe that leisure is more important than work. Others teach that the pursuit of leisure is the major aim of education. But of the four objectives listed above we are sure that recreation is not first.

When the body becomes tired and the spirit dull, then man needs recreation. Fortunate indeed is he who finds such interest in his job that he obtains his recreation in it. But not all jobs can carry high interest; and as compensation for the routine tasks that must be done, man builds a dream world. Even during spare moments on the job, his reveries furnish compensations for his physical and social restrictions. More important than these are the more purposeful recreations such as are provided in literature, art, music, and the other forms of culture. Such subjects are the basis of cultural education, and the aim of instructors should be to develop appreciations and interests which will make life more enjoyable.

Leisure should not be considered a time-killing vacuum, but an opportunity for creative achievement, social contribution and personal satisfaction. Play time is a cultural time, provided one has acquired sufficient capital to be able to purchase the tools of culture.

Play motives are complex, each having an individual interpretation, but for the most part they are compensatory. When satisfactions are low in our daily life, we play to find recognition, assertion, and muscular stimulation. Play provides expression for social and sex motives too. We expect everyone to have earned the right to play.

The Committee proposed four so-called educational objectives. It based these upon its understanding of the philosophy of democracy which it spelled-out in some detail. But merely identifying objectives is no guarantee that they will be attained. Objectives always contain an element of the new. Planning means new patterns are desired and those most active in the planning are most likely to accept the new patterns.[3] Persons associated with those who are changing are likely to change too. Persons who commit themselves when decisions are made are more likely to act than those not involved in the deciding. This means that group members should not be excluded from the planning.

Well integrated groups find no difficulty in formulating objectives. However in new groups it may be necessary to delay the all-out planning until a certain level of maturity has been reached. As a group enters the discussion of problems, and prior to the

    [3]Watson, Jeane, "Scientists and Sweetbreads," *Adult Leadership,* V2:No. 9, pp. 26, Feb., 1954.

time it ranks them, the leader should raise questions like the following:

1. Why is this problem important to us?
2. How will its solution affect our group and others?
3. What are the most important things in life?
4. What do all people deserve?

This sort of an exploration is sure to uncover controversial issues, and this should not distress us, for these are the kinds of issues adults want to discuss. Only a fearful chairman living under the false impression that differences always lead to hostility will skim lightly around them.

A group should select its own problems and it may do it more objectively by using a problem score card similar to the one below. Experience has shown us that problems scoring 80 or above generally challenge.

Problem score card	**Points**
1. Is the problem interesting or associated with interesting things?	20
2. Is it important and useful to me?	20
3. Is it urgent?	20
4. Is it neither too easy nor too difficult to challenge me?	20
5. Do I clearly and definitely understand it?	20

In using this score card each member should score each problem independently, the scores for each problem should be summed and the totals used in ranking. But before a problem is chosen it must be determined if it can be solved by a group; that is, is it a group or an individual problem.

2. Selecting the Important Problems and Placing Them on a Priority List

The second step in problem solving is that of deciding upon the order in which each problem will be attacked. Different problems carry different interests for different persons, but it is desired that all persons be involved in each problem. My interest is more likely on your problem if I know when to expect your interest on mine. Placing problems on a priority list is important in that it aids the flow of interests both forward and backward. As the group matures there will be less talk about "your problem," "my problem" and "their problem" and more mention of "our problems." When the "our problem" time arrives a priority list becomes less important from the interest-building aspect, nevertheless it is good planning to know what comes up next.

3. Formulating Hypotheses

The procedure to use in choosing the most probable of the several alternative hypotheses will depend upon whether or not the group possesses all the pertinent facts.

Suppose a problem has been introduced and accepted as "our problem." The chairman should immediately call for conclusions and advise against discussing any one until all possible answers have been given. This is the proper procedure in spite of the fact that we have been cautioned not to decide until all the facts are in. The natural way is to "jump to a conclusion" just as the man on the ferry boat did. The cautious thinker does this, but he holds his first conclusion as tentative until he has had time to test it.

MERELY SUSPEND JUDGMENT
DON'T ABDICATE IT

From this point the chairman should proceed differently depending upon which of the following circumstances exist:

1. If two or more answers have been given.
2. If only one answer has been given and the entire group agrees that it is the correct one.
3. If no answer of any kind has been given.

The first situation is the one most desired and usually it is attained if the problem was properly selected and adequately introduced. With two or more conclusions before the group, the chairman should ask for statements in support of each. When the ideas are contributed he should make it clear that they now are the property of the group and no longer belong to the person who contributed them. Thus, ideas rather than persons may be discussed.

The chairman should attempt to keep the arguments balanced by trying to draw out statements which reinforce the weaker arguments or which attack the weak places in the stronger arguments. As various statements are presented the group should be permitted to explain, comment, criticize and modify them, and this should continue until a trend in the thinking is evident or until some general idea appears.

If only one conclusion is presented then the chairman should introduce plausible alternative answers with arguments strong enough to establish doubt. Anyone who accepts the proposed alternative should then be allowed to argue for it. Here again the arguments should be presented in such order as to maintain a balance if possible.

If no answer is contributed, the leader should raise questions about various parts of the problem. This means that the leader will have to be prepared with questions that may serve as a basis for the discussion. If still no answer is presented, the leader may suggest two or more possible answers asking the group to test them. If the group is unable to test these the discussion should be delayed until the facts are obtained. Certain members may be delegated to gather the facts or to secure a "resource leader" who may present them.

Before proceeding it may be well to determine whether or not the problem up for discussion is one the group really wants to discuss at this time. If the decision is to continue, then those assigned to gather facts may proceed as follows:

1. Review the literature, or interview workers in this and related fields.
2. Work under pressure in order to become saturated with the subject matter.
3. Keep notes, classify and reclassify them; many times our best ideas come to us when we are merely sorting our ideas. Because facts are scanty and beliefs abundant in social-civic areas, it is well that we continuously question the various beliefs we hold. Such questioning frequently uncovers a new hypothesis.

Searching for facts. Reporters who seek facts through personal interviews have been instructed as follows: first, become familiar with the general topic; second, phrase specific questions about which you want information; third, be friendly, frank, and fair throughout the interview; and fourth, be a good listener.

Interviewers should be mindful of the fact that witnesses vary in their ability to observe and in their capacity to report evidence. They have a tendency to see and remember things according to their notion of what should happen. Thus we are apt to find conflicting statements between those interviewed.

Those assigned to search the writings of the experts will find that experts differ too. Thus they should examine the motives and the quality of the work of each authority. Statements by prestige persons are not in themselves proof.

The authoritative voice of the learned has many times delayed the acceptance of new ideas. Harvey's discovery of blood circulation was "laid on the table" for a generation just as Lister's discovery of antiseptics was opposed by early medical authorities. Many times "the voice of experience" has said, "My years of experience has shown how absurd are all new ideas."

In spite of this we must rely upon authorities because we know how impossible it is for us to know everything. Because scientists so generally are motivated to discover "truth" and because they so seldom refuse to retest their conclusions they have become our ideal authorities. Nevertheless their prestige has been used to influence us in unscientific ways. Advertisers sometimes say "Science says" without presenting evidence. Congressmen have been known to declare "I don't have to prove it, scientifically it's a fact."

When we attempt to get facts from lectures, meetings, demonstrations, exhibits, pictures and the like we must consider the motives of those who called the meeting or prepared the exhibits. The usual motives of those who call audiences together is to influence people. Skillful speakers using emotionally loaded language realize how they can make an audience vibrate to words. No harm is done if the audience realizes that it is being emo-

tionally aroused. We should approach audience situations psychologically prepared to evaluate the motives of the performers. We should realize that such statements as: "any informed person knows . . . ," "a farmer with his feet on the ground realizes . . . ," and "Aristotle said . . . ," are aimed to influence us. One bright boy realized this when he changed the quotation, "all right-thinking people will inevitably agree" to "all who agree with me will agree with me."

A third way to obtain facts is to enter a discussion. Herein we expect to see the interplay of ideas, with each person being given an opportunity to voice his agreement or disagreement and to give his reasons.

The fourth way is to plan an experimental project. Collecting

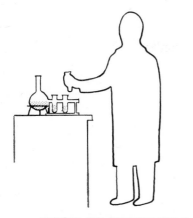

TEST OF TESTIMONY

data by means of experiments consists of at least two skills.

First there is the skill of observing similarities or differences. Observation must be accurate and this means reducing subjective judgments to objective measures. Observation must be extensive. Grain graders take many samples from different parts of a carload of wheat. The accuracy of the grade assigned depends largely upon the extensiveness of the sampling. Observation should include all typical cases, but debators and salesmen select only the favorable facts and ignore the unfavorable arguments, and this has given rise to the statement, "Each question has three sides, your side, my side, and the right side."

Classifying the facts. The second skill is that of arranging the data in orderly sequence. The mechanics of note taking is rather simple if the data is placed upon cards which may later be rearranged according to any classification scheme. Difficulties arise, however, when we set up classification schemes. Since new discoveries are continuously upsetting older classification systems we must keep alert to the newer evidence. Classification has its basis in definitions and a definition consists of two essential parts:

1. Include the term in a general class.
2. Exclude if from all but one subclass of the general class.

It follows, (a) that the subclasses must be mutually exclusive, (b) that all subclasses must be accounted for, and (c) that the controlling purpose must not be changed during the course of the classification. Classification is the key to the discovery of relationships, and skill in classification comes through practice.

Most groups have within its membership a great storehouse of facts and beliefs which should be classified before any outside facts are added. When a "resource person" who believes in group development is called in, he will act quite differently from those who consider themselves merely as expert "fact-givers." His strategy is essentially one of "pumping" all the ideas from the group before he adds his facts.

Below is an example of a fact finding, classifying and evaluating discussion taken from a "Future Farmers" meeting. The members, their teacher acting as the resource person, and several of their fathers were present to discuss the problem of selecting sows for their group project.

The president said the purpose of the meeting was to decide upon the purchase of some sows. He said, "We know of several for sale," and then called upon the teacher to tell about them. The teacher said, "Two of our boys were at Peter Granger's farm a few days ago and he asked if any of the class wanted to buy a couple of his gilts." The gilts were described and a number of questions were asked, which brought out the following facts. These were placed upon the blackboard.

	Gilt 1	Gilt 2
Age	7 mos.	6 mos.
Weight	210 lb.	190 lb.
Size of litter	12	8
No. raised to 6 mos.	10	7
Litter weight at 6 mos.	1800 lbs.	1530 lbs.
Dam came from litter of	8	7
Sire came from litter of	10	10

Which one of these is the best buy?" the teacher asked.

The vote favored Gilt 1, and all agreed it was the better because it came from a larger litter and a productive line. It had also made a satisfactory gain. The discussion appeared to be over.

"These figures indicate that Gilt 1 should have weighed about 180 pounds at six months and Gilt 2, 190 pounds," the teacher said. "That makes Gilt 2 the best gainer."

"But the litter was smaller," spoke up one of the dads.

"That's true, and I wonder why? Pete's a good feeder." The teacher paused. It was evident that everyone was trying to find the answer.

"Say!" exploded one of the boys. "Wasn't that gilt from the sow Pete bought at the Cravens' sale?"

"Yes, he brought her home just three days before she far-rowed," the teacher answered.

"What kind of feeder is Cravens?" asked the student.

"He doesn't pay so much attention to his gilts until the new corn comes in. Then he fattens them for his sale. His sales are always late," spoke another father.

"Then that accounts for it," the student said. "The smaller litter was probably due to the fact that the sow wasn't flushed before breeding," he concluded.

"Would you select Gilt 2?" one of the boys asked.

"I think so, provided . . . ."

"Provided what?" questioned the teacher.

"Provided she had ten well-developed teats," the student answered.

"Most of you will not be able to get as many facts and figures about the pigs you buy as we have here, so don't you think it would be a good idea to list the good points we want a sow to have?" the teacher asked.

The group summarized the facts that had been discussed and the teacher wrote the conclusions on the blackboard.

Whether or not we discover the right solution to a problem will depend upon our skill in fitting together facts that express orderly relationships. In all good reasoning, three fundamental conditions must be met.

They are:

1. Once a term has been defined, that meaning must be retained throughout the argument. We cannot understand an argument unless we understand the meaning of the terms, and it is trickery to change the meaning in the hope that the difference will not be noticed.

2. The relationships expressed in the argument must be real and significant. It is safe to argue from one set of facts to another only when there is a casual relationship between them. Objects and events are related in varying degrees. There are accidental or chance relationships; correlated, that is, occasional but not perfect relationships; and universal relationships. The inexperienced and uncritical often err in claiming an accidental or correlated relationship to be universal.

3. Only those relationships expressed in the premise may be expressed in the conclusion. In this way we maintain coherent fact systems. For instance:
   If Milwaukee is north of Chicago (premise)
   Then Chicago is south of Milwaukee (conclusion)

But if we should argue:
   If Milwaukee is north of Chicago (premise)
   Then Washington is south of New York (conclusion)
the system would be incoherent.

We err when we state a relationship that does not exist. This error is frequently found in "if-then" arguments. The argument, "If you wish to enter nurses' training, then you must graduate from high school," may be completed in four ways, only two of which are correct. For example, this conclusion is faulty: "I do not want to enter nurses' training; therefore I need not finish high school."

One must be careful in using "some-all" argument because there are so many combinations of the "all," "some," and "none" terms. In simple form the statements, "women are incapable of superior achievement" and "private industry stimulates initiative," are both in error because a part is mistaken for the whole. When caught making all-inclusive statements, many persons commit another error in claiming that "there are exceptions to every rule."

The common man has a tendency to classify his ideas into two opposing categories, for example, friend versus foe, rich versus poor, good versus bad, and theoretical versus practical. Here he overextends the "either-or" argument, because relationships are rarely so distinct. For instance, when is something hot enough to cease being cold or dry enough to cease being wet, or theoretical enough to not be practical? Darwin, was a great theorist, but he spent more than 20 years gathering facts before he stated his theroy of evolution. Every theory has its roots in some practice, every practice is based upon some expectation. Which is the most impractical: the man who develops the new idea or the generation which refused to accept it? Is it impractical

to be ahead of the crowd or to be behind the leaders?

By meeting the three fundamental conditions, we assure the soundness of our reasoning. When we are searching for and classifying facts we should be aware that, we are confronted with an accumulation of habits, hopes, hates, fears, superstitions, and failures which handicap our thinking.

Avoiding Common Errors in Thinking—Propaganda Tricks.[4]

Sometimes we substitute habits, hopes, hates, etc., for thinking. Sometimes they are called forth by those who would distort and influence our thinking to their ends. Consequently we must be on our guard against the common errors in thinking described below.

Rationalization.—Our intellect does not function apart from our personality. It is the whole person who thinks; consequently all of one's habits, experiences, emotions, and desires are involved in our conclusions. Because our habits permit us to act comfortably and easily, we often prefer to rationalize our behavior by searching for an ostensibly good reason for doing and believing as we do. A glance at the past may show how far we have gone in rationalizing our beliefs.

From the earliest days man has been a defeatist in his thinking about human life and social order. He has been repeatedly told, until he believed it, that he is helplessly in the grip of superhuman powers and natural forces. Wars, plagues, catastrophes, tyranny of rulers, and exploitation have been explained and justified by these beliefs. Indeed they have been interpreted as well-merited punishment or as happenings necessary to strengthen his character.

It has now become evident that these basic assumptions and the concepts of forces controlling social and economic behavior are but elaborate metaphors and are decidedly misleading. As the evidence increasingly shows, social order is not a part of nature; it is not a system out in space. Social order is in man; it is man's self chosen design for living. What he values and how he feels, what he chooses to cultivate or reject, constitutes his social order. Social order is not given, it is achieved.

It is easy to rationalize our hopes and beliefs into explanations of our behavior. It is easy to fall into error by declaring our beliefs to be facts. And it takes courage and imagination to unshackle our beliefs and remold our habits, and to face the changes in our modes of living that are warranted by the new knowledge which accumulates

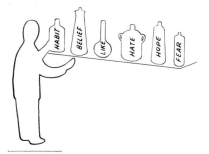

[4]See also Schramm, Wilber (Ed), *Mass Communications,* University of Illinois Press, Urbana, Ill., 1949.

during each generation. Change discounts experience, and those who are not honest often block progress because they fear they will loose status in the change.

Establishing a new idea has never been an easy process; consequently those expecting to bring about changes should design the learning situations as a series of climaxes because change occurs most easily in times of stress—when we are confronted with a crisis. They must think of changing attitudes as a revolution rather as an evolution of ideas, for life seems to move in discontinuities rather than in smooth, forward sweeps.

Superstition.—Superstitions are beliefs that have little or no factual basis. We seldom realize how we acquired them; we may even deny being moved by them. But yet we light a candle in a storm, or carry a four-leaf clover, or hang up horseshoes, or refuse to light three cigarettes with the same match. Because of our lack of facts, some persons attempt to take advantage of us

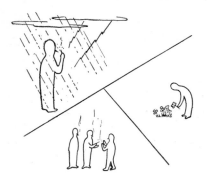

by playing upon our superstitions. Our protection is in facts, our duty is to experiment rather than to rely upon unproven relationships.

Fears.—Unwise parents and unscrupulous exploiters ply upon our fears by pointing terrible spectacles of bogeymen, radicals, reds, royalists, politicians, plutocrats, and plunderers. They threaten us with loss of job or social status, ill health or that an intruder will enter into our area of specialization.

Fear themes constitute a large proportion of all ads. Mothers have been told to fear germs, laxatives, constipation, and overweight. Father is made fearful of facing a room full of executives unless he is full of bran, iron or oranges. Brother is taught to fear his pink toothbrush and sister her B.O.

Here are some of the rules given to soldiers to help them overcome fear: (1) Perfect your training until you have confidence in your ability and skill. (2) Understand your objective and keep planning each move step by step to achieve it. (3) Admit the fact that you, your comrades, and the enemy are all afraid. These rules seem to apply equally well to all of us. One cannot think clearly when beset with fear.

Hates.—In hate we set out to injure and despoil; we become vindictive and distort our conclusions. Bigots use hate to obtain their end. It is easy to stir up hate; destruction is easier than construction. But there are times where hate seems justified— when the enemy must be destroyed—and then we must decide whether the object is worth fighting for and what some of the outcomes will be before we permit hate to stir us up.

Appeals to authority.—Children easily dispose of an argument by saying, "Mother said so." Adults dispose of their arguments less directly by introducing such statements as "everyone knows," "experience proves," "commonsense dictates," and "it is ridiculous to think otherwise." These are appeals to authority.

The patent medicine peddler, by dress and scientific jargon, seeks the prestige of an authority. Less brazen persons present their claims to authority by "my years of experience," "I have mothered three children," "speaking as an engineer," or "I have studied under . . . ."

Advertisers appeal to authority in such general terms as "science says," "business leaders know," or "the best people use . . ." and thus overextend the some-all argument. If educated to a point slightly below that at which intelligent criticism begins we become eager customers for "laboratory tested" tobacco, "scientifically blended" eyewash, "sanitary" cellophane wrapped string beans or "posture tested" bed springs.

It is not always easy to distinguish between false and true authority. A true authority keeps abreast of the most recent knowledge. He recognizes changes and does not fear loss of prestige because he changes his views. He does not consider himself competent in all fields because of his thorough knowledge in one. If an authority has a reason for a statement, then the reason rather than the person is the test. If reasons are not deemed necessary because the authority has insight, then the argument is circular; that is, authority makes insight and insight makes authority.

Restatement.—A hundred "wrongs" do not make a "right"—neither does one "wrong" repeated one hundred times. Nevertheless every day repetition is substituted and mistaken for proof in arguments and advertising. For instance, "If you want love interest, then try this dainty way. It's glamorous! It's feminine! It's alluring! Men love the fragrance of Linderence." The politician who claims loudly, "Relief destroys character. If you give a person something for nothing, it is bound to destroy his character," is not presenting proof; he is repeating himself. Many persons have learned that loud and insistent talk gets action, but it takes more than noise to make a truth.

Compromise.—It is arithmetically correct to let an average figure represent group data. But is is not correct to use the concept to resolve an argument in which two extreme views have been contrasted and no agreement seems possible. On such occasions someone not particularly interested in the outcome offers to compromise the differences by claiming that the true answer lies midway between the extremes. This argument fails if another view is introduced, for a mid-value may then be found between it and either of the other two views; thus we have two middle of the road values.

A compromise is not honest because it sacrifices the integrity of the individual. A person has the right to be right even though he be in the minority. A compromise is insincere, and those who propose it err in thinking that differences are undesirable. A compromise is only temporary. Rebalancing power offers no solution; it creates no new values; it only postpones the fighting.

Even when it is legitimate to use the concept of an average value, we should examine the reference data, for the unscrupulous often select their cases in order to prove their point.

Analogies.—Argument by analogy is not necessarily a dishonest argument, although it always requires careful scrutiny. If one ball is glass, red, and large and another ball is glass, red and small, it can be argued that the first is like the second, only in respect to material and color.

To argue that instincts, like steam, must have an outlet, otherwise they burst forth, is to argue by analogy. To argue, "Why should congressmen be elected? We don't trust children to elect their teachers," is false analogy. Likewise it is false to argue, "You can no more analyse love, patriotism, and religion than you can dissect a body without killing it."

Scientists use analogy with considerable success, especially when developing a new generalization. For instance, because elm, oak, maple, and many other trees have leaves, we assume all trees have leaves. But after developing this hypothesis, the scientist diligently seeks an exception, and in this respect he differs from the ordinary thinker. The fact that one dog finds his way home does not prove that dogs possess a homing instinct. Many become lost.

Emotionally colored words.—There is no argument against using emotionally colored words nor against being swayed by them upon occasion. Emotions are a proper part of appreciation, and it lends interest to our discourse. Our error is in not knowing when we are so swayed or in using emotions to promote a measure that will result in harm or injustice.

Once we are on the lookout for the difference between "objective" and "emotional" meanings, we begin to notice how frequently emotional terms are used in controversial issues. Note the differences in feelings attached to the following sets of words when they are used to characterize human beings:

dog	half-breed	mongrel
firm	obstinate	pig-headed
bad	ugly	repulsive
stern	mean	vicious

In attempting to decide a question of fact, it is wise first to reduce any highly colored words to neutral terms. Snarl words like **red, filthy, crackpot, scoundrel;** purr words like **charming, brilliant, progressive;** and action words like **come here! hart!** are phrased to influence us. But unless our discourse carries effective terms, it is not interesting, and unless it is accurate it is not informative.

There are times when speakers deliberately use affective terms to convince or confuse the listener. Ridicule of an opponent by use of emotionally colored words is not only bad taste; it is bad thinking.

CAUGHT BY CATCHY PHRASES

Catchy phrases. — Complicated problems seldom have easy answers, and yet many people demand that each problem be reduced to a simple formula. Instead of taking time to understand a proposition, they ask us to substitute a slogan. They reduce Darwin's complicated theory to "man from monkey" and Einstein's mathematical physics to "everything is relative." Advertisers seeking sales invent such action terms as the "American way," "free enterprise," "milk for health," and "social security" which disregard many of the finer meanings. Such expressions serve useful purposes as summary statements, provided we have complete understanding of the meanings implied. But if they become merely catchy phrases with uncertain meanings, they are apt to confuse and lead us into error.

Words are not things—they are symbols; and they become nonsense symbols when their meaning is not clear. It is rather difficult to find meaning in the following statement: "The adviser has more power than he could use, even if he had the authority."

Purposive judgments.—Many of the difficulties we encounter in reaching agreements are due to differences in values which different persons hold. We can not ignore values, so we must view all judgments in the light of the purposes behind them.

We can best deal with our own desires by admitting them, just as we deal with our fears. The admission, however, is complicated by the fact that we do not always recognize our particular prejudices because they have become so much a part of us. Nevertheless we must understand how wishes influence our thinking. They lead us, for example, to detect errors in argument against our beliefs more readily than errors in favor of our beliefs. They help us to remember favorable facts and forget unfavorable facts. Many of the things we see or remember are things we

want to see or remember and things we don't want to see or remember we just won't see. We should always be on guard against our desires.

Every day we meet persons who try to convince us to believe as they do. In the absence of real relationships, they turn to the devices just discussed. They plant the seed of suspicion, they mock a movement with scorn, they stir up hates, they dismember a cause with ridicule, they call upon authority, they repeat themselves, they try to strike a middle ground that does not exist, they invent catchy phrases that do away with the need for thinking, or they cover their desires with odds and ends of thought that clutter up our thinking.

Our ability to evaluate their arguments depends upon our knowledge of the relationships expressed and our resistance to being swayed by emotion.

How to Decide. Most of our decisions are made without any conscious effort. This is because they are based upon beliefs or theories which serve as standard patterns or guides to behavior. These beliefs if strongly held permit of no exceptions. In order to maintain these beliefs we may even go so far as to ignore data contrary to them.

When we see alternative answers our decisions become more difficult. Then the first step is to trace the consequences of each alternative. Rather than to ask ourselves, "What shall we do?" it is better that we ask, "What will happen if we do this? Or that?" This opens the way for us to estimate the probability of each action contemplated. Then we may examine the desirability of each and choose between them.

If we can't decide and let the matter drift we become distraught with tensions. Under pressure to decide, we may come to think that any decision is better than none and throw ourselves forward with a fatalistic hope that the outcome will be favorable. Or we may dodge our responsibility to think, by hiding behind a majority vote and thus have others to blame if the outcome is adverse.

There are two reasons for indecision: fear of others and fear of ourselves. Fear of others forces decision in accordance with their wishes. We may fear our ability to decide because we have always had to conform. Being thus intimidated we may reject our own wishes and desires and develop into a neutral personality.

Scientific thinking is a method of thinking. One who expects to do it must hold himself ready to change. And when he undertakes the study of any phenomenon he must ask clear questions, report unprejudiced observations, revise unsubstantiated assumptions and submit his conclusions to retesting. It is desirable that

he apply the method "across the board" but often we find him
only a part-time scientist, fulfilling his obligations to his pro-
fession but failing to put the method into operation in his every-
day thinking.

When a group must decide it is important that we use
consensus* devices which permit everyone to express himself on
each issue without being "stampeded" or "railroaded."

SUMMARY

Problem solving has been emphasized in this section, and
the first three steps have been discussed in detail. They are concerned with the determination of objectives and the ways and
means of attaining them. Understanding clearly what we are
trying to do and why, has a tremendous influence upon speeding
up the action processes. Becoming skillful in the methods for
gathering and analysing data should increase the accuracy of the
solutions proposed. But no matter how good the thinking, group
problems cannot be solved without a group. Consequently we
must be concerned with group processes as well as thinking
processes. This will be the subject matter for the next section.

SECTION IV

*Group Maturity*_____

The topics for this section are those concerned with the growth and maturity of a group. They are the last three items on the Problem Score Card.* They are necessary in the solution of a group problem, for without a group no group problem could be solved.

Chapter 10 is titled "Integrating Persons and Agencies into Task Forces." This brings the factors of change into focus. We form a group to initiate some change; consequently, the organization should be designed with respect to the type of change anticipated.

Groups need officers and officers need skill. The skills of the leadership team are discussed in Chapter 11.

Participation is the key to all group work. High quality participation can be learned only through practice. Getting participation is the topic for Chapter 12.

Probably nothing distinguishes a mature from an immature group any better than its ability to look critically at itself, its goals, its skills and its processes. Evaluation is the fifth step in problem solving and the subject matter for Chapter 13.

The final judgment of a group's maturity is its willingness to spread the benefits of its action to other persons. This will be the topic for Chapter 14.

Morale is hard to get and easy to lose

Chapter 10.

INTEGRATING PERSONS AND AGENCIES INTO TASK FORCES

Ever increasing amounts of work are being carried on by teams. Teams design plans, conduct research, extend knowledge, implement programs and evaluate results. Even in the Armed Forces where we thought that the General made all the decisions and issued the orders, we find staff teams are planning the strategy and task forces are taking the objectives. The outcome depends upon the degree of integration, that is, upon the processes which strengthen, regulate and perpetuate the group.

Teamwork is here to stay and fruitful cooperation will depend upon our skill both in matching men to jobs and in matching men to men. Whether it be a new job or a new group, we will have new things to learn, and for most of us it will mean a change in our behavior.

HOW TO CHANGE BEHAVIOR

Change isn't easy, its just inevitable; but it would not be as difficult, according to Dr. Wm. A. White, the noted psychiatrist, if we were taught the history and growth of ideas and knew more about the changes which have occurred in law, politics, science and religion in the past.

Social change is man made and the events follow each other in the following sequence:[1]

1. Invention is the first g r e a t disturber, but there is time to anticipate its impact. It usually takes about 30 years from the birth of an idea until it is accepted and put into general practice.

[1] Ogburn, Wm. F., "Technological Trends and National Policy," *Nat. Res. Comm. House Doc. 630*, 75th Cong. 1st Session, Washington, D. C., 1937.

2. Next come changes in the economic organizations most closely associated with the invention. For instance, railroad financing was an important change which followed the invention of the steam locomotive.

3. Next come changes in the social habits of persons closely associated with the economic organizations.

4. Then, these changes bring about changes in social organizations one step removed, such as the family, the school and the church.

5. Finally we make changes in our philosophies and codes.

The great number of new discoveries and inventions with which we come into daily contact make it relatively easy for us to change our ways of living. We know the facts about the changes in rocks, plants, soils, buildings and equipment. We know how civilization has risen and fallen because of changes in natural resources. We have had much success in controlling nature here in America, and we look upon technological change as something desirable.

But when it comes to social change we have an altogether different idea. Sociologists discovered our resistance and called it cultural lag. Some even go so far as to advise that we hinder the faster processes rather than hasten the slower ones.

This dual attitude regarding change is a tremendous handicap to achieving the better life in the atomic age. Students of

sociology find the newspapers, the schools, the state and the church are as often as not opponents to new ideas. They at times provide censors against those things that force us to question our old beliefs. Mort and Cornell[2] found that there was a lapse of about 30 years between the time the first person got a new idea and the time the first school did anything about it. There was another 30 year period before as many as 50 per cent of the schools took up the idea.

Those of us concerned with social change are confronted with three problems. The first is to marshall the facts. Knowledge*

[2]Mort, Paul R., and Cornell, Francis G., *American Schools in Transition,* Bureau of Publications, Teacher's College, Columbia University, New York, 1941.

has been placed in three catagories (1) scientific, (2) practical and (3) intuitive. These include what we know, but there are other states of nature about which no one knows.

Because in the Western civilization we are accustomed to discovery, invention and rapid technological change, most of us have no difficulty in making adjustments to scientific knowledge. Because practical knowledge comes into daily use and is frequently checked against our experiences, we find no great difficulty in changing it. But intuitive knowledge offers us more difficulty. If we liberally supported persons playing philosopher roles and more diligently studied their philosophies we might find it easier to negotiate changes in these fields. At any rate, group leaders should explain the different kinds of facts and discuss the difficulties encountered in substituting a new fact for an old one in each category.

The second problem, that of negotiating change in the area of attitudes and feelings is much like the first problem. Take for example one's dislike for milk. The facts about milk should convince anyone that milk is good to drink but some still refuse because they don't like it. Lewin[3] described change tactics in three steps.

1. Unfreeze the present level.
2. Move up to the new level.
3. Freeze at the new level.

And he said that a considerable degree of emotional stir-up may be necessary to unfreeze the present and refreeze at the new level. Furthermore he said that any change has a better chance of succeeding if the step-up is great rather than small. It seems that when a person gives up a belief he gives it up lock, stock and barrel.

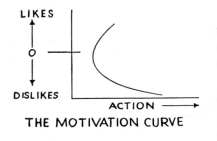

THE MOTIVATION CURVE

Scherwin[4] verified this by showing that actions increased as both likes and dislikes increased.

Both facts and feelings have been used in health education. First we used lectures, posture pictures, films, stories, clowns,

[3]Lewin, Kurt, "Frontiers to Group Dynamics," *Journ. Soc. Issues* 1:5, 1948.
[4]Foreman, Bob, *Listening in Advertising and Selling,* May, 1949.

and sugar coated songs. Then we tried fears, horror scenes, naked truths and awful consequences.[5] Nothing much happened. There is no denying the importance of facts and feelings but even so, used alone or together they are not enough.

The third problem is the one of getting action. Three media have been used.

Mass media which seems the natural means for reaching many people do at best little more than change "verbal sentiments."[6] Propaganda is more effective in reinforcing our prejudices than in giving us new facts. This comes about because we remember best those things with which we agree and forget those things with which we disagree.

Individual means have long been used by teachers. They form classes of individuals, ask for individual work, expect individual decisions, and give individual rewards. The ability to surpass is their criterion of the method. But the results have been disappointing. We get competition instead of contribution.

Group methods indicate that the force of a group are about the most effective means for changing behavior.[6] Involvement is

the key, but involvement is not attained by individual or mass approaches. Both of these place a person in a psychologically isolated position. Involvement takes place within a group and it includes group planning, group decision, group action and results in a feeling of we-ness." After the members have committed themselves they seem unwilling to depart from the standards of the group. Not only does a group decision produce a new idea, it produces a new feeling-tone, too. It produces the satisfactions of having passed through the verbal level and onto the action level.

As group workers we are in fact "change agents" and should use the forces of the group as well as mass and individual forces.

[5]Goldston, Iago, "Motivation in Health Education," *Journ. Am. Diet. Assoc.*, 25:745, 1949

[6]Lewin, Kurt, and Grabble, Paul, "Problems of Re-education," *Journ. Soc. Issues* 1-3, Aug., 1945.

Let us summarize these forces.[7,8,9]

1. People act in accordance with the patterns which they have found make sense in their over-all design for living. Culture serves to keep life in a groove and we repeat the behavior we have found satisfactory in solving our problems.

2. People do not change their patterns of behavior unless they feel a need for things not satisfied by existing patterns. New problems produce new tensions and groups under tension are ripe for change.

3. People act as members of a group. They do pretty much as those in their group think they should. Persons may be changed deeply and suddenly by changes in the group atmosphere. To change the group atmosphere, we must upset the present constellation of forces which hold it in balance and then immediately liberate the forces of the new pattern. Change should be planned with the group concerned. Thus the group will understand the nature of the change and the change-agent the nature of the group. Any amendments to the program should be communicated to the group with the reason. Administrative leaders do not need to fear admitting their errors. It is better to have the people believe the administration honest than infallible. They never believe the latter anyway. The re-educative process takes time—it must change the groups value-structure, its knowledge and its motor reactions.

From the above list it seems clear that the patterns of change should be discussed with the persons concerned. Such a discussion should include the following:

1. Should life be considered a series of problems?

2. Can we learn to act in the drama of life as both an actor and an observer?

3. Can we be happy in the experiment?
    Do we understand why change is desired?
    How does change take place?
    How can we overcome the obstacles to change?

Had these things been discussed it might not have been necessary for Moses to have kept the children of Israel in the wilderness for 40 years until those who had lived in slavery had died and a new generation had learned to live as free men.

[7]Lewin, Kurt, "The Special Case of Germany," *Pub. Opin. Quart.*, 7:555, 1943.
[8]Lewin, Kurt, and Grabble, Paul, "Conduct, Knowledge and Acceptance of New Value," *Journ. Soc.*, Issues 1:53, Aug., 1945.
[9]Leighton, Alexander H., *The Governing of Men*, Princeton University Press, Princeton, New Jersey, 1945.

For those interested in examples of the influence of the group at work in effecting change, reference should be made to Erasmus.[10]

Why we join a group. A group, according to Cattell,[11] is a collection of individuals in which the existence of all is necessary for the satisfaction of certain needs of each. Thus it seems useless to attempt to organize unless we can make our coming together satisfactory. This means that satisfactions must flow in all directions. We form a group expecting it to serve us but unless we serve it, it cannot serve us. The action is reciprocal.

Different groups provide different kinds and amounts of satisfactions. Our hope in joining a membership* group is that therein we may find the solution to our more personal and intimate problems. We join reference groups largely because of the prestige, the security or the opportunity they offer to solve problems too big for us alone.

We voluntarily enter some groups, but are inducted into others. In voluntary groups we conform to the group's standards because we desire approval. The group is attractive to us if we help set up its standards, select its problems and make its decisions. [12, 13] In nonvoluntary groups our decisions to conform are based upon our own motives rather than upon any desire to satisfy those having power over us. These groups become attractive as they satisfy our self-oriented needs, as identified by Fouriezos.[14]

1. Dependence—both generalized dependency and dependency upon authority.
2. Status—prestige in the power heirarchy.
3. Dominance—intellectual and social dominance as distinct from dominancy demanded by our responsibility to act.
4. Aggression—both generalized aggression and aggression against authority.
5. Catharsis—personal unburdening.

Usually a group is attractive to its members as it provides affirmative answers to the following questions.

1. Does it assist the members in attaining some object of importance to them?

[10]Erasmus, Charles J., "An Anthropologist Views Technical Assistance," *Scientific Monthly,* March, 1954.
[11]Cattell, Raymond B., "New Concepts for Measuring Leadership in Terms of Group Syntality," *Human Relations,* 4:161, 1951.
[12]Gordon, Raymond L., "Interaction between Attitude and the Definition of the Situation in the Expression of Opinion," *Am. Soc. Rev.,* 17:50, 1952.
[13]Sherif, M., *The Psychology of Social Norms,* Harper Bros., N. Y., 1936.
[14]Fouriezos, Nicholas T., Hutt, Max L., and Guetzkow, Harold., "Measurement of Self-oriented Needs in Discussion Groups," *Journ. Aborm. and Soc. Psychol.,* 45:682, 1950.

2. Does it show that it values the membership of each?

3. Does it provide each with status and functions? For example, if a person joins the "Louisiana Tigers," its past becomes part of his past. This organization began as "Wheat's Tigers," in Civil War days. The legacy was carried on by Major Boyd who became the first president of the University of Louisiana. More recently, the tradition was transferred to China by General Claire Cheunault, a native of Louisiana, in the form of "Flying Tigers."[15]

4. Does it approve the specific contributions of all? Coch and French[16] gave recognition* by telling a group of its past achievements and by setting a slightly higher goal each week. The production increased from 25 to 100. Another group was told how far below expectations they were and at what point they would have to be in 10 weeks. Its production increased from 24 to 65.

5. Does it provide member support?

To make a group more attractive we may do the following:

1. Make it more effective in solving its important problems.
2. Provide more status and recognition for the members.
3. Make interactions within the group freer, more friendly.
4. Make relations cooperative rather than competitive.
5. Favorably evaluate the group's activities.
6. Attack the group.

An attractive group is a cohesive group but cohesiveness cannot develop without a group. Consequently there is no alternative but to organize and then to try to make the group cohesive.

Organizing a membership group. Selecting members is a real problem because group members must be both alike and different and they cannot know their similarities in interests nor their differences in skills and abilities until they have become rather well acquainted. Of course their similarities make it easy for persons to assemble, but it is their differences which make their coming together fruitful. Too many group workers abhor differences as if they were something bad, something to be avoided. But it is these differences which permit specialization and efficiency. Consequently we should cultivate them. We want them neither annihilated nor absorbed, just integrated. If you give of your differences and welcome mine and if I can do likewise we

---

[15]*Time,* 63:8, Feb. 20, 1954.
[16]Coch, Lester, and French, John R. P. Jr., "Overcoming Resistance to Change," *Human Relations,* 1:512, 1948.

both can learn. But if we can discuss only those things about which we agree there is no use talking.

In spite of the value of differences there is always strong pressures toward uniformity, because one's security depends upon his ability to predict how other members will react toward him. One cannot predict unless the members assume certain stable relations. Pressures toward uniformity arise from two sources.[17]

1. Reality or lack of reality—If opinions and beliefs rest upon physical reality a person has little need to depend upon the beliefs of others for validity. For example—If I believe an object is fragile and I break it with a hammer, my belief is clear. But should I believe in a principle about which few facts can be marshalled, my tests of validity must then be anchored in what others believe.
2. Group locomotion toward the goal—Pressures to comply are greater when the group must depend upon other members to help it reach its goal.

Since group members must be both alike and different and also involved in the problem, we see how difficult it is for a group to select its own members unaided. The solution to this problem is to seek the aid of a resource* person. But no resource person can or should do more than to help the members do their own choosing. And even then he will need some form of group selection blank.

The Neighborhood Group Survey Form (on the next page) was designed for Extension Agents to use in the following manner.

Should a person bring a problem to the Farm or Home Adviser, he or she playing the resource person's role should attempt to determine whether or not it is a group problem. He asks, "Do you think your neighbors may have this same problem?" and then explains that helping a group makes his job more efficient and that better solutions are generally found in a group. If the person responds favorably the adviser asks him to name the neighbors who have the same problem. He fills out the Neighborhood Group Survey Form and promises to take steps toward forming a group.

He then proceeds to visit those persons named in the blank telling them about the problem. If they are interested he fills out a form for each by asking them to name other neighbors who might also be interested.

---

[17]Festinger, Leon, "Informal Social Communication," *Psychol. Review*, 57:271, 1950.

NEIGHBORHOOD GROUP SURVEY FORM

Interviewee Mr. Mrs._____   Location:
     Twp._____   Sec._____   Acres_____

Address _____   Are you the owner?_____

Interviewer _____ ___   Date_____   County_____

Codes for columns below:

Neighbors—Give names of those with whom you neighbor.

V — Check each family with whom you visit, that is, spend the evening or go over for dinner.

C—Check the families that attend your church.

T—Check the families who are on your telephone line.

Kinship — Indicate relationship of man or woman to you.

Work—What kinds of work do you do together?

Social—What social or recreation activities does your family do with these families?

Notes—Indicate which of these persons you would go to for what kinds of information or help.

Names of neighbors	V	C	T		Kinship	Work	Social	Notes
1.				M				
				W				
2.				M				
				W				
3.				M				
				W				
4.				M				
				W				
5.				M				
				W				
6.				M				
				W				
7.				M				
				W				
8.				M				
				W				
9.				M				
				W				
10.				M				
				W				
11.				M				
				W				
12.				M				
				W				
13.				M				
				W				
14.				M				
				W				
15.				M				
				W				

Expand upon notes: ,

1. _____
2. _____
3. _____
4. _____
5. _____

Note: Evidence of isolation

GROUP SELECTION BLANK

Instructions: Below are the names of persons who have been suggested as possible members of the group described in the accompanying letter. There are too many names for one group, so we will have to form two or more groups.

1. Will you place "1" in Column C for each person whom you would prefer as a member of your group (check about 5 or 6 persons).

2. And place a "2" in Column C for each person who would be your second choice as a member of your group (check another 5 or 6 persons).

3. Then place an "O" in Column C for those who you think should be placed in groups other than yours. Every person should be marked 1, 2 or O in Col. C.

4. Now place an "M" in Column V for those persons who you think will be most valuable in helping your group do the jobs which have been described in the letter. Only those marked 1 in Column C need be marked in Column V.

Your Name ＿＿＿＿＿＿＿＿＿＿＿＿＿＿＿ Address＿＿＿＿＿＿＿＿＿＿＿

(This information is only for our use and will not be shown to others.)

Family Names		C	V	Family Names		C	V
1.	Mr.			17.	Mr.		
	Mrs.				Mrs.		
2.	Mr.			18.	Mr.		
	Mrs.				Mrs.		
3.	Mr.			19.	Mr.		
	Mrs.				Mrs.		
4.	Mr.			20.	Mr.		
	Mrs.				Mrs.		
5.	Mr.			21.	Mr.		
	Mrs.				Mrs.		
6.	Mr.			22.	Mr.		
	Mrs.				Mrs.		
7.	Mr.			23.	Mr.		
	Mrs.				Mrs.		
8.	Mr.			24.	Mr.		
	Mrs.				Mrs.		
9.	Mr.			25.	Mr.		
	Mrs.				Mrs.		
10.	Mr.			26.	Mr.		
	Mrs.				Mrs.		
11.	Mr.			27.	Mr.		
	Mrs.				Mrs.		
12.	Mr.			28.	Mr.		
	Mrs.				Mrs.		
13.	Mr.			29.	Mr.		
	Mrs.				Mrs.		
14.	Mr.			30.	Mr.		
	Mrs.				Mrs.		
15.	Mr.			31.	Mr.		
	Mrs.				Mrs.		
16.	Mr.			32.	Mr.		
	Mrs.				Mrs.		

The information you give is only for our use in forming the groups. These blanks will not be shown to any others.

Visiting in homes is generally one of the most enlightening experiences an adviser can have. Those who have done it feel that it should become one of their major activities. In counties with more than one organized group the Membership Committee* may help do some of the interviewing.

As the interviewing proceeds two or three times as many persons will be named on these sheets as should ever be organized into a group. This is desirable and when it happens it is time to select the group members.

The names of all persons on the Group Survey Forms are placed upon the Group Selection Blanks and a copy is sent each with a letter outlining the problems and stating that more per-

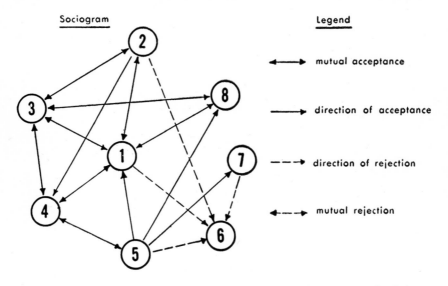

sons have shown an interest than can possibly be handled in a single group. The instructions give an easy way to reject unacceptable persons. Since many may refuse to reject their neighbors unless it is done in confidence, these blanks are held in confidence by the resource person. When resource persons are not used, we find some groups refuse to select members and consequently fail to get the right combination of persons.

From the choices expressed on the Group Selection Blanks the resource person should draw socio-grams like the above which shows how eight persons accepted and rejected each other.[18]

---

[18]Moreno, J. L., "Contributions of Sociometry to Research Methodology in Sociology," *Am. Socio. Rev.*, 12:287, 1947.

Persons 1, 2, 3, 4, and 8 appear acceptable enough to each other to compose a group. Persons 5 and 7 no doubt would be fringe members if they were included. Person 6 should go into another group. Persons 1, 3, and 4, have been chosen more times than any other. This may indicate that these are the most acceptable leaders. However we prefer to include information about the person

thought to be most valuable in helping the group solve its problems (See instruction 4 on Group Selection Blanks) before we identify the leadership team. This plan being based upon likes and dislikes may produce an attractive group but it may fail to produce all the roles needed in group life. It will provide much valuable information but it does not guarantee the right combination of people. (See Appendix B.)

With the sociometric information at hand the resource person should ask one of the most accepted members to invite the chosen persons to an organization meeting. The agenda should include a discussion of problems, some instruction on group atmospheres* and membership roles.* The election of officers might be delayed until the members have met together several times.

Organizing a reference group. Generally at the center of every reference group is a membership group. Although it need not be so, this inner circle usually operates in a dominative manner. It usually decides what it wants to put over on the larger group and then proceeds to sell its ideas in a sweet-dominative fashion. In most cases participation is low because people do not like to be handled in this manner.

The Federation of Civic Clubs, a democratic reference group, took the following steps in organizing. A number of persons had become aware of certain community needs and of the ineffectiveness of the many existing small groups in meeting them. They decided to call a meeting and agreed to attempt to organize a large reference group to help integrate their various activities into a community program. Three possible procedures had been discussed, namely: (1) ask each interested agency to appoint delegates (2) ask competent persons, regardless of their affiliations, to represent a geographical area; or (3) ask competent persons to represent a particular point of view.

The advantages and disadvantages of each of these procedures had been discussed and three conclusions had been formed. (1) The agency-representative plan suffers from possible hazards of push-and-pull tactics. The work of the delegate is considerably hampered if he must return to his agency for instructions before he can speak. Then, he may fear being repudiated if he does not win for his group, or he may fear being declared non-cooperative if he fights too strenuously. However, this plan does have the advantage of being fairly easy to mobilize into action. (2) The area-representative plan has a broader interest base than the agency-representative plan, particularly if there are many occupational and social patterns in the group. There is a danger, however, that some minor interests may not be represented. Mobilization for action may be difficult under this plan. (3) The point-of-view plan may provide the broadest interest pattern of all, as well as the most competent workers, but it is the most difficult one in which to get action. In this plan, as well as in the area-representative plan, the loyalties of the group members may be directed towards the person who selected them rather than towards the persons they are to serve.

The organizing committee decided to invite agency representatives and other interested individuals and to attempt to build a point-of-view organization. About 40 were expected to attend. The chairman began as follows:

"This meeting has been called because some of us thought we could solve the problems confronting us if we united our forces. I've been asked to serve as temporary chairman and when I began to think about what I should do, it occurred to me that we had two jobs. First we will have to explore our problem, determine its importance and define its limits. Then we will have to decide what kind of an organization we want to build. I think I have stated them in their order of importance but we can reverse

the order if you want." There was no comment and the chairman continued.

"We will have difficulty in expressing and recording all our ideas in this large a group, so I want to suggest that we form a number of smaller groups, say eight. Let us discuss, decide and record our conclusions. Each group should have a chairman and a recorder. These you should select. The committee that called this meeting thought there were at least three specific points which we should discuss. I've written them on the blackboard.

"Won't you now break up into groups of 5 or 6 persons merely by rearranging your chairs so that those in one row face those behind. Should those in any group be from the same organization won't some of you move? Then decide which problem seems the most important and report back in 10 minutes what you think we should do about it."

As soon as the buzz groups had assembled the chairman of the meeting gave to each recorder a Buzz Session* Discussion card. After about 10 minutes he asked the recorders to come to the platform and report. The items they reported were written under the three questions already on the blackboard:

1. What problems do we want to solve?
2. Why do we want these changes made?
3. What obstacles must we overcome?

The chairman then asked for an opinion poll as to whether or not these problems were important enough to deserve an organized effort to solve. There were both "yes" and "no" opinions but more "yes" votes.

"It's no secret" said the chairman "that I favor an organization. That's one reason I was picked to chair this meeting. The committee said, 'let's get someone who's interested.' I hope no one holds this against me anymore than I hold it against you that you may differ. If we didn't have different ideas we never would learn anything new. Even though the majority favors organizing, let's not proceed until we consider whether or not we have all the skill we need.

"The kind of an organization we build should depend upon the abilities of the persons expected to become members. During this meeting you have been getting impressions about the skill and abilities of those present. You may have thought we can't do this or that because we haven't the time or the know-how. But there may be persons who do have. This may make us want to search our community for others who can help and bring them in prior to the time we form an organization. But we may not know who we need until we speculate about the kind of an organization we want to build."

No doubt the chairman hesitated to undertake a discussion of the fundamentals of a good organization because he at this point called upon a resource leader who had been invited to attend. Actually resource persons are essential to organizations. They are permitted to do things no member could do even though he was more competent. We need to understand the role of resource leaders* and their place in the leadership team. A resource leader at this point might tell the story of the Atomic Energy* Commission or discuss the topics of "atmosphere" or "roles" or the "functions"* which groups must perform. The resource leader in this case was a professor from the state university. He was introduced as a person who had helped other communities organize. He began by saying:

"The kind of an organization you build should depend upon the abilities of the members, but I rather think its success will depend upon their skill. I make this distinction to emphasize the fact that skills in group activities can be learned.

"You can build either an authoritarian or a democratic organization. If you decide to give the leaders the right to make your plans and tell you what to do, everything will proceed smoothly, if they are skillful and if you are submissive. If you decide to build a democratic group, your success will depend upon the skill of a lot of people. The officers will have to be skillful but in a different way than dominative leaders. The chairman will have to know how to maintain a permissive atmosphere and to play group building roles. The recorder will have to be skillful in problem solving so as to keep record of the points at issue. The observer will have to be skillful in helping you manage your group. These officers are important. But more groups fail because of members than because of officers. Before you select officers you must decide whether you want a democratically or an autocratically controlled group. This may seem trite but it isn't, for many people declare that they are for democracy, but fail when it makes demands upon their time. "Let George do it," is more than a saying. It actually happens. Before we stand up for democracy we must be sure we know what it means. We must agree to what we affirm about democracy as well as to what we deny about it. Therefore we should discuss both what it is and what it isn't. And we must be sure just how a democratic group should function."

This resource person then proceeded to discuss the twelve functions* outlined in Chapter one, saying that eight of them should always be maintained for the group itself and should never be assigned. He then discussed in more detail the four which may be assigned for limited periods. These are described below.

Representation*—duties delegated for a period of one year. A regent is elected by each membership group to head that group's delegation to the County Assembly. His major responsibility is to act as a contact man for the group, to receive and transmit all incoming demands to the appropriate action committee. When issues arise which demand a decision he is to poll the delegation or transmit the decision of his neighborhood group to the County Assembly. He presides at his membership group's meetings.

Expedition—a committee of three or more appointed or elected for one year. This committee arranges for meeting places, notices, materials, and any other thing requested to expedite the business of the group. The chairman of this committee serves as recorder for the group, and maintains custody of the records and prepares reports, agenda, and other documents for the group.

Recruitment—a committee of three or more elected or appointed for a period of one year. This committee shall solicit new members, receive applications, and instruct candidates in the rules and cooperative procedures of the group, during their probationary period. This committee shall help new neighborhood groups to organize and shall assist them to understand cooperative procedures.

Action—the function of action is assigned any individual or group who will undertake to solve a problem considered important by the group. Problem solving consists of two acts, the first is arriving at a decision, and the second is action based upon that decision. The first part is the responsibility of the group although

it may need the help of a discussion leader in following through
the steps of deciding, or a resource person to gather the facts and
materials needed. The second part is frequently assigned to action
committees which may be classified under any one of the several
working objectives.*

The resource leader concluded his discussion by advising
the appointment of temporary chairmen for several meetings
thus giving time for the members to become acquainted with
each other before the final election. A steering committee was
appointed and, assisted by the resource leader, it prepared the
organization chart shown on the next page. This was adopted by
the group, at a later meeting as the blueprint for the organization.
The group is not yet functioning in each category, neither is it
discouraged as many organizations soon become. This no doubt
is due to the fact that it has a plan and knows how to fit the
parts together.

A number of critical points in the organization deserve
special emphasis. These were discussed by the steering committee
and later reported to the group by resource leaders as follows:

The county was chosen as the base because so many activities and authorities are county wide. Delegates were chosen from
both neighborhood and special interest groups, and their qualifications were designated as competency, vision, and community
interest. The point-of-view plan was emphasized in order to avoid
a conflict of opposing pressures, which generally results in loss
of confidence and public interest. The chairman of the County
Assembly was not the chairman of the Executive Council.

A rather large program committee was suggested and sub-
divided into four committees each designated by one of the four
objectives. Each sub-committee was charged with the preparation
of a detailed plan for attaining its objective. These plans were
to be integrated by the Executive Council whose responsibilities
were to facilitate planning and to integrate action-decisions. Any
member of the program committee could call for a vote of confidence in the Executive Council. Lack of confidence was cause
for the reorganization of the Executive Council.

Two activities, training and evaluation overlap somewhat the
recruitment and the program committee functions. Special committees operating through the County Assembly and responsible
to it were set up because these activities generally need the help
of resource persons.

CHART OF THE FEDERATION OF CIVIC CLUBS

Functions	Authority	Duties
General functions (Unassigned)	Neighborhood group	Policy making
Representation	Regent	Intercommunication
Recruitment	Recruitment committee	Recruitment Initiation and Training
General functions (Unassigned)	Assembly	Policy making Decision making Delegation of action
Program building (6 steps)	Program committee	Policy execution
Expedition	Executive Committee	Integration
Action		Problem solving

Neighborhood membership groups

Com-mittee

County Delegate Assembly
A reference group

County Program Coordinating Committee

Executive council

Action committee

CHART FOR PROGRAM BUILDING COMMITTEES

ORGANIZATION AND FUNCTIONS

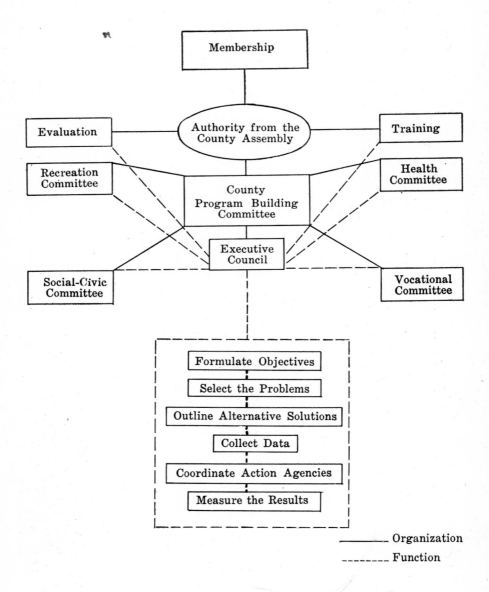

The recruitment function was assigned to a special committee responsible to the County Assembly. What groups should hold membership? Where should new groups be organized? How shall their members be recruited and inducted? These are some of the problems for this committee. The organization plan provides for open membership but it did not leave membership acquisition to chance.

Every reference group, if it decides to perpetuate its organization, must soon begin the search for new members. It may select a recruitment committee which systematically organizes every step in the acquisition process or it may leave the matter to chance. Those who believe that a group, in order to succeed, must be composed of the right combination of people will favor the systematic plan which includes both the needs of the group and the needs of the new members.

The first big problem in membership acquisition involves an analysis of the needs of the group. This should include a review of the goals and purposes of the organization. What are they? Have these changed since the organization was founded? Are they consistent with the times? A more embarrassing question which nevertheless must be answered is, **Is the organization necessary?** Then there arises a number of more specific questions:

1. Has the organization a special clientele, or should it attract persons from the entire community?
2. Are the members chiefly interested in becoming informed, or do they want to undertake an action program?
3. Do the people want an intensive or an extensive program?
4. What different kinds of members are needed, and what proportion should each kind be of the total membership?

An organization must stand for something. It cannot go in all directions, nor can it mean all things to all people.

The second big problem is to find the new member and induce him to join and to participate. The person who is asked to join usually asks himself, "What is going to happen to me?" "What do I expect of this group?" and "What does this group expect of me?"

People join groups for a number of reasons.

1. Because it is the thing to do; it is expedient. At a low interest level the reason may be merely to conform, but at a higher level it may be because the things people want are found in groups and the things they want done are done by groups. Actually, our society operates on a group basis.

2. Second, because it provides status, superiority, and prestige, or a chance to extend one's ego. A joiner so oriented has little interest in the contributions he can make. His interests are mainly in the rewards he can reap.

3. Third, because it provides an opportunity to extend one's vision, to enlarge one's circle or to serve one's fellow. These members are less concerned with rights than responsibilities.

People refuse membership because it calls for too much effort or because they fear to be involved or because they do not understand the processes through which democracy operates.

Our aim should be to seek out new members to meet the needs of the group, and to avoid the situation in which the group finds itself with a wrong new member, or in which a new member finds himself in the wrong group.

Chapter 11.

HOW TO GET SKILLED OFFICERS

Ask anyone—your friend, your neighbor, the man on the street, what he thinks about the way groups are led and you'll get all sorts of answers. Some will say "leaders should know and do," while others will say, "leaders should confer with the group." You will get demands for a "strong man," and complaints about dictators. And there will be advice about unfriendliness. The topic will stimulate much discussion and many disagreements.

If you ask administrators, or sales managers about leadership you no doubt will be instructed at length about discipline, prestige, tact, authority, knowledge, praise, skill, and influence, which these folks claim distinguishes a leader from followers. If you ask executives they may point out the ideal leader as a vigorous, assertive individual who was taught in a leadership course "how to make friends and influence people." If you ask a foreman he may refer to himself as a self-made man who has learned to get what he wanted by "suggestion" or by showing those about him that they serve themselves best by serving him. If you ask teachers they may go so far as to write out "His unique behavior consists of (1) analysing the situation and (2) initiating the action required."

These statements represent the popular concept of strong-man leadership saturated with domination and oozing with diplomacy. It is a combination of individualism and groupism for it means imposing ones personality upon his friends, associates, customers and students.

And to keep all the rest of us happy the big-time leader is advised to reinforce his position by hiring a publicity agent who will build-up his benevolent and paternalistic qualities in an effort to convince us that he is a good fellow, who upon occasion will even "sit down at the common table and share our simple meals."

A new and quite different concept of leadership has been developing based upon studies of group reactions. These show that leadership consists of a number of roles, the playing of which depends upon the group and the situation. These roles differ if the leaders are officially designated or group chosen, and if the group expects authoritarian or democratic rule. They differ also as the tasks differ.

Cattell[1] describes leadership as (1) acts which help a group decide upon its goals and (2) acts which help it achieve these goals. From this it is clear that leaders depend upon groups and that a leader in one group may not be acknowledged as a leader in another group.

In membership groups, interpersonal reactions are intimate. If the group is personality-satisfaction-centered as are hobby groups or card clubs it may expect the leadership to be shared and leader functions to be not much different from member functions. If the membership group is task-centered it may permit more direct guidance to the problem-solving procedures and more differentiation in the leader functions.

In reference groups with officially designated leaders the groups may expect more or less authoritarian leadership. The leader functions may be differentiated with leaders giving direction to roles which facilitate control, such as originating action, giving only those orders which will be obeyed, using established channels, holding their distance both socially and psychologically and living up to the group norms.

In more democratically oriented reference groups the leaders are more permissive over content, permitting wider member par-

ticipation, and attempting to build cohesiveness by generating a pleasant atmosphere and by giving member satisfaction in the kinds of decisions made, in the kinds of group practices adopted and in less dominative leader behavior.

Recent studies bring into serious question the "follow the leader" theory for getting action. Followers have not been inspired by leaders "richly endowed" with abilities or facili-

---

[1]Cattell, Raymond B., "New Concepts for Measuring Leadership in Terms of Group Syntality," *Human Relations* 4:161, 1951.

ties. Followers will not "try" to copy leaders unless they consider their situations to be similar. Tasks too easy or too difficult cause followers no concern. For example, demonstrations[2] set up on land belonging to a farmer considered by his neighbors to be on a higher socio-economic level failed to motivate the neighbors. Demonstrations conducted with equipment much better, or on soils much better, or with funds much greater than those possessed by the persons expected to be influenced, lacked in effectiveness. Experiences in sections of India and China indicate there is a greater tendency for improved practices to be copied from persons lower on the economic ladder than from those higher. These reports indicate that leadership resides more in the situation than in the person.

However, there are persons at the center of each activity whose skills focus the behavior of other persons. These were found, in the Peckham Experiment,[3] to hold their position by virtue of their performances rather than their attributes. Since all levels of skill were present, the groups formed themselves into a sort of graded series about leaders only slightly more skillful. They had no leadership problems at Peckham when the group and the task were permitted to determine who should lead.

Rather than a single leader these studies place emphasis upon a leadership team, playing roles which seek the answers to

three questions: 1. What is the problem? 2. What shall we do about it? How do we feel about it?

The answer to the first question demands someone or several persons to play the orientor's role. The answer to the second question will demand the facilitator's role. These persons need the chairman's help in directing the group's attention to the matter at hand. Because they tend to upset the traditional patterns of thinking and

[2]Matthews, M. Taylor, Jenkins, David R., and Sletto, Raymond F., *Attitudes of Edgefield County Farmers Toward Farm Practices and Rural Programs.* South Carolina Agric. Experiment Station, Bulletin 339, 1942.
[3]Pearse, Innis H., and Crocker, Lucy H., *The Peckham Experiment,* Yale University Press, New Haven, Conn., 1945.

doing; because they force the group to re-examine their beliefs and readjust their behavior, they create tensions and arouse negative feelings toward themselves. Nevertheless these roles must be played if problems are to be solved and the players must expect not to be the "best liked" members of a group.

The answers to the third question are obtained by the help of persons playing the encourager-harmonizer role. These players are usually warm friendly individuals who "have to be liked." They avoid conflict and task functions, and concern themselves with the social-emotional problems of the members. They approve traditional patterns and dominant values, because approval generates positive feelings. They even avoid the thought that they can't like some as well as others and as a consequence they develop ingratiating skills. They become the best-liked members of the group because they seldom take a stand. At this point we should note clearly the distinction between "liking persons" and "having to be liked."

The evidence indicates that both orientor-facilitator and harmonizer-encourager roles are needed in all groups. The division of time will depend upon the problem at hand[4] and upon the players obtaining their major satisfactions from playing their own role.[5] In task centered groups those persons who push for a solution are the most prominent participants; the "best liked" individual plays second fiddle.

Suppose the "best liked" is not willing to remain second man in participation, but wants to be the most prominent. He may gain considerable support from the group in any attempt he makes to upseat the top man, merely because he is so well liked.

If he succeeds and takes up the role of guiding the group he will in all probability lose his "best liked" position because he either must push for a solution or become impotent as a leader.

Suppose on the other hand that the top man in participation wants to become "best liked." The chances are that he will lose his prominence as a

[4]Carter, Launor F., Haythorn, William and Howell, Margaret, "A Further Investigation of the Criteria of Leadership," *Journ. Abnorm. Social Psychol.*, 45:350, 1950
[5]Bertowitz, Leonard, "Sharing Leadership in Small, Decision-Making Groups, *Journ. Abnorm. Social Psychol.* 48:231, 1953.

participator if he becomes "best-liked," for seldom can a leader push the group for a solution and be "best-liked" at the same time.

Slater[6] was able to differentiate roles into chairman, technical specialist and best-liked on the basis of replies to five questions as follows:

1. Who talked most? (participation rate)
2. Who contributed the best ideas? (specialist role)
3. Who did most to guide the discussion? (chairman role)
4. How well did you personally like each member? (best-liked role)
5. Who received most of the communications?

Fiedler[7] found that teams composed of players who did not discriminate between their best-liked and least-liked member were not the winners. These players accepted all comers; they probably felt a need to be "best liked." Their relationships were "buddy-buddy," a thing coaches have called team spirit. But winning teams and productive work groups were composed of persons who could see differences between their best-liked and least-liked co-workers. They held certain persons at a distance.

In another study Fiedler[8] found that leaders who were so close to their groups that they could not criticize the behavior of the members, lead unproductive groups. Effective leadership requires a certain optimum psychological distance between leader and co-workers. This distance is composed of two units, one is discrimination as measured by ability to identify differences between best-liked and least-liked co-workers. The other is measured by the preference for a certain key worker. The sum of these units may be too small, too large or just right for a highly productive group.

The usual pattern for a successful group is to have a discriminative leader who has a high preference for his keyman. The accepting, non-critical leader with high liking for his keyman may be so closely attached (the psychological distance is too short) that he has difficulty in making decisions involving his subordinates.

The discriminating leader with a low liking for his keyman is too far removed for effective communications. It would

[6]Slater, Philip E., "Role Differentiation in Small Groups," *Am. Soc. Rev.,* 20:300, 1955.
[7]Fiedler, F. E., "The Psychological Distance Dimension in Interpersonal Relations," *J. Pers.,* 22:142, 1953. Fiedler, F. E., "Assumed Similar Measures as Predictors of Team Effectiveness," *Journ. of Abnorm. Soc. Psychol.,* 49:381, 1954.
[8]Fiedler, F. E., "The Influence of Leader—Keyman Relations on Combat Crew Effectiveness," *Journ. Abnorm. Soc. Psychol.,* 51:227, 1955

seem possible to have an accepting leader with a low preference
for his keyman and find a successful group; the distance being
just right.

Two conclusions may be derived from these studies. First,
it is important that members and leaders become skillful in playing their respective roles. The second is that leaders must maintain the optimum psychological distance between themselves,
their keymen and the group. These skills may be learned. Let us
turn our attention to further analysis of the three major roles
on the leadership team.

CHAIRMAN DUTIES

The chairman is by far the most strategically situated official in a group. His position permits him to regulate the rate of
activity, the kind of subject matter discussed and the manner
in which it shall be discussed. He, in a large measure, may
determine the atmosphere and the kinds of roles played.

A good chairman has many skills. He knows the steps a
group must take to solve a problem.* He knows how to proceed
when either one, several or no hypothesis* has been suggested.
He knows how to use parliamentary rules to facilitate decisions
and how to prevent them from hindering consensus. [9, 10, 11]

Then, too, he knows how to help a group service itself.
Realizing that there can be no growth without differences he
knows how to draw them out and how to integrate them. He
knows what roles* are needed at various stages of group growth
and how to cause these to be played.

He knows that group members must learn their skills;
consequently, he places training aids in their hands. For example, some leaders have distributed a card "The Techniques for
Group Discussion" to each member to hold in hand and they
frequently point out the steps shown thereupon.

Stage 1: The "Bright Idea" Stage.[12] (Finish Stage 1 before going
to Stage 2.)

    a. *Get acquainted.* Get more than the person's name. Find
       out why he is here, what he expects to get from the
       meeting, and what he can do to help the group. But don't
       expect him to tell much about himself unless you ask

---

[9]Henderson, Melvin and Rucker, Herbert J., *Guide to Parliamentary Practices,* Interstate Publishers, Danville, Illinois.

[10]Knowles, Malcolm S., "Move Over Mr. Roberts," *Adult Leadership,* 1:2, June, 1952.

[11]Robert, Frank L., "Using Discussion Techniques Under Parliamentary Procedure," *Journ. of Communications,* 5:149, 1955.

[12]See "Bright Idea" suggestion sheet Appendix C 5.

questions. Be friendly and permissive. No domination, please.

b. *Hear e a c h member.* When your turn comes, share all your thoughts and feelings, and give suggestions for improvement freely. Be sure to give reasons why you think as you do. Let down the bars so that we may look into your personality.

c. *When others have the floor, do not criticize or contradict.* Ask questions merely to get a better understanding of their statements. Do not offer your own ideas until it is your turn. Do not start or continue any arguments. That is part of Stage 2. Do not by question or facial expression show doubt or criticism; radiate encouragement and that *only.*

d. *Keep a record of every suggestion given.*

Stage 2: Discussion and Evaluation

a. After all have been heard, *consider each idea the property of the group* and no longer belonging to the person who stated it. Discuss ideas, not persons; criticize, comment, explain, modify, and try to develop a better conclusion by putting all of the ideas together.

b. *Continue the discussion until a trend in thinking is evident,* until some general idea appears, or until it seems that there is a need for additional facts not possessed by the group. Then make plans to get the needed information. We do not need to have unanimous agreement, but we do need to understand what others think and feel.

c. *Do not go back to Stage 1 after entering Stage 2* unless the group agrees that it has overlooked some new idea.

Stage 3: Decision and Report.

Near the end of the discussion, *decide upon the most important problem or conclusion,* and ask your recorder to report it to the group. Be sure this statement covers the issues fairly.

Stage 4: Future Plans.

Decide what you should do next and when you should do it. Vote—don't try to railroad any action.

This card emphasizes the fact that each member has a unique contribution to make, and that we can get his bit and work it into the general conclusion only if we listen with our minds open. This makes it possible for him to lay his suggestion

upon the table, content to let it become the property of the group, and willing to let it stand or fall by the test of truth. Only then can we expect consensus. Consensus is too important to be attempted by the usual bag of tricks included in many books written for presiding officers. Sutherland[13] goes beyond these tricks and lists the skills needed by chairmen in various types of meetings.

Several of these skills are illustrated in a report of the first meeting of the Central States Employee's Club, which follows. Those assembled were elected representatives from each department. The chairman began:

"I am happy to be here to take part in this discussion. We have been given the responsibility for working out the details of the monthly programs for the next year. You no doubt have examined the official objectives of our club which were sent you

with the notice of your election. Extra copies have been laid out before you along with cards, note paper and pencils. The objectives should guide us as we do our planning.

"But before we start operations, let us be sure that we are all acquainted." He wrote his name on a card and set it up on the table. Each person did likewise. "Now," he continued, "will each of you tell us why you are interested in a program for our club and what part you think you can best take in promoting it? Tell us why you are here and what you hope to accomplish." Each made a brief statement and the chairman encouraged when necessary by asking questions about interests and skills. Then he continued:

[13]Sutherland, S. S., *When You Preside,* Interstate Printers and Publishers, Inc., Danville, Illinois, 1952.

"None of us would like to see our program fail, but we know of instances where the same program failed in one club and succeeded in another. There must have been reasons, and if we can discover these reasons we may be able to avoid another failure. As we look over the objectives won't you tell us what activities you think we should plan which will further these objectives?"

At this point several members gave examples of activities that had succeeded or failed and others began to declare their preferences. Then one man began to argue the merits of the various suggestions. "At every meeting someone gets up and says, 'We've planned this,' or 'We've planned that for you to-night.' They never ask us what we want to do."

His neighbor continued, "I'm getting all fed up with this planned economy."

Then the leader cautioned, "Planning is a device for releasing rather than restricting people's actions. Of course, poor planning can restrict. A poor traffic plan will tie up traffic rather than help it to move along."

"What can we do but plan? Someone has to make the arrangements and get the refreshments. Someone has to decide the time and place," spoke up the secretary.

"Good planning," continued the leader, "is merely looking backward for experience, looking around for facts, and looking forward for guidance."

A period of silence followed. It was broken by a thoughtful member who questioned, "What are we trying to do in planning these programs?" This question caused the members to refer again to the card.

"If these are the objectives," said one woman as she tapped her card, "and if we build programs which will interest people in attaining them, I think we should begin by asking the people what things they want."

"I am in favor of asking our members," spoke up one member, "but I think we will get more answers if we suggest things for them to vote on." Thereupon the committee proceeded to prepare a ballot.

The group decided to prepare a list and ask the total membership to vote their preference for each item.

Let us pause to examine both the methods and the ideas produced by this group. The chairman without difficulty led the group into the "Bright Idea" stage. It then undertook the discussion stage and advanced to the point where it needed additional information from the membership (Stage 2b). Intermixed with problem-solving steps were group building activities.

In attempting to involve all members the chairman spoke of "our club," "we," "you," and only once said "I." He could have said, "I placed extra copies," "I laid out the cards, paper, and pencils," "I don't want the program to fail," and "I'll read the objectives." He could have used several "you's" when he was cautioning, but instead he talked about "planning" as if the ideas were the property of the group rather than the person who suggested it. Then the secretary could have questioned "you" instead of "we" when she spoke.

The chairman introduced himself as a participant to help rather than to boss. He introduced the members by means of the name card which enabled them to associate names with faces.

He had materials and the official objectives ready so that there would be no delay when he called for suggestions from the group.

The "thoughtful person" played the role of an orientor as he called the group back to the subject. Note also how easily the secretary stopped the gripers when she played the harmonizer role.

RECORDER SKILLS

The recorder's role is essentially one of communications, although frequently it includes representation and expedition.* Because he has custody of the records he is the logical person to become chairman of the Expedition Committee.* Whenever he needs to transmit records between groups he serves as the groups' representative. Having the constitution and the agenda at hand he is often called upon to orient the group. Then, too,

because he keeps the records, he is in position to facilitate the problem by pointing out the steps that have been taken. His role is much broader than record keeping.

These examples show the recorder's place in the communications network. All of us are communicators if we communicate meanings, but just because we "told him" is no reason that he understands. Understanding is best when two-way communication exists—when sending and receiving responses alternate.

There are two types of communications,* (1) instrumental, aimed at changing the receiver, and (2) expressive, aimed at relieving the sender. The choice of a receiver will depend upon the sender's motives, the discrepancy between the sender and receiver about the item, and the extent to which the receiver is perceived as being able to be changed.

During the "Bright Idea" stage when various members are trying to express their feelings and opinions and later during the "Evaluation" stage when senders are attempting to change receivers the recorder may serve as the center of the communications network by recording and classifying ideas as "pros" and "cons." Then, too, he may summarize the suggestions presented or the conclusions drawn on the basis of his records. His work may be made easier if he uses the "Buzz Session Discussion" card which permits problems to be ranked in much the same manner as a proportional representation ballot permits nominees to be ranked.

The instructions call for the card to be passed around, but each person may be given a card and their rankings summarized by the recorder if the problem is such that the voting should be secret.

It is important that all members of a group have a voice in deciding the issues, but mere voting does not guarantee intelligent choice or democratic control. The voter should be given a part in determining what issues he must decide between. Only when the issues are made clear can he accept or reject intelligently. Furthermore if he is presented with only one issue he has no choice. Some persons are concerned with the small proportion of voters, but why should we vote if we have no choice, or if we haven't enough information to vote intelligently? The recorder may help us here, first by holding out for sufficient candidates or for several issues, so that there can be no "railroading," and second by helping us follow the steps in problem solving so that we will become informed.

We should not accept the arguments that "they don't know enough to decide" or that communications are too costly. If we want an organization we must provide good communications.

FRONT

Buzz Session Discussion

Instructions to Recorder-Spokesman: Write on the reverse of this card all the questions suggested by your group. Then pass the card around and ask each to rank the questions in order of importance to him. Then add the rows and get a total score. The lowest score indicates the most important problem. Now write out fully and clearly this most important problem in the space below and report it to the main group.

Our most important problem is:

BACK

Questions or problems suggested by the members of this group.

Each person must rank each question in order. If there are 5 questions, rank 1 to 5.

	Persons										Total Score
	1	2	3	4	5	6	7	8	9	10	
	RANKS										
1.											
2.											
3.											
4.											
5.											
6.											

A good system carries messages in all directions. It fails unless it carries all the kind of information needed and desired. It fails unless it carries clear and adequate information about policies, procedures, and results to every person concerned and unless it transmits the reactions of those at both ends of the line to the other end.

A poor system is too long, too devious, and too easily jammed. It does not tell us who should start nor who should relay messages. It may be easily blocked by someone failing to give the facts on policies, procedures or progress, or by failing to express feelings. Most grievances arise over day-to-day feelings about one's job. Feelings that we are mere cogs or complaints about lack of interest could be dispelled if we would pull up the iron curtain which separates workers from each other and from their supervisors.[14]

---

[14]Bakke, E. Wight, "Teamwork in Industry," *Scientific Monthly*, 66:213, 1948.

The recorder's job is important. He is at the center of the communications network and in the middle of the problem-solving process. We should do more than choose a "mousy" little person who will stay in her corner for our secretary.

OBSERVER'S JOB

One major contribution which came from the study of group dynamics was the identification of the observer's role. The observer was introduced as the third member of the leadership team, and his role promises to accelerate group growth faster than almost any other role. Even though all group members may observe, it is common experience that they rarely do unless given the responsibility and then an opportunity to report. We do not expect every member to record the business, neither

should we expect every person to observe the group processes. Generally we get too busy participating to have time for observing and recording.

Because the role is so new, and in spite of the fact that it promises so much, some persons advise against playing it because they fear the group cannot examine its own behavior. And some groups can't. Neither can most children because of their immaturity. Acquiring ability to objectively examine one's behavior is part of the process of growing up. Persons who feel superior, and see no need to change, even though they admit "we could be wrong," should be reminded that "you can't be any better than you are unless you *do* change."

We should not postpone the selection of an observer because we find no one adequately trained. Even trained observers are not all-wise, they too must ask "How do you feel about what happened?" By all means, new observers should stick to questions. They should ask "How do you think we did?" "Did we get off the subject?" "How could we have gotten back sooner?" "What role was needed?" "What was blocking us?" or "When were we making good progress?"

Two sources of data are available to the observer. One is his record of what happens, the other is the record of what the members feel, desire and believe. Both involve verbal statements. The observer can't record and report overt behavior except through words. And when he asks others, both they and he must use words in expressing and recording how they feel, what they desire and what they believe. Thus it is exceedingly important that we use common understandable words in our reporting. Some of the problems of verbalization have been pointed out by Friedman.[15] She defines value behavior in both positive and negative terms and shows how an observer can learn what a person values by observing the time, money and energy he

Time begin *8:08PM* Time end *8:31 PM* Time elapsed *24 min* Recorders Report No. *1*

Minutes

Persons	Summary Questions	Statements	Time
1. Ben	0	4	4.5
2. Dora	0	2	1.1
3. Joe	1	4	3.1
4. Ed	1	5	3.6
5. Mabel	2	5	2.5
6. Alice	1	4	3.3
7. Evelyn	1	5	3.6
8. Everett	0	2	1.3
9. D. T.	0	0	0
10. Olive	0	1	1.0
			24.0

devotes to obtaining or avoiding various objects. Let us leave this matter to those who wish to devise questionnaires and turn our attention to the common observer record forms.

Observations. One of the easiest records to keep is a simple tally of the number of times each person participated. A more informative report is a record of the time devoted by each member to raising questions or supplying answers. This record is kept on the following form.

[15]Friedman, Bertha B., *Foundation of the Measurement of Values*, Bureau of Publications, Teacher's College, Columbia University, New York, 1946.

The group members are identified by number. As each participates, the time consumed is indicated on the graph along with his code number. If he asks a question, a question mark (?) is added. Whenever another person participates the graph line is changed to a different level, so that the distance between the vertical segments show the time used. Person 5 was chairman, the other officers might have been identified too. The summary shows the number of questions asked, the number of statements made, and the time used. Number 9 did not contribute. He may have been a thinker and not a talker.

Several more complete and more complicated observation forms have been devised.[16] For example Bales[17] classifies behavior into the twelve categories below:

1. Shows Solidarity: raises others' status, gives help, rewards.
2. Shows Tension Release: jokes, laughs, shows satisfaction.
3. Agrees: shows passive acceptance, understands, agrees.
4. Gives Suggestions: gives directions implying autonomy for others.
5. Gives Opinions: evaluates, analyses, expresses feelings and wishes.
6. Gives Orientation: gives information, repeats, classifies, confirms.
7. Asks for Orientation: asks for information, repetition, confirmation.
8. Asks for Opinions: asks for evaluation, analyses expression of feelings.
9. Asks for Suggestions: asks for direction and possible ways of acting.
10. Disagrees: shows passive rejection, formality, withholds help.
11. Shows Tension: asks for help, withdraws "out of field."
12. Shows Antagonism: defames others, defends self, asserts self.

Categories four to nine are verbal communications. They answer the questions of: who talked (sent) most and who received most. Categories one to three are group building activities except that joking may show antagonism as well as solidarity— it depends upon the joke. Categories ten to twelve are group destroying roles, except that too low a tension rate may indicate indifference or a difference so great that some members feel it

---

[16]Miel, Alice, "A Group Studies Itself to Improve Itself," *Teacher's Coll. Record*, 49-31, 1947. Carter, Launor; Haythorn, Wm., Meirowitz, Beatrice, and Lanzetta, John, "A Note on a New Technique of Interaction Recording," *Journ. Abnorm. and Soc. Psychol.*, 46:589, 1950.

[17]Bales, Robert F., *Interaction Process Analysis*, Addison-Wesley Press Inc., Cambridge, Mass., 1950.

PARTICIPATION REPORT
(for small groups)

Group_____ Date_____ Observer_____

Purpose of the meeting (A code)_____

Seating Chart   Person Code:

Person Code:

1. _____ 6. _____
2. _____ 7. _____
3. _____ 8. _____
4. _____ 9. _____
5. _____ 10. _____

Instructions: Use "X" after task and role codes to indicate that the task or role was needed but not undertaken or that its opposite was used. Use "in" for reference to in-group and "out" for out-group.

Time ¼ min.	Task Code	Sender-Actor Person	Sender-Actor Role	Receiver-Object Person	Receiver-Object Role	Time	Task Code	Sender-Actor Person	Sender-Actor Role	Receiver-Object Person	Receiver-Object Role
1	A1	2	0	in				4	E 2		
						11		2	O 2	5	F1
2		2	0	in		12					
3		1	B 3	out				several	D 3		
		5	S 1	out		13					
4		3	A 1	out		14		2	E 1x	several	D3
5	P1. 1	6	O 2	in				5	B 3		
		2	O 8x			15		3	F 5	5	C 3
6		6	O 2					4	B 1		
						16			B 3	out	
7		2	O 1	in					A 1	7	B 1
		4	02	5		17		several	S 5		
8	P1. 2	several	O 2	in	O 2			2x	F 3x	in x	
						18			O 7x		
9		6	F 1	8	O 3	19	P2.1	2	F 2	4	F 2
10		1,2,5	F 2	8	F 4		P2.2	2	F 8		
						20		3	F 2	10	F 2

If time extends past 20 min. use another sheet

not worthwhile to attempt to change others. No doubt a medium rate of tension is desirable in that it shows the group is striving to overcome some problem.

The Bales classification seems to provide no place to record a person's efforts to improve himself or to raise his status without being autocratic. This is a group building role.

The Participation Report was designed to permit an analysis of different parts of the agenda, the different problem-solving steps as well as the different roles.

Four codes are given:
    Person code
    Agenda code
    Problem code
    Role code

Until the observer becomes familiar with these codes it may be advisable to have two observers, one to use the Agenda and Problem codes, the other to use the Role code. The first step is to make a seating chart in order to identify each person. Numbered cards may be attached to each person. Usually one agenda code number will serve for the entire meeting. The problem code numbers may need to be changed several times and the person and role codes many times during a meeting.

Column one of the Participation Report provides for a time record. The second column permits entries under the agenda and problem codes. The third and fourth columns show the sender and the role he played. The fifth and sixth columns show the receiver and the role he played, if any.

PERSON CODE—Number each member of group and draw up a seating plan. Use "in" if a remark is addressed to the group in general. Use "out" if a remark is addressed to objects or persons outside the group.

AGENDA CODE—An agenda is a list of things to do or the order of business. It serves to delimit or control the group. The agenda code permits one to record the major item of business for the group. Problem solving is part of the agenda but because it is so important it is given a separate code.

A1.0 Organizing a group
A2.0 Selecting and initiating members
A3.0 Routine business
A4.0 Educating members (lecture, movies, trip, etc.)
A5.0 Recreation
A6.0 Training leaders

PROBLEM-SOLVING CODE (The significant terms in the outline are defined at various places in the text. See the index.)

P1.0 Formulating general objectives
    1.1 Orientation
    1.2 Specific plans, goals, and procedures
P2.0 Selecting problems
    2.1 Problem acceptance
    2.2 Problem census devices
P3.0 Discussing and evaluating problems
    3.1 Formulating hypotheses
    3.2 Collecting and classifying data
    3.3 Determining the value of the arguments
        3.31 Identifying propaganda tricks
    3.4 Holding fast to the topic
    3.5 Decision making
        3.51 Proposing solutions
        3.52 Consensus devices
P4.0 Acting upon decision
P5.0 Evaluating the results

ROLE CODE

Group Building Roles

O Orientor
O.1 Reviews past
O.2 Inventories expectations, abilities
O.3 Encourages change—differences
O.4 Seeks concensus—vote
O.5 Divides up duties
O.6 Balances sides
O.7 Calls for a return to subject
O.8 Disciplines

F Facilitator
F.1 Acknowledges—recognizes
F.2 Asks for or gives facts
F.3 Defines, interprets, evaluates
F.4 Outlines, organizes facts
F.5 Determines obstacles
F.6 Sets up standards
F.7 Provides tools and supplies
F.8 Summarizes

E Encourager—Harmonizer
E.1 Invites participation
E.2 Offers help
E.3 Supports, defends others
E.4 Gives ground
E.5 Admits error
E.6 Uses humor to detense

R Recorder

Ob Observer

Group Destroying Roles

A Aggressor—Dominator
A.1 Threatens
A.2 Manipulates
A.3 Boasts
A.4 Tries to influence
A.5 Defends self

C Censor—Blocker
C.1 Blocks
C.2 Ignores
C.3 Withholds
C.4 Asks group to surrender rights
C.5 Interrupts

B Blamer—Dodger
B.1 Lacks involvement
B.2 Fails to do part
B.3 Blames others
B.4 Tries to influence

S Submisser
S.1 Fears
S.2 Nervous
S.3 Scapegoat
S.4 Curries favors
S.5 Plays for sympathy

I Isolate
I.1 Apathetic
I.2 Barrier of indifference

Group Dependent Roles

D Dependent
D.1 Passive, drifting
D.2 Helpless, needs reassurance
D.3 Off subject, such as visiting, several talking at once, noise, disturbances

Below is part of the recorder's narrative report of the meeting.

"We began as many groups do, by complaining about our competitors and by patting ourselves on the back. Then suddenly, one person said, 'We're not getting anywhere by always telling ourselves how good we are, how long we have lived, and how much we deserve the territory. The next most important thing after knowing we are right is to know wherein we are wrong. I don't think anyone of us will claim that we are perfect. So let us look at our faults for a while.'

"Then we began to look at ourselves and we made progress for a time. But when it began to hurt, we turned about and began to defend ourselves. We went only half way . . just until it began to hurt. Immature groups often project their shortcomings onto others and thus show their unwillingness to accept responsibility. Mature groups can be objective and critical and can profit from their mistakes."

The recorder could have reported in greater detail. Let us decode his record to get an understanding of the amount of information he recorded. The meeting opened with the selection of officers. This took merely two minutes. Thereupon person 1 began to blame others for their failure to appreciate the values of adult education. Then person 5 expressed his fears and person 3 attempted to manipulate the group, probably trying for a position for himself. Number 6 undertook the orientor's role by beginning an inventory of expectations or abilities. At the 5th minute the recorder thought that the chairman failed to show leadership in not disciplining because some members were off the subject or were making disturbances. However, the chairman may have been waiting for someone else to play the orientor's role as members 6, 2 and 4 did during the next two minutes. Apparently things were happening too fast for the recorder because he reported that several told of their expectations between the seventh and tenth minutes. At eleven minutes number 4 offered help to number 5 who accepted it.

The record continues at the fourteenth minute with the leader failing to invite participation when several were engaged in off-subject conversation. This appears to have set off a cycle of blaming, threatening and some lack of involvement. The value of the arguments was not determined at minute eighteen and the group should have been called to return to the subject according to the recorder.

There are two kinds of cues an observer should use, verbal cues and behavior cues. For example, early in the above report the observer saw behavior which he identified as an immature group projecting its shortcomings upon others. Later he saw submissive behavior. It may take considerable practice for an observer to become skillful in noting and recording these cues, and for that reason training sessions should be arranged. Friedman[18] showed how an observer can learn what a person values by noting the time, money and energy he devotes to obtaining or avoiding various objects.

All group developmental processes need not be left to the observer. Feelings may be revealed in small groups by holding evaluation and planning meetings. At that time the following questions may be pursued.

1. What do you think this group should do?
2. Do you feel it has made progress toward its goal during the last year?
3. Why did you join?
4. What does the group mean to you now?
5. How can you best help the group?

There is always a hesitancy for some members in new groups to contribute until they discover the lay of the land. Their first contributions generally are questions rather than statements. In this way, they do not expose their inner feelings and  they offer nothing they feel obligated to defend. Soon, some brave soul will say, "I'll stick out my neck," or "I'll show my ignorance," and follow by letting down the bars a little, thus permitting us to glance behind his exterior at his feelings and motives. Discussions in certain respects resemble icebergs, most of which are under water. Hidden away in tacit assumptions are the things which really count and unless these are brought to the surface and made explicit, discussion remains a sort of shadow boxing.

During these discussions the observer might make a record of all "should" and "ought" statements and all expressions of guilt, shame, or self-depreciation if they seem real. Expressions of what members work for and of how they spend their time, money and energy are evidences of things they value.

[18]Friedman, Bertha B., *Foundation of the Measurement of Values*, Bureau of Publications, Teacher's College, Columbia University, New York, 1946.

Statements of things they approve or disapprove, or of things that frighten or threaten are indications of attitudes or cathectic orientation.

Attitudes may be obtained by questionnaires and surveys. One survey is similar to the usual membership data card upon which new members write what they can do and what they want the group to do. This then becomes a resource file for the membership and program committees.

SURVEYS. The only way to know how members really feel is to ask them. One form called the "End of Meeting Evaluation" contains the following four questions:
1. How did you like the meeting today?
2. What was the group trying to do?
3. Did you contribute all that you could?
4. What improvements can you suggest?

The answers should be summarized and reported at the next meeting.

For special occasions one or two questions from the list below may be selected by the observer.

Replies may be either written or oral, and the results should be summarized and used as the basis for a discussion. This type of procedure will become more valuable as the group becomes better acquainted with the roles* described earlier, and with the functions* the group should perform.
1. Did the group have an agenda?
2. How closely did it follow it?
3. What problem-solving steps did the group undertake?
4. Was it handicapped by lack of facts?
5. How did it go about getting the facts it needed?
6. Did it use consensus devices to come to decisions?
7. How general was the interest?
8. Were the needed roles played?
9. What roles were lacking?
10. How permissive was the atmosphere?
11. Was the group dominated by the leader?
12. How much did the recorder help the group?
13. Did the observer help the group to understand group processes?
14. Were the members frustrated?
15. How do the members get along together?
16. Is there much "crabbing" outside of meetings?
17. Do you think the group can handle the problem it undertook?
18. Does the group mean more or less to you than formerly?
19. Was there too much "horseplay"? What was the cause?

20. Does the group plan its future programs?
21. Does it devote time to educating its members?
22. Does it do anything but talk?
23. Does its committees function?
24. Does the group have a membership committee?
25. Do new members join?
26. Does it delegate duties to different members?
27. Are some members inactive? Why?
28. Does the leadership change?
29. Do you think the group is worthwhile?
30. Is it living up to its possibilities?

Some of these questions have been placed in check sheets and included in the appendixes. One such questionnaire was aimed at obtaining information about group organization, another at problem-solving activities, and the third at inter-group relations. These might be administered at different times during the year.

Many groups never undertake opinion surveys, nor observer reports and consequently never experience the satisfactions which follow discussions of group relations. Of course a group wants to solve problems, but unless it develops satisfactory relationships it may never live long enough to solve a problem.

Some groups become discouraged and abandon ship because they do not understand the developmental stages through which groups usually pass. There is a time when frustration and discouragement is high but this usually is followed by a period of harmony and integration.

STAGES IN GROUP DEVELOPMENT

There are four stages in the development of the group.[19]

1. **Self-centered stage.** At first members hesitate to share their feelings and beliefs. They ask questions rather than make statements thus showing their unwillingness "to stick their necks out." During this stage each will be sizing up the situation and attempting to establish himself.

2. **Frustration and conflict stage.** Because authority has not yet been established, hostility will arise between the emerging leaders. These conflicts must be resolved before members can feel secure. The first solutions proposed are seen as either A or B, and permit no C solution nor any combinations of A and B. This is fruitless thinking and it would be better if the

---

[19]Thelen, Herbert, and Dickerman, Watson, "Stereotypes and Growth of Groups," *Educ. Leadership,* 6:307, Feb., 1949.

problem were stated as "What would be the results should we adopt A or B or any other solution?" Many groups collapse at this stage because they do not realize that stage three is coming.

3. **Consolidation and harmony stage.** Soon some persons find each other. This may split the group into cliques or consolidate it into a whole. Either the members develop skill in playing the different roles or the differences are glossed over and complacency follows. Permissiveness may develop and the group may move on to control its own behavior, or it may not develop and then the group will never pass the stage of verbalization but continue to fight out a sort of polite cold war.

4. **Individual self-assessment.** It may be quite a while before members become objective and self-critical. Then they emphasize problem solving and control of group processes. This does not mean compromise and submission, for the members may accept partial success, and move on to find improved ways. Because a group expects its members to change, it sets up training activities and undertakes frequent evaluations. It evaluates the program and the behavior of the group, then it evaluates the behavior of individuals.

No group can grow through these four stages unless it can establish and maintain a non-threatening atmosphere. Each new member joins expecting to conform to the expectations of the group. But only after he feels accepted and secure will he begin to explore his own feelings and desires and this leads to shifts in his behavior toward the group's standards. Most persons would rather be approved by their group than be right by the standards of the world at large. This shows how misleading a recommendation can be unless we know the standard of the group.[20]

It is natural that group leaders hesitate to undertake discussions of group maturity and integration. There are some roles that neither officers nor members can easily perform.[21] Thus it is important, even necessary that a place be reserved for a resource leader.

RESOURCE PERSONS

It may well be that the resource person is the key to successful group life. For example, during its organization, particularly when the Neighborhood Survey forms are being

[20]Taylor, Gordon R., *Are Workers Human?*, Houghton Mifflin Co., Boston, 1952.
[21]Lewin, Kurt, "Cultural Reconstruction," *Journ. Abnorm. and Socio. Psychol.*, 38:166, 1943.

filled out and later when the Group Selection blanks are being summarized, an outsider is needed to do some of the work.

At this time it is impossible to get a true expression of likes and dislikes, or of acceptances and rejections unless the neighbors are able to talk in confidence to some outsider. We have uncovered instances in rural areas where seemingly needed groups were not even formed because they had no way to select and reject members in confidence.

Training tasks, particularly leadership training seldom is undertaken without outside help. When training is undertaken by resource persons as it is in the Boy Scouts, and the Extension Service, strong organizations result. But when it is neglected as it so often is by cooperatives, many failures result. A resource person has priviliges not granted any group member, to recommend procedures and point out the errors made.

A resource person may be the preferred leader for a discussion of goals and purposes. Thereupon he may help sharpen and clarify the objectives of the group without doing its thinking. By being present he helps members to think differently than they would were they alone.

There are other times when he may be called upon to help solve human relations problems. Then he must cause members to face problems they deny exist. Sometimes members deny the very needs they want satisfied. Sometimes they want change but fear the consequences. At these times a resource leader must prevent the group from running away from fears, pain and the conflicts in feelings.[22] A resource leader should bring out differences in feelings but see to it that they do not destroy the group. For unless a group has differences it has nothing.

There are times when a resource person should be called in to marshall facts and present arguments. If he is skillful he may be the most important factor in the final action.

But contrary to the common belief, mere fact-giving does not lead to action. Lectures had practically no influence in

[22]Cantor, Nathaniel, "Focus and Function in Group Discussion," *Teachers' Coll. Record,* 53:375, 1952.
[23]Lewin, Kurt, *Studies in Group Decision,* See chapter 21, in *Group Dynamics,* Cartwright, Dorwin, and Zander, Alvin, (Ed). Row, Peterson, and Co., Evanston, Ill., 1953.
[24]Levine, Jacob, and Butler, John, "Lecture vs Group Decision in Changing Behavior," *Journ. Appl. Psychol.,* 36:29, 1952.

changing food habits[23] nor in changing supervisor's rating.[24] Knowing that a practice is in error, even knowing that one is responsible for correcting the error was not sufficient to cause a change. The acquisition of knowledge does not automatically lead to action.

There are other times when a resource person may be called to act as the spokesman for the group. He then serves the representation function. His role is acceptable if he becomes a member of the leadership team and cautiously holds to the limits established by the representation* function.

There are other places where resource persons may help, but rather than attempt to list all of them, let us instead list the skills and insights which characterize a mature group and let you determine the occasions when your group needs outside help.

Characteristics of a Mature Group.

1. Skill and facility in building programs to solve problems
2. Skill in managing the group's environment
   a. ability to set up a suitable organization
   b. ability to select the combination of persons who can form a group
   c. ability to develop sufficient cohesion to permit the assimilation of new ideas without group disintegration, the profiting from failures, the holding of long range goals, and the detection of tension, fatigue, or changes in tempo
3. Skill in solving problems
   a. ability to inform itself
   b. ability to seek out real relationships
   c. ability to detect false analogies, loaded words, fears, prejudices, hates, hearsay, or rationalization
   d. ability to render decisions
4. Skill in making adjustments in group processes
   a. ability to maintain a permissive atmosphere
   b. ability to collect appropriate information on group behavior
   c. ability to make and accept interpretations about member and group functioning
   d. ability to plan future activities
5. Skill in training members to participate
   a. ability to seek out differences
   b. ability in role-identification and role-playing
   c. ability to delegate authority
   d. ability to use consensus devices
   e. ability to determine progress made

In contrast to these skills which are often called signs of group maturity, there are other signs which indicate immaturity. Some of them are:

1. Failure to outline purposes or objectives for the group.
2. Establishment of an organization based upon seniority only.
3. Members forming into cliques, refusing to participate with each other or attending merely to block others.
4. Members refusing to be involved.
    a. Appointment of committees in order to evade work
    b. Inconsequential discussion, frequent changes in topic or frequent dropping of issue for fear of having to decide
    c. Time spent in self-admiration and complaining about others
    d. Aggressive tendencies vented upon a straw bogeyman
5. Election of "strong man" chairman to rule.
6. Failure to evaluate group activities.

It is strongly recommended that every group seek alliances with a resource person or persons who can serve it in the many places where it stands in need of help but who will not do for the group the things that the group should do for itself.

At present we appear to be attempting to solve all our problems by external means. We form health organizations to provide us with health, recreation organizations to teach us how to play, art leagues to show us beautiful surroundings, employment services to find us jobs, and associated charities to give us relief. We even employ truant officers to lead us off to school. All this provides us with a corps of experts who rob us of some of our most precious possessions—our responsibilities. We need the skill of experts but they must not relieve us of our responsibilities.

I think of the resource person as being an important, even an essential part of the leadership team for nearly every group. But there are persons serving in professional capacities as specialists, staff members, executives, managers, and the like, trained and paid to render certain services, who have not thought of themselves in the role of resource person. In order to clarify the role and in hopes of making the services of professional leaders more effective, let me state the major concepts of the role as a sort of code for resource leaders.

A Code of Ethics for Resource Leaders

1. We are in the business of helping groups to help themselves and we should avoid making ourselves indispensable.

2. We must have a genuine, deeply emotional belief that people can work out the problems they face together. This makes us co-workers with the group rather than outside experts.

3. We should consider "values" to be evolving concepts. More important than what we hold as values at present is our attitude toward the development of values. The group's values are best determined by it deliberately discussing the various outcomes to be expected if this or that course of action is pursued.

4. Adult learning takes place in the community and the community should always be the focus of our attention. This means that we should try to understand the needs and wants of the people and the problems they face in trying to satisfy them.

5. We must be committed to the scientific method of problem-solving. This means we must gather facts, all the essential facts and then apply them to the problem. This means strengthening the hands of the people in their formulation of policies and in their rendering of decisions. Furthermore it means that we must not abdicate our position as a resource person merely to court the good will of the community.

6. Since education means solving problems we must face squarely the responsibility of action. People must think together but they must act together too. We need to study the cooperative process and help make it operative in solving problems.

7. Education is the essential instrument for the development of democracy. We know that democracy cannot be imposed or handed down. It can only be learned by being experienced. Cooperative education implies a philosophy which begins with individual differences, which affirms the right of each person to develop his individuality, which appreciates that growth is accomplished through human associations and which sees these associations as basically free and voluntary.

Chapter 12.

HOW TO GET PARTICIPATION

Almost every group worker stresses the importance of participation. Participation is something a group does but to some it doesn't matter what, so long as there is action. To others it does matter and they complain because the group gets nowhere.

Participation is defined as sharing in common. This means that there is a giver and a receiver and we assume that sharing is important on the basis that something will happen to both. Perhaps both will be more favorable to the task at hand, more inclined to work, more willing to accept the group decision, more ready to change their own behavior.

Let's not forget that we behave as we do for three reasons:

1. We act in accordance with habit. This means that former experiences in solving problems causes us to repeat former behavior.
2. We do not change our patterns of behavior unless we have new problems.
3. We act pretty much as those in our group think we should.

In discussion groups we encounter both over and under acting. This raises the questions: "Why do people talk?" "Why do they participate?"

There are two kinds of talk, namely instrumental and expressive.

Instrumental communication is aimed at producing a change in the other person. The desired change may be in information, (cognitive) in feeling (cathectic) or in values (evaluative). Whenever the desired change has been produced there is no need for more talk. For example, in groups, relatively little talk is directed toward the member who agrees. The talk is directed toward the person who disagrees, unless he appears stubborn and unwilling to change, then communication ceases.

Expressive communication is used as a means of self-expression. We talk because we have some feeling, some tension which we want released. If our need-disposition involves building up our status we may overtalk to make ourselves feel important. This frequently occurs in competitive and threatening situations.

The solution for those who overtalk instrumentally, is to call into action mechanisms which show when others agree, or when  others do not consider the issue important enough to disagree. Then there is no need for further talk. Every group should upon occasion pause and ask, "Are we agreed?" "Is the issue important enough to disagree about?" Generally more persons overtalk expressively when the atmosphere is dominative, and competitive. The remedy is to change to a warm supportive atmosphere, then much of this kind of talk would be unnecessary.

Other groups are plagued with under-participation. Some persons remain silent because their idea has already been expressed and they see no need for repetition. Others may remain silent because they do not want to become involved. They reject group membership. Still others may fear to stick out their necks because of ridicule. Then there are those who do not speak up until they have learned where the prestige leaders stand. None of these feel an immediate need to express themselves. Then, there are persons who do not talk because they feel they have no influence.

The best general solution for under-participation is a permissive atmosphere. The leader may help by repeatedly calling  for alternative views and demanding serious consideration for each one offered. Then too he should point out the value in differences and resist all attempts at "scapegoating." He should be cautious not to overplay prestige persons but should call frequently for the encourager role.

Of course there are conditions which make participation impossible. If the group is too large or if the topic is beyond the knowledge of the members some persons just can't participate.

UNDER-PARTICIPATION

Bradford[1] points out five reasons for under-participation. They are:

A. The goal seems unimportant.
B. There is fear in working or fear of the solution.
C. The group lacks skill in solving problems.
D. The members feel their work will be useless.
E. The group is involved in conflict.

A. Because something was important to a certain group is no reason that it is still important. Traditional goals should be re-examined at intervals because times change and new members enter the group. Planning is a group function that should never be delegated, and if it seems too difficult, a resource leader should be called in to assist. When members raise questions such as "What does it mean?" "What is it worth?" or "Is this all we have to do?" they are thinking the activity is unimportant. When they suggest that "we hurry on" or "work on something else," or when they engage in side-talk, jokes or horseplay they indicate lack of interest. When there are no volunteers for additional work or when they want to refer the matter back to a subcommittee, they may consider it unworthy of their attention.

B. Fears are powerful motivators, but they are defensive. We fear to act because we are insecure or have been punished or ridiculed because of former mistakes. Fears are frequently concealed under boasts, consequently we must look carefully for cues.

Some of the most obvious cues are:

1. Unnecessary delays in getting started.
2. Embarrassment or reluctance to discuss a problem.
3. Undue emphasis upon consequences, or errors.
4. Statements like "We haven't the facts," or "It can't be done."
5. Alternatives proposed but hesitancy to choose between them.
6. Questions about what the "higher-ups" think.
7. Psychological blocks such as aggression, regression, rationalization, repression and sublimation.

---

[1]Bradford, Leland P., Stock, Dorothy, and Horwitz, Murray, "How to Diagnose Group Problems," *Adult Leadership*, 2:12, Dec., 1953.

C. When members lack skill in problem solving we find behavior patterns as follows:

1. No one is able to suggest how to start.
2. Members shift from one point to another, and fail to follow the sequence in problem-solving steps.*
3. There are no summaries, no evaluation, no calls to return to the topic, no forward movement.
4. There are subgroups, private discussions, and little attention.
5. There are attempts to get the leader to decide.
6. There are decisions, then retreats from them.
7. There is stampeded voting, where those in agreement have overridden those in disagreement and ignored those who have not yet had time to make up their minds.

D. Members become apathetic when they feel powerless in the final decisions. Committees soon become dormant when they are set up to pacify or divert. Such committees see no point in "knocking themselves out" merely to have their work ignored. The quickest way to produce apathy is to ask for a suggestion, then to ignore it. Members may feel frustrated when they behave as follows:

1. Members say their work will be pigeon-holed.
2. There is much talk about power, prestige, and influence.
3. Doubts are voiced about "wasting our time."
4. There are complaints about the important people not being present.
5. The group lacks responsibility, it wastes time and makes no effort to decide.
6. It is suggested that the "higher-ups" are only pretending to be democratic.

E. There are four important causes of conflict, but only three of them are considered bad. They are:

1. *Frustration.* A group is frustrated when its instructions are inadequate and when it is given a job too easy or too difficult for it. Under these circumstances five different behavior patterns may be observed.

a. There are different and conflicting ideas about what the group is supposed to do.
b. There are declarations that the group is too small and hasn't the time, ability, or experience to do the job.
c. Suggestions made for solutions are declared impossible, impractical, or unsatisfactory. The blocker* role is frequently played.

    d. Members are impatient with each other, and have no faith in themselves.

    e. Members make excuses to withdraw from the group.

The solution is to make a better inventory of the competencies of the group and then consult with it about those things it considers important before making an assignment. The assignment and any alternatives which might be undertaken should be made clear. Then ample time to complete the job must be allocated. Importance and difficulty are two considerations a group should give a problem before it assigns it to itself.

    2. *Status seeking.* Struggles for power and prestige throw a group into conflict. The behavior cues are as follows:

    a. Ideas are attached before they are completely expressed.

    b. There are arguments about inconsequential points.

    c. There are arguments about rules and procedures. Parliamentary rules are strictly enforced.

    d. There are no attempts to find goals.

    e. Random suggestions are offered, many of which are beside the point.

    f. Members form cliques, demand support for special issues and refuse to compromise.

    g. The most talkative monopolize the time.

    h. There are subtle attacks upon persons.

    i. The leadership is attacked. There is "jockeying" for power.

    j. There are frequent references to "I" "me," "mine," to "my training," "my age," "my experience," etc.

The remedy for these conflicts lies in a cooperative atmosphere wherein each one can find satisfactions for his own needs while letting others satisfy their needs too. It helps if we let each one know that his views count, that his value is more in what he does, than in what he is. We should not name committees as "Mr. Clark's committee" but give them meaningful names which include all members.

    3. *Outside loyalties.* The manner in which a group is organized will give rise to or hinder conflict due to outside loyalties. We note the following behavior patterns.

    a. References are made to outside groups possessing the field or being better able to solve the problem.

    b. Certain members claim that they can't act until they consult some outside group.

    c. Goals are stated in too general or in non-operative terms.

    d. Suggestions are not built upon prior suggestions, each one seems to start from the beginning.

e. Members do not listen to each other, each seems anxious to force through his own pet plan.

The best remedy is to give a committee both authority and responsibility. Planning an inclusive program and developing methods for coordination will help also.

4. *Problem worth fighting for.* A certain degree of tension is desirable because it indicates a group is striving for a solution. It shows involvement. The behavior cues are:

a. The members have identified their goals and they understand and talk about them.
b. Most of the suggestions made are relevant and build upon each other.
c. Members disagree over suggestions made but not on a personal basis.
d. Suggestions are classified and acted upon rather than being ignored.
e. There are frequent expressions of interpersonal warmth.
f. Members frequently become impatient because there are delays.
g. There is general movement toward the solution.

There are two keys to participation; one is knowledge of the things that need to be done, the other is recognition for one's efforts. We can't act if we don't know the issues, and we won't act if we think our views don't count. When we are excluded from the planning, when our proposals are ignored, when our duties are not defined, when our representatives are shunned—any tactic which sets others "up" and us "down" will cut short our participation.

Although recognition is good we must be careful not to overdo it. We need some but not too much. Too much is bad for both us and the group. Some persons in their eagerness to give recognition overbuild the "expert" and the "practical man" as "top-flight" or "outstanding" and start a vicious circle. There are examples in cooperative groups when the directors, having lost the support of the membership, call in a firm of experts to tell them what they should have known—for a fee. To make it seem worth what it costs, the "experts" tell the directors that they are "practical" men because they called in the "experts." This combination of the "expert" who *knows* and the "practical" man who *does* has about crowded the rest of us out of participating. They make it almost impossible for us to be trusted with responsibilities and to feel worthy. There are kinds of recognition group members need but they are quite a different kind from that lavished upon prestige leaders by their stooges.

In fact some of those who complain about participation really want participation limited to the approval of "my" plans. They truly fear membership interference, and in some large organizations these prestige persons hire public relations experts to tell us only what they want us to know.

A smile, a nod, a pat on the back is recognition to team members who stand well together. To be told that she was big enough to help was enough to make a participant out of six-year-old Marcia, in helping Daddy prepare the dinner and to wash the dishes when Mother was away.

Large quantity participation is not enough, we need a high quality participation too. Both could be achieved if group members had knowledge of and skill in playing group building roles. To increase knowledge about group building roles the education committee might conduct a discussion centered about the 13 happenings outlined below:

Happening	Role Needed *How It Is Played*[2]	
1. A fact is given		
(a) It is clear, concise	Encourager	— acknowledges, nods, smiles
	Orientor	— verifies, interprets, shows relations
(b) It is not clear	Facilitator	asks for clarification tion
2. Two or more ideas are given in the same contribution	Orientor	— distinguishes between facts
3. An unrelated idea is contributed		
(a) It is off the subject	Orientor	— asks for a determination of the direction of the discussion
(b) It was an opinion given as a fact	Recorder	— asks where to place idea in the outline
4. Facts are needed, but not given	Facilitator	— asks for the fact or where it can be found. Calls upon the resource person
5. Fragmentary fact given, but overlooked by the group	Encourager	— asks for elaboration
6. Wasteful repetition of facts	Recorder	— shows the fact is already in outline
	Summarizer	— ties all ideas together to show idea is present
7. Signs of lack of interest	Encourager	— invites participation tion

---

[2]See the index for definitions of these roles.

(a) a non-contributing member	Facilitator	— asks for an example
8. Two talking at once	Facilitator	— keeps communication from becoming jammed
	Harmonizer	— detenses or asks for consideration
9. Disagreement	Harmonizer	— asks that differences be stated
	Orientor	— asks for consequences if one or another view prevailed
	Facilitator	— ask group to undertake role playing
10. Signs of tension (a) dominative behavior	Observer	— asks group to express its feeling as to motive
(b) aggression	Harmonizer	— asks for understanding
11. Recognition is sought	Facilitator	— suggests that contributions are property of the group
	Encourager	— gives recognition if deserved
12. Attempt is made to block	Harmonizer	— asks for motives, disciplines
13. Signs of fatigue	Facilitator	— checks ventilation, asks for change in tempo

Skill in taking[3] these roles may be gained through an educational device known as role playing. In role playing,[3] sometimes called sociodrama, psychodrama, or reality-testing, certain members merely slip into another person's shoes and act out his part. Then the group discusses the problem and tries to find a better solution.

Role playing is simply the spontaneous dramatization of some realistic human problem. It permits the group to look back over a situation or to look forward to what might happen. Our purpose in using it is to deal with human problems in a straightforward manner, and this includes diagnosis, treatment, and education.

Should we wish to uncover a member's real feelings, in order to discover if he is ready to take his part, we merely set up a situation with the required degrees of realism and let the group or individual play it out.

Should we desire to make adjustments in practices of living, we dramatize, then discuss, those problems which seem to be

---

[3]Moreno, J. L., "Sociodrama," "Psychodrama," *Monograph No. 1,* Beacon House, New York, 1944.
: We want to distinguish between role-taking, the actual assumption of a role as prescribed by the situation and role-playing, the dramatization of a situation for purposes of learning.

causing the trouble. We provide a chance to face conflict and to practice finding the solution.

Should we desire to change behavior in some respect, the players are asked to play out the present situation under observation. Then the inadequacies of the outcome are discussed and the scene is replayed until the desired proficiency is reached.

In each of the above situations the players are allowed freedom to be expansive and natural, without fear of failure or punishment. Learning is facilitated because the players identify with and become involved in the particular roles. Role playing permits action-learning with its freedom of emotionalization. Educators have intruded into our lives with content-learning almost to the exclusion of action-learning. They have separated thoughts from action and forced us to live in two worlds. They have separated mind from body, thinking from feeling and this brings on emotional disturbances of various kinds. Role playing permits us to associate learning with feeling and this makes it too valuable a device to ignore.

ROLE PLAYING

Role playing needs direction, someone who understands the problem and can guide the group in clarifying the situation and in producing insights. The director needs to protect the players by not letting the scene go so far as to hurt. He should understand how to develop skill by using the following devices:

1. *Role reversals.* The usual roles of the players are reversed. For example, a parent takes the child's role and the child the parent's, at the table and at piano practice afterward. After the usual pleadings, balking, and interruptions the child may speak out "Children can be such brats, can't they?"

2. *Soliloquy.* Between certain scenes the characters speak out their real feelings in soliloquy.

3. *Recast.* The characters are recast in more desirable roles, for example, from fighter to mediator.

It seems wise that directors should have participated in role playing themselves and that they understand the essential steps the group should take.[4]

---

[4]Writings on the subject include: Cook, Lloyd A., *Sociological Approach to Education,* McGraw-Hill, N. Y., 1950. Jennings, Helen H., "Sociodrama as an Educative Process," *1950 Ybk. of Assoc. for Supr. and Curriculum Develop.,* pg. 260. Haas, R. B., *Psychodrama and Sociodrama in American Education,* Beacon House, N. Y., 1949. Maier, Norman N. F., *Principles of Human Relations,* Wiley and Sons, N. Y., 1952. *Role Playing in Human Relations,* 2 reels, Columbia Univ. Bureau of Publication, 525 W. 120th St., New York 27, N. Y.

The Steps in Role Playing Are:

1. Select the situation, which should be limited to a specific problem, that is clearly understood by all present. The problem should be real and have significance for the group. The group should be made ready by means of a discussion of the importance of the situation and its problems. Not every situation is suitable for role playing.
2. Assign the roles according to the understanding of them by the players and according to their interest. Start people in roles familiar to them so that they will not be constrained. Select persons who want to explore the situation. Be sensitive to interpersonal relations within the group. The director or some status person may be able to carry an unfavorable role easier than other members.
3. Briefing the players and the audience. Instructions should be clear, complete, and brief. One must decide whether players should be instructed in private or before the group. Assign the group to observe certain players or to watch for interaction and be prepared to suggest improvements. The group may be able to brief itself. Rehearsals seem to dull the spontaneity.
4. Enact the situation which involves tension and conflicts. Cut the scene when players have exhausted their resources and before anyone may get hurt. It is a common error to let the action go on too long. Role playing is not for entertainment; it is for learning.
5. Analyse pattern of conflict. Ask the players what they learned, then ask the audience. Then seek suggestions for improvements.
6. Replay the situation. Act upon the suggestions given. Some roles may be recast or reversed. It may be that the same person may replay his role in order to show improvement.
7. Discuss the new patterns of adjustment.
8. Arrange additional training if necessary.

Role playing may be useful in discovering attitudes and feelings, in changing attitudes, in developing permissiveness, in building morale, in repairing damage done to the inter-group relations, and in training both officers and members. It is a valuable device but it is not sure-fire. It is spontaneous but should never be unplanned.

Before you attempt role playing, plan it out in considerable detail and make clear to yourself just why you are using it. Then do not despair if it gets away from you, it has from many. Read what happened to Mrs. Cole[5] on her first attempt to introduce the device.

[5]Cole, Natalie Robinson, "Role Playing Children's Concern," in Haas, R. B., *Psychodrama and Sociodrama in American Education,* Beacon House, N. Y., 1949.

Here are some thoughts about my first attempt with fifth grade kids. It began by my wanting as big a pile of papers as the next teacher. The paper drive was on and each grade was in competition. The kids didn't like to push door bells so I thought they needed a little role playing to desensitize them. So I said, "Morty, what are you going to do for the paper drive?" "Go next door and ask Mrs. Hamberger" he replied. "All right, you choose someone to be Mrs. Hamberger, and let's play-practice asking for paper."

He chose Sandra and then without any question went outside. We heard a knock and the following exchanges took place.

"Well, what do you want?"

"Good evening, Mrs. Hamberger. Our school is having a paper drive and . . ."

"I'm sorry all our papers are high up in the garage."

"I could get our ladder."

"I'm too busy."

"But I could do all the work."

"No, my husband said if anyone went into the garage we would have to go with him."

"I could wait for him. Isn't that your husband coming up the street now?"

"No, that's the Fuller brush man."

"It looks like the man I see coming here all the time."

This last nearly took the roof off. Ten-year-olds. Could you beat it? Now I knew this wasn't psychodrama it was melodrama and the kids had taken to it like ducks to water. They begged for more as they laughed their heads off. I felt helpless as I chose others to play.

Finally one housewife affecting a high-pitched English voice exclaimed:

"Oh, these American schools. A lot of new-fangled slosh."

"Oh, yea," said the other kid drawing himself up for a snappy comeback.

Then it came to me. Then I got my little bit of insight.

"Just a minute," I said, my confused impotence dropping away. "Just why are we pushing door bells?"

"To get papers," they answered feebly.

"Then are we just going to show how clever we are or are we going to do things which will *get* paper?"

"Get the paper," they shouted.

"Let's go over that scene again."

This time the reply to the English woman was, "Yes, I hear the English schools are marvelous, but we're working very hard on the paper drive."

Another lady who said she didn't have any was told, "I'll be around tomorrow night in case you happen to find some."

One thanked his neighbor for the papers and said, "I'll be glad to help repay you if you have any ashes to carry out."

I was thrilled. Here were children facing the fact that they must summon skill in dealing with people. They were holding the goal in mind and weighing their behavior and sentences in order to get paper.

HIGH QUALITY PARTICIPATION

High quality participation comes easiest in a permissive atmosphere. Therein we have no fear and consequently we try even though we have but little skill. Therein we receive recognition, and stimulated by the feeling that our efforts count, we become eager to increase our skill. Any program designed to increase skills in participation should follow the principles outlined below.

1. **Members want to design their own plans.** Since most of us demand a part in determining our own destiny we are not easily integrated into your nicely designed plans. Planning should be face-to-face rather than behind the scenes.

2. **Plans should grow out of members' needs and wants.** Problems rather than topics should be the basis for discussion and the problems should be those of the group rather than of the leaders. You can't get real action from imaginary problems.

3. **Plans should be based upon facts.** Too often groups fail to search for facts not possessed by their members. If we hold a group responsible for its acts we are better able to force it to gather all the facts and then think them through.

4. **Professional leadership** is important but it is not the whole solution. Groups need something to do for themselves. Nevertheless there are things groups do much better when guided by resource leaders.

5. **Groups must make steady progress** from problem selection to problem solution; otherwise interest will lag. There are certain steps which should be followed in problem solving.*

6. **Every group should take time to evaluate** its plans, its processes, and its products. Evaluation restricts a group to the facts discovered and costs a group the right to exist by opinion. These are restrictions which aid in producing clear-cut plans, and in building interest. The basic rule for building interest in

any activity is to give those concerned a means for measuring the progress they make.

Generally it is more difficult to achieve high quality participation in a large group than in a small one. This has led some group experimenters[6] to search for devices which will permit large groups to reap the benefits enjoyed by small groups.[7] Some of the devices described below have rather limited use and should be selected on the basis of the step they can best serve.

Fifteen Devices Effective in Stimulating Group Participation

1. **Interest approach.** Not all problems will arise from the grass roots. We may be unaware that a certain situation presents a problem. Others may see it and feel obliged to communicate it to us, but their problem will not become our problem until we understand it and accept it as ours. The responsibility for pointing out problems belongs to the experts who see them approaching. Their task is to present the problem in an interesting manner making it clearer, more specific, and more understandable. What should they do?

They might organize a tour so that the group may go and see, they might bring in a movie or a resource person or arrange a discussion. In these ways the members may project the situation into their own lives and determine whether it is important or not. In most cases there should be attempts to emotionalize the situation, but we should use group-building rather than group-destroying emotions.

2. **Questionnaire.** Questions are answered and the summary is presented to provide the topics for the discussion. This device is valuable in discovering problems (Step 2) and particularly in measuring the results (Step 5). (See problem solving steps*)

3. **Quiz.** The quiz may be either written or oral. It serves to explore the problems and discover interests and attitudes of those quizzed (Step 1). It may be valuable in getting agreement (Step 3d).

4. **Forum.** Several speakers present different aspects of the problem, and their presentation is followed by questions from the audience. This is essentially a device for discovering problems (Step 2) or for obtaining facts (Step 3). It seems more satis-

[6]Bradford, Leland P., and Corey, Stephan M., "Improving Large Group Meetings," *Adult Educ.,* 1:122, 1951.
[7]Hemphill, J. K., "Relation between the Size of Group and Behavior of Superior Leaders," *Jour. Soc.,* 4:11, 1950.

factory to have each speaker sit in the audience after completing his speech.

5. **Panel.** Panels differ from forums in that there is more discussion between speakers, fewer formal speeches, and a discussion leader who attempts to clarify the issues. Panels generally merely open up a topic (Step 2) which should be continued in smaller groups. If audience questions are permitted, the chairman may open the questioning by stating "I am not going to interrupt your thinking for one minute during which time I hope you will be phrasing the question you wish to ask. You may be assured that our speakers will treat kindly all questions which raise doubts about their view points. I hope, however, you do not aim to embarrass the speaker by your questions."

6. **Hearing.** A judge and jury listen to witnesses who give testimony on both sides of a question. An attorney may question the witnesses, and the jury then renders the decision. The jury may discuss the issues before the entire group in order to permit the group to evaluate the thinking that is being done. After the decision, smaller groups may discuss the justice of the decision. The hearing may be aimed at discovering the important problems (Step 2), at giving facts (Step 3a), or at the critical evaluation of proposals (Step 3b).

7. **Clinic.** Experts hear a case and prescribe a remedy or treatment. This may help in formulating objectives (Step 1, or in Steps 2 and 3), but it does have a special place in evaluating results (Step 5). Small groups should take up the problem after the clinic.

8. **Group interview.** Several persons who are qualified to speak upon a specific topic are assembled and interviewed before the group. The interviewer should ask pointed questions, ask for differences or confirming statements and ask questions which bring out all sides or issues. He may ask the audience to submit questions either orally or in writing which he relays to the experts. This procedure permits an interviewer to develop the problem in a clear and logical fashion.

9. **Interview play-back.** If the problem is of a personal nature and the interviewee might do better without an audience, the interview might be recorded and played back to the group. This device permits the group to gain insight into emotional problems, unexpressed desires, and conflict situations.

10. **Soliloquy.** One or two persons less timid than the rest may be stationed behind a screen to tell what goes on in their minds, as the meeting proceeds. It is a sort of stage aside or conscience which gives insight to unexpressed thoughts. Considerable expert skill is demanded. The voices may better be carried over a loud speaker.

11. **Buzz sessions.** The group is divided into smaller groups of about 6 or 8 persons each. One or two definite questions are proposed, and each group is asked to find the best answer and report back in about ten minutes. This is really a small group discussion, but the method is limited to the discovery of problems, to listing them in order of importance (Step 2), to collecting suggestions (Step 3a), and to obtaining a vote (Step 3c). Doing these things does not guarantee that the problem is solved.

The chairman of a buzz group may use a roll call device to get contributions. In so doing he may introduce it something like this, "Make your statements brief and to the point. In fact, the more pointed they are the more they will stimulate discussion. You need not explain why you believe as you do. It will be fun for us to try to figure that out. It will even be fun for us to figure out whether or not you have something up your sleeve."

12. **Listening teams.** There should be a purpose in the giving of a report. It should contain facts that confirm former decisions or that point out problems needing solution. Unless the audience is informed about former decisions or about present problems, it may not see the significance of the particular facts that are presented. The appointment of listening teams is a device that will focus the attention of individuals upon a particular issue. The program chairman should divide the audience into about four groups by means of numbered cards. The particular topic each person is to look for and evaluate while the reports are being given may be typed upon the cards. Some of the topics are:

a. Have the policies outlined by the members been carried out during the year?
b. Has the business grown stronger or weaker? In ownership? In patronage? In membership information?
c. What are the critical operational problems? Into what areas should we expand?
d. Are the abilities of the board members balanced? Are officers active and well informed? Are their decisions democratically arrived at?

These or other questions may be written on cards, one question to a card. Six cards carrying the same question may be given the same number. The cards may be distributed as the group assembles. After the reports, buzz groups consisting of persons holding cards numbered alike are formed. These groups then discuss the problems and arrive at a set of recommendations. One person is appointed from each group to meet and compare notes and to select an audience report panel of four to six members.

13. **Audience report panel.** This panel may be selected from the listening teams, or the chairman my designate only six persons from the audience to listen for specified topics. This panel is given the responsibility of discussing the reactions of the listening teams, or their own reactions if no listening teams were designated, and to report to the entire group. A report panel is a device for identifying important problems (Step 2), and for evaluating (Step 3b), for deciding a plan of action (Step 3c), and for measuring results (Step 5), but it cannot easily do all these things at the same time.

14. **Sociodrama.** Sociodrama is an extremely useful device in formulating objectives, in building morale, in evaluating proposed solution and in training leaders. It has already been discussed.

15. **Surveys.** By taking a survey the group may learn much about the interests, attitudes, and abilities of its members (Step 1) and about the progress made during the year (Step 5).

One type of survey is a sort of association test. The chairman arranges a list of ten words which have some meaning to the discussion topic. He asks each person to check each word as to whether it is pleasant, neutral or unpleasant in meaning. He then records the number of responses to each word. The questions might be alternated between pleasant and unpleasant aspects of the problem or the leader may inquire as to why certain words carry neutral meanings. A list of questions which might be checked true or false are included in the appendix.

Although variety is important in any program it would be a mistake to select these devices merely for the sake of variety. Each should be selected on the basis of how well it will advance the specific step which needs to be taken. For example, the buzz session has become a popular device. It has been over-used, even abused because it was expected to serve where it could not serve adequately.

Participation is the reason behind forming a group, it is the reason for selecting and training officers and leaders, it is the reason for building a program and having meetings. If we don't get participation all our efforts are futile. High quality participation is a skill that can only be learned through practice. And it will not be high quality unless it produces results.

A caution should be introduced here. The various techniques and gadgets suggested in the last two chapters may be seized upon as escapes from discomforts and responsibilities if they become formalized procedures. There is a lure in formal procedures, such as selecting an observer, planning an agenda, conducting a survey, holding buzz sessions, filling out end-of-meeting evaluation sheets or in role playing which should be recognized and guarded against. These devices are not cure-alls, they have a place but that place should be determined on the basis of how well the particular device will serve in the particular situation.

Chapter 13.

EVALUATION

It is no problem to get people to evaluate. That they do easily and naturally. They evaluate whenever they render judgments, whenever they say, "That was a good job," or "What a lousy time," or "You shouldn't do that," or "It costs too much." Whether right or wrong, such judgments are important because they influence future events. The real problem is not evaluation but better evaluation.

Better evaluation depends upon two things:
1. A clearer understanding of the standards by which objects should be judged.
2. A more dependable factual base.

Both are difficult for individuals and more difficult for groups. Most standards have evolved unbeknown to us. They are usually highly charged with feeling, even with fear and they seldom are questioned. For a group to decide between several hazy and highly charged standards* is indeed a difficult task. Furthermore evaluation is difficult because dependable facts are hard to get.

In addition to overcoming these difficulties, those who seek to evaluate must overcome opposition too. Evaluation is opposed because it circumscribes freedom. So long as the value of a piece of work is unknown, its advocates are free to make claims and assumptions, but once it has been evaluated the workers are no longer free. Evaluation costs a movement its right to exist by opinion.

Those who dislike these restrictions may even attack evaluation as they attack the Character Education Inquiry.[1] The study was well designed and ably executed but it showed that boys and girls who belonged to the so-called character building agencies were no better than those who didn't. In fact those who had moved up the achievement scale of these agencies were more disposed to be dishonest.

---

[1]Hartshorne, Hugh, and May, Mark A., *Studies in the Nature of Character,* Teachers' College, Columbia, Univ., Macmillan Co., N. Y., 1928-30.

In spite of all these difficulties, those who seek to know and profit by their mistakes must evaluate.

"The most important step in any science," said James Clerk Maxwell, "is measurement of quantities. Those who observe what happens have occasionally done service by directing attention toward the phenomena, but it is to those who endeavor to find out how much there is of anything that we owe all the great advances in our knowledge." So long as education is considered an art, its results are spoken of as intangibles, but when it is considered as a science, measurement becomes essential. The scientist believes that any thing that exists (empirical beliefs), exists in some amount and can be measured. Furthermore, he believes that measurement is indispensable to progress.

The scientist applies measuring devices to his work because he wants to know not only how, but *how much*. He believes that, next to knowing he is right, the most important thing is to know he is wrong.

Administrators usually want measures of work done for two reasons: (1) to justify the expenditures made and (2) to furnish facts which may be useful in making decisions. They want facts for building programs, and facts which will enable them to select the best methods or procedures. Unless they have facts, decisions must be based upon tradition or opinion. Reason and judgement cannot be rendered without facts.

Personnel workers see a third reason for evaluation; that is, its high learning value. To have a part in gathering the facts and in rendering decisions based upon them is important as a learning situation. Furthermore, interest grows and integrative feelings evolve as one has a part in making the decisions for one's group. Any program which ignores this fact suffers a serious handicap.

From the viewpoint of the program builder, evaluation is a splendid aid in building interest. Clearly the number one principle for building interest is recognition, recognition which has an objective basis. Stated otherwise, "Give a person an objective means for measuring his progress if you want him to remain interested in any activity." This is a very important law.

From the viewpoint of the project leader, evaluation permits him to test the methods used, and it gives him facts for seeking financial support. Measurement permits him to know when he is right, and he cannot choose except by chance unless he knows. Evaluation permits him to correct his mistakes promptly. Experience is such a good teacher that we should take every possible precaution to avoid experience in error. The rule "trial and error" is better stated as "trial and success."

From the viewpoint of the local program expediter, adviser or leader, evaluation will help him to select the more important from among the lesser tasks. It will enable him to select those jobs which give the largest returns, and to apply himself more diligently to those that get results.

From the viewpoint of the clientele, evaluation is an important integrator. Our efforts increase when we realize that we are appreciated and that the rewards for achievement are rightly granted. Our morale is destroyed when we see rewards being arbitrarily or subjectively distributed. There is no greater administrative skill than that of distributing rewards on the basis of merit, objectively determined. But we have not yet developed objective measures for some activities. This deficiency permits some officials to use the term "merit" as a device for "lining up the loyalties" behind themselves. The task of distributing rewards justly is difficult and the instruments available are crude, but its importance should motivate us to vigorously and objectively pursue the job.

Evaluation is not an end in itself. It is a means. It is a means for causing us to more carefully consider our objectives, a means for holding us more closely to the task of attaining our objectives, a means for determining the effectiveness of our various methods and procedures, and a means for permitting us to distribute the rewards for achievement more equitably.

The best measures of any program are its results. A measure of what a person has purposefully accomplished includes what he knows, what he does, and what his feelings and values are. More important than our motives and knowledge is what we do, and more important than that are the results we obtain by doing. If we can't find measures of results, we are forced to step back and measure activities or take the second step back to measure facts, manual skills, thought skills, interest and attitudes or habits. Too often evaluation stops with a listing of time spent and activities undertaken. This only tells us that the group went through certain motions, it tells nothing of the results attained.

There are four well-defined steps in the process of evaluation. Whenever a person is asked to help measure he first must ask "What are you trying to accomplish?" This means that we must agree upon a set of values and then describe them in terms of the behavior involved. These descriptions become criteria by means of which we determine (1) the level of behavior at the start, (2) the progress made up to any time and (3) the final attainment. For example, nearly all will agree that everyone should be healthy. But health consists of a number of things so we must set up a number of criteria. Suppose we state one criteria as "What is the standard score for any boy or girl on the 600-yard endurance test?" This permits us to collect several measures of progress during a period of time.

The second step is to set up test situations which will give a chance for the behavior to operate. If our criteria for the vocational efficiency of a hog farmer is—"How many pounds of pork did he produce per sow in six months?" the test situation might be a pork production contest which will enable us to collect the data from the kinds and numbers of persons we desire. If we have decided reading is an important skill and have found that reading consists of both oral and silent reading of which speed and comprehension are recognized parts, then we will have to set up test situations for word recognition, sentence understanding, paragraph comprehension, and speed. All these will have to be tested.

The third step is to obtain an accurate record of the behavior that took place. A lack of rapport or a strong desire for approval will bias the results. If we are measuring agility by means of the time taken to run 60 yards and the runner doesn't try his best, our results will not be an accurate test. An adequate and typical sample of the behavior must be recorded to enable us to evaluate the data. The evaluator wants to know how

> Tradition speaks quickly.
>
> Opinion speaks loudly.
>
> Evaluation does not speak—unless it has the facts.

valid are the results, how reliable are the data and how dependable is the sample. He applies statistical techniques to assist him in drawing conclusions.

The fourth step is to re-measure after a period of time during which we have been attempting to apply certain methods or practices. It takes more than one point to determine a direction. A compass does not point the way, neither does it tell us where we've been nor where we are going. It merely points north. We must take our bearings on two occasions for us to tell where and how far we have gone.

Most of our efforts should be expended upon people, for it is through people that we change physical and social environment as well as psychological behavior.

When working in the educational area our objectives are people and we expect to see desirable changes in people as the ends or goals of our efforts. Our facilities for effecting changes in people are the resources, the plants, the animals, the buildings, the equipment, the machines, and the supplies. Our tools are the facts, interests, and skills. Our problem as group leaders is to become skillful in using our facilities and tools to develop interests and skills in people and to teach them to think straight. Subject matter is only our tools, method is our skill in using our tools and our goals are certain desirable changes in people.

Because there are so many goals it seems appropriate here that we list only a few criteria hoping that they may suggest others. We shall classify them under one or another of the broader objectives outlined previously. Our classification is not exact, there may be several criteria for the same objective and any one criterion might be placed under more than one objective. For example suppose a community attempts to solve its parking problems. Three criteria are suggested. One might be, "what are the number of parking spaces added?" A better one would be, "What are the number of parking spaces within a certain area on December 31st each year per 1000 cars registered within the trade area?" This same problem might be approached by asking a representative sample of the car owners to indicate their satisfaction in finding a parking space on certain days of uniformly congested conditions before and after parking conditions were changed. Here we have both a physical and psychological criterion for an objective which might be classified as social-civic.

CRITERIA FOR OBJECTIVES

Here are other criteria, some of which are not completely stated.

Health Criteria:

1. What proportion of the school children in a certain district has been immunized against smallpox?
2. What is the average standard score of any 12-year-old boy on ten fitness tests? (The tests must have been carefully selected and validated.)
3. What is the incidence of (any important) disease per 1,000 persons per year?
4. What per cent of the families live within 20 miles of an approved hospital?
5. What is the number of persons per doctor or per dentist within the county?
6. What is the per cent of youth between 10 and 20 that can swim 100 feet?
7. What is the per cent of herds of cattle free from Brucellosis?
8. What is the number of various kinds of accidents per 1,000 persons within the county?
9. What per cent of children of each age group are growing according to standard? (There are body growth charts upon which growth may be plotted. From these, above or below standard growth may be determined.)
10. What per cent of school children show the common signs of malnutrition?

Vocational-efficiency criteria:

1. What is the average pounds of milk produced per dairy cow per year in the community?
2. What per cent is this of the average production of farmers in the cow test association?
3. What is the average yield of corn per acre per year when compared with the 10 year average or with a good management standard?
4. What per cent of men 20 to 50 years of age are gainfully employed per year?
5. What is the distribution of scores for a representative sample of the community on Sims' Socioeconomic Scale?
6. What is the average farm family index on Sewell's Socioeconomic Status? (See Okla. Agri. Exp. Sta. Bul. 9.)
7. What is the total volume of business done by cooperative organizations each year?

Socio-civic efficiency criteria:

1. What is the number of public library books per person over 15 years of age in the community?

2. What is the per cent of children 15-19 years of age in school?
3. What is the per cent of farm homes having electricity?
4. What is the average score on Sewell's Family Socio-economic Status Scale for families of the community?
5. What attitudes are held by persons of different ages who hold membership in different groups? (Tests can be prepared for such attitudes as dependability, determination, flexibility, social effectiveness, and civic responsibility. If these are administered from time to time we may obtain facts regarding the development of civic attitudes.)

Recreation:

1. What is the number of library books per person in the county?
2. What is the attitude of the different age groups with regard to the adequacy of recreational activities of various kinds?
3. What do the people of the community do in their off-duty hours?
4. What is the number of recreational activities undertaken by different groups of persons?

No group having objectives broader than self-enjoyment can afford to go without evaluation. It's much too important to any program to be overlooked. Evaluation generally starts with a feeling of dissatisfaction and this same feeling is behind the building of every program. Consequently evaluation is a splendid point of departure for any program building or rebuilding project. The more objective the evaluation, the better it will help define the goals and purposes; and an exact statement of objectives has many times been found of tremendous influence in speeding up problem solving activities. Furthermore an objective evaluation helps in decisions regarding methods of procedure.

Since evaluation tasks are often too involved and too time consuming for many groups, it is strongly recommended that every group seek alliances with a resource leader who may help point up the procedure for measuring results, and help make the objectives more specific. When we understand the objectives we gain a deep sense of the importance of the matter at hand. To be important the problem must be useful and seem within the ability of the group to solve. Furthermore a resource leader can help make meaningful the methods to be pursued and when a group understands the reasons for doing a thing it is better able to make minor adjustments as conditions change.

Group leaders like other humans have limited skills compared with the great demands placed upon them. Therefore, they should expect to spend considerable time in training or learning. In the Army, teachers spend about one-fourth of their time on further training and it seems no less important to have men efficient in peace than in war.

Chapter 14.

EXTENDING THE BENEFITS

There is an ancient philosophy which declares that it is natural and good for men to fight. It states that competition is the life of business and that mankind's present high position resulted from conflict. There is a modern philosophy which teaches that mutual aid is beneficial and had it not been for man's ability to cooperate the human race would have perished long since.

In competitive society the hope is that the contending forces will balance each other. Merchants and customers, manufacturers and laborers, lawyers and criminals, soldiers and enemies are all engaged in a great game of give and take. They choose sides and business becomes a battle, with the rewards going to the victors.

Around these contending interests are myriads of agencies serving minorities of individuals through programs tailored to fit the needs of housewives, bankers, laborers, farmers, even religious and cultural groups. Over and against these aggressive forces have been a multitude of societies formed to promote the public safety and the general well-being. The tendency in America has been or organize. Over 100 years ago a French visitor, Tacqueville wrote of our "let's get together and do it ourselves" philosophy. He said that in no country in the world has the principle of association been more successfully used.

We have groups organized both *for* and *against*. The greater number are against. They are protest movements, formed to protect the organizers. Tacqueville saw and we later recognized the inevitable confusion, conflict and factionalism which resulted from groups organized to get ahead by overcoming, defeating or destroying.

A more positive expression of the human need for getting ahead is in cooperation—cooperation *for* rather than *against*. In fact, the answer to our central dilemma both economically and politically lies in responsible participation in cooperative enterprise.

This is the essence of Dewey's social philosophy.[1] Cooperation to him is both intelligent and good. It is intelligent because
modern industry has been built upon it, because it puts government in its proper place as a helpful resource available to people
as they need it and because society itself could not survive without it. The fittest to survive are those able to find their strength
in cooperation, able to build organizations based upon mutual
helpfulness and responsibility for one's fellowmen. And it is
good because it is intelligent, because it prevents society from
hardening into classes or castes
and because it liberates the
minds of individuals to make
creative contributions to the
common life. Humans need not
only to be helped but to be helpful. Mankind advances as it adds
to the past and gives to the
future.

> Democracy is an all-out activity!
> The world cannot live by halves:
>   half-well, half-sick
>   half-educated, half-illiterate
>   half-fed, half-starved
>   half-rich, half-poor
>   half at work, half idle
>   half-clothed half-naked
>   half-protected, half-neglected

The first appeal of coopera-
tion is that it permits us to obtain more goods and services
than we could enjoy individually. Witness our schools, roads,
sewage disposal plants, our fire and police protection, our art
galleries and museums, our parks and playgrounds, none of
which we could afford alone. Cooperation permits one to have
things which he could not provide for himself.

The second appeal is in its service to others. If I would live
a fair and honest life I must give to society in return for what
society has given to me. No individual is genuinely and lastingly
happy until he has something beyond—something greater than
himself—to care about, to work for, and, if need be, to die for.
The fact that a community is a community of interests is the
most important thing about democracy.

This sharing of interests is the indispensable condition for
achieving a level of development above the brutes.

Democracy is a tired word, but it stands for a new idea. It
stands for creating a new potential for humans just as technology has created a new potential for industry. Democracy is a
moral idea, in it we see humans not fixed but flexible; we see
experiences not distinct, but as something which happens to
humans; we see thinking not as the voice of reason, but as a

---

[1]Nathanson, Jerome, *John Dewey, the Reconstruction of a Democratic Life*, Charles
Scribner's Sons, N. Y., 1951.

method for solving problems; we see knowledge not as something immutable, but as dependable propositions about a changing world; and we see education not as a body of facts, but as a process in which all social institutions take part.

Spiritual acts are realized by a person when he operates as an agent of the ideal community of persons created equal. He may act against his individual conveniencies and stand up for universal interests because he feels he is a part of a group superior to his particular individuality.[2] The merchant who uses weights, measures and tests because he believes that is the way to be fair to his customers executes a spiritual act.

Of the democratic trio—liberty, equality, and fraternity—the greatest of these perhaps is fraternity. Liberty matured to the left becomes laxity and license, to the right dominance and monopoly. Equality prevents us from misusing our liberty and forces liberty to mature as equalized access to the benefits of the social order. And equality saves fraternity from fanaticism. The brotherhood we want is of the equally free; free men equalized to the burdens as well as the benefits. Freedom makes brotherhood tolerable and equality makes it possible.[3]

Any action system designed to place emphasis upon the community is duty-bound to extend the benefits to the entire social group. Wealth would be worthless without people. It is human wants and desires which makes a product valuable. We would be nothing were it not for the people about us; in fact, we could not persist. The individual organism does not reproduce its kind as a rule, the organism does not evolve. It is the breeding population, not the individual, not the species, but the natural self-generating groups which actually do interbreed; these are the groups which persist. And there is a good deal of evidence to show that when benefits become so few that the population decreases below a certain point that population does become extinct.[4]

A Co-operation Fable

Said a wise old bee at the close of day,
"This colony business doesn't pay.
I put my honey in that old hive
That others may eat and live and thrive:

---

[2]Romero, Francisco, "Man and Culture," In *Ideological Differences and World Order*, F. S. C. Northrup (Ed), Yale Univ. Press, New Haven, 1949.
[3]Smith, T. V., "Methodological Equality and Functionalism Idealism," Chapter 18 in *Freedom and Authority in Our Time*, Lyman Bryson (Ed), Harpers, N. Y., 1953.
[4]Miller, Hugh, *The Community of Man*, MacMillan, N. Y., 1949.

And I do more work in a day, by gee,
Than some of the other fellows do in three.
I toil and worry and save and hord;
And all I get is my room and board.
It's me for a hive I can run myself,
And me for the sweets of my hard earned self."
So the old bee flew to a meadow alone,
And started a business all his own.
He gave no thought to the buzzing clan,
But all intent on his selfish plan,
He lived the life of a hermit free—
"Ah, this is great," said the wise old bee.
But the summer waned and the days grew drear,
And the lone bee wailed as he dropped a tear;
For the varmits gobbled his little store,
And his wax played out and his heart was sore,
So he winged his way to the old home band,
And took his meals at the Helping Hand.
Alone, our work is of little worth,
Together we are the lords of the earth;
So it's all for each and it's each for all—
United stand, or divided fall.

—Author Unknown

Shared experience is the greatest of human goods.

John Dewey

Appendices

General Information

These appendices contain suggestions of things leaders may do. Some are discussion outlines, some are check sheets, some are evaluation forms and some are facts which may be useful in preparing talks. They are coded as follows:

A = materials on objectives, goals, or policies.

B = materials on membership, attitude and information.

C = materials on problem solving

D = leadership materials

E = materials on group processes

F = materials for evaluation

A Table of Contents

Appendix A1.

OUTLINE FOR DISCUSSION OF GOALS FOR PROGRAM COMMITTEE

Problem: What rules should guide a Program Committee?

> Note: This problem may be introduced either by the president or the chairman of the Program Committee. He might repeat the parts in quotation. This discussion is aimed at developing the idea of *our* program vs. *your* program.

"We are expected to prepare a program for our group. This means that we should consider not only what to do but also where will it get us. Back of this are the objectives of our group, that is, where do we want to go. I wonder—Won't you write three little sentences on the note paper before you?

1. Where to go?
2. What to do to get us there?
3. Who will we do it to?

"After deciding where to go we then must decide what to do unto others. I saw a statement about the Golden Rule which I should like to read.

"The Golden Rule is, 'Do unto others as you would have them do unto you.' We can't do without doing something and the rule says do just what we like for ourselves. That's sort of selfish isn't it? If we state it differently and say, 'Do something other than what you don't want done to you,' we are still intervening in the affairs of others. If we think we shouldn't push others around and state it in negative terms such as, 'Don't do what you would like others to do to you,' we've only changed from action to inaction. If you want to eliminate the idea of intervention you might like it stated, 'Don't let others do to you what you would do to them.' But to be neither selfish nor intervening, to be truly altruistic you would have to state the Golden Rule, 'Do to others as they would have you do to them.'

"Can we follow this last statement and build a program that will get us along the road toward our objectives?"

> Note: As program suggestions are offered each should be evaluated as to "where will it get us" and "who will do it."

Appendix A2.—————————————————

OUTLINE FOR A SERIES OF DISCUSSIONS OF POLICY FORMULATION

Problem: How may an organization formulate a set of policies?

Introduction: Some organizations fumble about and become impotent because they fail to consider their policies. Some members even say that it takes too much time.

Progress means movement in some known direction, and unless we know where we want to go we do not know in what direction to "take off."

Note: Below are questions which should be discussed by the group. It seems better to divide the group into buzz groups and ask each to report on the following questions:

1. Who should determine the policies for a group?
2. What problems do the members say they have?
3. What problems do they see in the community?
   a. Can an organization discover the things its members think are important without asking them? Is it worth the time it will take to send out a questionnaire?
   b. Suppose members differ regarding the things they think are important? How can these differences be clarified? Should it be done publicly or privately? Are differences bad?
4. Who should determine whether or not the projected solution is within the province of the organization?

Problem: How can an established policy be revised?

Note: There comes a time when every group needs to consider revisions. New members have been added and they may be unaware of the original goals and times may have changed so that new goals are in order. The task of proposing revisions may be assigned a committee composed of both old and new members. The following questions should be discussed and the committee report to the whole group.

1. Have new problems arisen since the original policies were established?
2. Was any provisions for revision made in the original plans?
3. Will basic aims be vitiated by proposed revisions?
4. Will revisions upset the present power structure?

5. Will certain persons suffer because of the revisions?
6. Would a trial revision be acceptable?
7. Why is the change urgent to some persons?
8. What things in the world are unchangeable?

Problem: How can vague policies be made clear?

These questions might be considered by planning committees.

1. Do vague policies serve a purpose for some persons?
2. Have you tried having the members write out a set of policies?
3. Are some persons using the group for a personal satisfaction of which the members are unaware?
4. Should policies be based upon actual issues?
5. Are issues disguised for selfish desires?
6. Is there any disposition to cut short discussion on issues?
7. Do you think a policy can have 3 sides: your side, my side, and the right side? Have you tried to state the 3 sides?

Appendix A3.

A CHECK SHEET OF GROUP FUNCTIONS FOR OFFICERS

Officers should give a certain direction to the group activities. There are five functions outlined below with steps to take or activities to perform listed under each. These may help officers determining whether or not important things are being done. This check list should be reviewed rather frequently.

Planning functions:

1. Has the group determined its broader objectives?
2. Does it have more immediate goals for this meeting? Does it decide what to do now?
3. What has been done to find out whether all the members are in accord?
4. Has the group set up a priority list of its problems, made a step by step plan?
5. Does the group consider complaints based on value-attitudes?

6. Does the group consider the probable sources of resistance to its plans?

7. Are goals adjusted when need arises?

Fact-finding functions:

1. Did the group assess the competencies of its members as they relate to the problem at hand?

2. Has it set up mechanisms to make the various abilities known to all the members?

3. Does it proceed to get all the "nuggets" contributed from each member?

4. Is each idea contributed considered thereafter as group property?

5. Does the group slow up its tempo to give time for thinking?

6. Does it call up resource persons?

7. Does it form small work groups into which members feel free to move and work in order to collect necessary data?

8. Are the members free to contribute? Do they hedge in expressing themselves in questions or are they able to make straight-forward statements?

Evaluating-data functions:

1. Are differences cherished? Do members tell of their differences without hesitation? Do they welcome opinions of others?

2. Are facts evaluated distinct from the person who contributed them?

3. Do members express fear of being misunderstood?

4. Are definitions called for? Do persons understand each other?

5. Are alternative propositions set up?

Decision-making functions:

1. Are parliamentary rules evoked in order to make decisions a necessary part of the procedures?

2. Is the group able to close the discussion on one step and move to the next in problem-solving?

Putting-the-plan-into-action functions:

1. Does the group set up an administrative organization?

2. Does it delegate responsibility and authority?

3. Does everyone know the part he is to play?

Appendix A4.————————————

PHILOSOPHY TOPICS FOR DISCUSSION

On occasion some informal groups get into a speculative mood. If the group is small, a good deal of satisfaction may come from a thoughtful consideration of the four questions below:

1. Which way is man headed?
2. Which way should he be headed?
3. How far can he go?
4. How far will he go?

Appendix B1.————————————

MEMBERSHIP COMMITTEE CHECK LIST

Too often new members are recruited and then left to sink or swim. Usually members want to join to gain status; consequently, they want to conform if they only know how. The induction and training of new members is a neglected responsibility of membership committees.

Status and cohesiveness seem to increase together except that the inner circle of low status groups are very cohesive.[1] Then, too, as conformity increases, the more the members try to influence each other and the stronger is the rejection of nonconformists.[2]

These findings make it seem important that the membership committee undertake activities which would cause members to consider the following questions:

1. Why am I in this group?
2. What do I expect to get from this group?
3. What is the group trying to accomplish?
4. What am I trying to learn?

[1]Thibaut, John, "An Experimental Study of the Cohesiveness of Under-privileged Groups," *Human Relations,* 3:251, 1950.
[2]Festinger, Leon, "Current Developments in Group Dynamics: Social Work in the Current Scene," *1950, 77th Annual Meeting of National Conf. of Soc. Work.,* Columbia Univ. Press, N. Y., 1950.

5. Where am I in my stage of learning?
6. Do I want to change?
7. Do I need encouragement and friendship?
8. Will strong opposition force me to examine myself?
9. Does the group accept me?
10. What can I do for this group?
11. What can the group do for me?

Appendix B2.——————————

SOCIOMETRIC QUESTIONNAIRES

Groups fail unless they are composed of the right combination of persons. Selecting the personnel is an important task for officials and for membership committees.

Personal liking is one basis for selection but it is not the only basis. We enjoy different persons for different reasons and this makes it important that we know the purpose of the group when we propose questions of personal likes. Below are a few examples:

Whom would you like:

a. to room with   d. to care for if sick
b. to eat with   e. to travel with
c. to work with   f. to dance with
            g. to chum with

Abilities or competencies are needed too. In discussion groups two ability patterns stand out. The first is the technical specialist's role, that is, the person who supplies the facts or the "know-how." The questions **a** to **g** below attempt to discover the technical specialist. Here again the special ability may differ depending upon the objectives of the group. The following questions are suggestive:

a. Whom would you rather have on a committee to manage a bake sale?
b. Whom would you rather have on your baseball team?

    c. Whom would you rather have in your 4-H club?

    d. Whom would you rather have to help build a parade float?

    e. If you needed facts about (some subject) to whom would you go?

    f. To whom would you appeal if some dangerous job needed to be done?

    g. To whom would you go for a loan?

The second role needed is the chairman's or the person who guides the group through the problem-solving steps. Questions h, i and j are aimed at discovering the person who provides the guidance.*

    h. Who in your group best guides it through its group activities?

    i. Name five persons in your group without regards for their official position whose value, importance or contributions to the group you think is:

        1. Outstanding _____

        2. Superior _____

        3. Average _____

        4. Fair _____

        5. Slight _____

    j. Now rank the outstanding (and/or superior) individual on a 6 point scale (1=high; 6=low) on each of the following items.
       Rank

      _____ Skill on the job

      _____ Knowledge of his subject

      _____ General knowledge

      _____ Range of interests

      _____ Value to the community

      _____ Ability to cooperate

      _____ Recognition by others for his ability

      _____ Rate of growth in knowledge and skill

      _____ Ability to stimulate, encourage, and harmonize differences.

Appendix B3. ─────────────────────

GROUP AND COMMITTEE SIZE — FACTS FOR OFFICERS

Studies of the size of different kinds of groups may be helpful in the selection of a committee for planning or for action.

Informal work groups ranged from 2 to 7 members.[1]

Action-taking committees averaged 6.5 members.[1]

Sub-committees of the U. S. House of Representatives averaged 7.8 members.

As discussion groups increased in size from 5 to 12 members, the degree of consensus decreased when time was held constant.[2]

Appendix B4. ─────────────────────

MEMBER CHECK LIST OF OWN MODE OF ORIENTATION

Three modes of orientation have been described in Chapter 2. Answers to the following questions will give a sort of rule of thumb analysis of the mode receiving the major emphasis in the life of a particular member.

Do you enjoy life?
Do you let your feelings often get out of control?
Do you enjoy expressing yourself?
Do you have "ups" and "downs" in moods?
Do you enjoy meeting and talking with people?
Are you impartial?
Do you like nearly everyone?
Are you able to control your emotions?
Do you question your beliefs?
Do you enjoy studying?
Do you keep extensive notes of your studies?

─────

[1]James, John, "A Preliminary Study of the Size Determinant in Small Group Interaction," *American Soc. Review,* 16:474, August, 1951.
[2]Hare, A. Paul, "A Study of Interaction and Consensus in Different Sized Groups," *American Soc. Review,* 17:261, June, 1952.

Do you reorganize your notes?
Do you plan your attack upon a problem?
Are you able to size up a problem?
Do you size up your abilities?
Are you scientific?
Do you like figures?
Have you thought out your goals?
Do you like to take responsibilities?
Do you welcome new ideas?
Do you choose between things before doing either?
Do you have goals worth fighting for?
Do you give up easily?

Appendix C1.

PROBLEM SOLVING FUNCTIONS — FOR PROGRAM COMMITTEE

The following questions may be found useful in provoking discussion in a planning committee.

Planning functions:

1. Does the group use procedures for discovering its real problems?
2. Does it select immediate goals which are consistent with its broader objectives? Does it have a priority list of problems?
3. Are the members able to state the group's objectives without hesitation?
4. Are the goals reviewed and adjusted at regular intervals?
5. Does the group use devices to learn the members' value-attitudes?
6. Does it determine how many members are in accord with its goals?
7. Does it consider probable resistance to its program?

Fact-finding and evaluating functions:

1. Does the group have ways for getting contributions from every member?
2. Does it assess the competencies of each member?
3. Does it have means for making these known to all?

4. Does it call in resource leaders?
5. Does it form small work groups to collect data?
6. Does it give time for thinking?
7. Does it select a recorder to help it contrast and compare facts?
8. Does it avoid the common errors in thinking?
9. Does it follow a step-by-step procedure to advance the discussion?
10. Are facts evaluated distinct from the persons who contributed them?
11. Are definitions called for?
12. Are alternative propositions set up?
13. Do members express fear of being misunderstood?

Decision-making functions:

1. Are parliamentary rules evoked to advance but not to hinder group decision?
2. Is the group able to decide one issue and move on to the next? Does it railroad any decisions?
3. Is it able to report its decisions with arguments for and against?

Action functions:

1. Does the group set up organizational procedures suitable for the action required?
2. Does it delegate authority and responsibility?
3. Do members understand the part each is to play?

Appendix C2. ──────────────

HOW TO BECOME A SOUND THINKER

The list of statements below may be duplicated and placed in the hands of every member of the group as a means of teaching procedures for problem solving. Ask members to note when violations of the statements are made.

1. Be sure you understand what problem is being discussed.
2. Hold close to the meanings expressed in the problem. Do not change the meanings of terms as the discussion proceeds.

See Douglas, Jack, "Problem Solving Evaluation," *Journ. Comm.* 3:20, 1953.

3. Search out real relationships. Beware not to declare an accidental or chance relationship as a universal case. Give chief consideration to the typical rather than the exceptional case.

4. Remember that only those relationships expressed in the premise may be expressed in the conclusion.

5. Revise or relinquish former hypotheses whenever they have been found in conflict with a single new fact and accept the new conclusion willingly.

6. Beware that you do not rationalize your prejudices, hopes, or beliefs into an argument for or against a proposition.

7. Disregard heresay and superstition.

8. Overcome your fears by admitting their source, then plan your steps to take your objectives and perfect your skill so that you can.

9. Seek to understand what you hate and why you hate it. (Is it an impersonal act?)

10. Search out the most competent authorities to quote.

11. Remember that it takes more than loud and insistent talk to make a truth.

12. Beware of compromises, they discount differences and differences are the real values in arguments.

13. Beware of false analogies.

14. Beware of loaded and colored words.

15. Look for the full significance of catchy phrases.

16. Seek out the purposes behind arguments.

Appendix C3.

MEMBER CHECK LIST IN GATHERING AND EVALUATING FACTS

	Yes	No
1. Do I read other things than my favorite paper?	___	___
2. Do I check the sources of the story?	___	___
3. Do I examine the qualifications of the author?	___	___
4. Do I question the conclusions drawn?	___	___
5. Do I look for false generalizations?	___	___
6. Can I distinguish between fact and fancy?	___	___
7. Do I give new and strange ideas a fair chance?	___	___
8. Am I aware of my own prejudices?	___	___

Appendix C4.

IN THINKING — BEWARE!

1. of your rigid assumptions
2. of your passions, they befog
3. of your stereotypes
4. of your tendency to consider human conflicts as unimportant, transitory and unreal
5. of guesswork
6. of over generalization

Appendix C5.

TO UNDERSTAND ANOTHER'S FRAME OF REFERENCE

Choose a topic for discussion; a more or less controversial one. Then adopt a rule: Before any of us replies, he first must restate the statement made by the former speaker accurately enough that he agrees it is a satisfactory statement of what he said.

This will demonstrate how difficult yet how important it is to understand what each other intended to say. The group should be limited to three or four persons.

Appendix D1.

LEADERSHIP BEHAVIOR PATTERNS

Three types of behavior are described in the following paragraphs. One way to use these is to play a sort of "Guess Who," game. Select three persons giving each a copy of the four statements under one heading. Ask them to come before the group and have each read statement 1. Then in rotation read statements 2, 3, and 4. Ask the members to hold up their hands as soon as they identify all three types of leaders as portrayed.

Laissez-faire Leader:

1. I allow complete freedom to the group to formulate its own policies. I maintain a "hands-off" position.
2. I offer advice, and materials, only when I am asked. I take no part in discussion, or decision making.
3. I take no part in assigning work, or allocating time. I maintain no pressure toward achievement, industry, and enter into disorder only when there is personal danger involved. I believe in freedom.
4. I make no judgments of praise or criticism except when asked and then I maintain a sort of passive attitude.

Autocratic Leader:

1. I determine the policies because I am the chosen leader.
2. I determine all techniques, procedures and activities one at a time. The future steps are uncertain but I don't want to confuse the group.
3. I appoint the committees and determine the work task and the time and place.
4. I give my own "personal" praise because I am a benevolent leader. However I give criticism because I am the leader and have status as a judge and parent-ideal.

Democratic Leader:

1. I encourage and assist the group to discuss and determine all policies.
2. I help the group to formulate its own goals, and to point out alternative consequences. I supply technical advice or facts when needed but permit group choice.
3. I permit members freedom to work with whom they choose, and to divide the tasks as they see fit. However I maintain pressure toward achievement, industry, and against disorder. I react as if I were a member of the group.
4. I try to be "objective," and "fair" in praise and criticism and do not hold myself up as the final judge or "all wise" being.

Appendix D2.————————————————

LEADERSHIP QUESTIONNAIRE

Below is a sort of attitude test which was found useful in opening a discussion on "Leadership," with a group of 4-H leaders. Each leader was instructed to place 40 numbers on a sheet of paper in two columns of 20 each. Then as the words were read rather rapidly each was asked to put an "L," after the number if the word suggested was pleasant, a "D," if it suggested unpleasant things, and a "O," if neither reaction was present. No time was given for writing down the words because we did not want the group to deliberate on words nor to be able to change answers when a summary was made. The summary was made on the blackboard by asking for a show of hands to question 1 for answers "L," "D," or "O." Then the words were discussed. The words were:

_____ 1. Meetings	_____ 21. Swimming
_____ 2. Pigs	_____ 22. Health
_____ 3. Home	_____ 23. Attention
_____ 4. Town	_____ 24. Citizen
_____ 5. Show	_____ 25. Outstanding
_____ 6. Kids	_____ 26. Adult
_____ 7. Chores	_____ 27. Cooperation
_____ 8. Leader	_____ 28. Independence
_____ 9. Parents	_____ 29. Prize
_____ 10. Demonstration	_____ 30. Last
_____ 11. Sewing	_____ 31. 10 years
_____ 12. Fruit	_____ 32. Girls
_____ 13. Garden	_____ 33. Record book
_____ 14. Weeds	_____ 34. Community
_____ 15. Noise	_____ 35. Roads
_____ 16. Boys	_____ 36. Social
_____ 17. Big	_____ 37. Hogs
_____ 18. Finish-up	_____ 38. Milk
_____ 19. Judging	_____ 39. Award
_____ 20. Fair	_____ 40. Boys

Appendix D3.

TEST FOR IDENTIFICATION OF LEADERSHIP TYPES

Note: The correct answers are given, but these should be omitted when the questionnaire is reproduced.

Instructions

Place a "D," before each item characteristic of a **democratic leader.**

Place an "A," before item characteristic of an **autocratic leader.**

Place an "L," before each item characteristic of a **laissez-faire leader.**

D _____Gives credit for achievements

L _____Allows complete freedom

A _____Asks for indefinite postponement

L _____Offers no advice

A _____Defends self

D _____Offers his service

D _____Admits his error

D _____Confirms views of another

L _____Maintains a hands-off policy

A _____Talks about "I," "me," and "mine"

L _____Gives no praise

D _____Accepts obligations

A _____Gives credit for attributes

D _____Invites participation

A _____Seeks praise

L _____Assigns no work

L _____Maintains no pressure to achieve

A _____Determines details

L _____Assumes an "it's up to you" attitude

A _____Lectures the group

D _____Gives an example

L _____Offers no materials

D _____Offers suggestions

A _____Demands cooperation

D _____Impartial but not uninterested

A _____Discourages

L _____Takes no part in discussion

L _____Passive

A _____Threatens

L _____Takes no part in decision

A _____Rations materials

L _____Neither guides nor directs

L _____Offers no criticism

D _____Encourages

A _____Partial to group

A _____Directly refuses requests

D _____Seeks and uses advice

A _____Demands approval for acts

Name_____

Group_____

Date_____

Appendix D4.———————————

SHARED LEADERSHIP — THOUGHTS FOR LEADERS

Is the leader permissive about the content of the discussion?

Does the leader control the manner in which the group goes about its business?

Does the leader take over the problem solving functions like a parent does?

1. Does he propose the solutions?
2. Does he enlarge upon the proposals?
3. Does he seek comment from the members?
4. Does he summarize?
5. Does he set the goals?

What proportions of the talking does the leader do?

Are the various abilities (both task and social) of the members allowed to be expressed?

Appendix D5.———————————

FUNCTIONS OF BOARD MEMBERS

Ten activities have been identified as essential functions for a board of directors of a business organization. They are:

1. Sees that legal requirements and by-laws are followed.
2. Helps determine ideals, goals, and objectives for the organization.
3. Formulates guiding policies.
4. Sets up safe guards of assets.
5. Decides upon facilities.
6. Selects the manager.
7. Approves operating budget.
8. Approves operating program.
9. Checks conformity.
10. Evaluates own performances.

Appendix D6.

MOST FREQUENT ERRORS OF BOARDS OF DIRECTORS

1. Fail to provide adequate objectives.
2. Fail to set up strategic points of check.
3. Tend to take over management functions.
4. Pay too much attention to dollars and too little to human relations.
5. Fail to take action when personalities are involved.

Appendix D7.

CONTROL — A DISCUSSION OUTLINE

In our discussion of control it is imperative that we recognize two distinct types: (1) facilitative, and (2) preventive.

Facilitative:

How are we doing with respect to plan?
How are we coming along with respect to rate?
What should be changed?
What do we need that will help in replanning?

Preventive:

How can we prevent unauthorized actions?

To answer the above questions we must:

1. Set up specific standards
2. Establish strategic points of control
3. Establish danger signals
4. Fix responsibility
5. Require records that reveal opportunities and prevent surprises

Appendix E1.————————————

ATMOSPHERE QUESTIONNAIRE

The atmosphere questionnaire shown below might be reproduced and a copy given each member of the group. It is useful in teaching group members to identify behavior patterns and a summary of the replies on several different occasions will show any trend toward one or the other types of atmosphere.

Three types of atmospheres are briefly described below. As you read the three sections, check those terms which you think describe the behavior of both the group and the leader during the discussion period today. Then count the checks and record the numbers in the squares.

Autocratic ☐.   Laissez faire ☐.   Democratic ☐.

Autocratic Atmosphere

____Leader used pleasant mannerisms to "sell the group a bill of goods"

____Leader put over own ideas

____Leader monopolized the time

____Members' abilities not recognized

____Leader favored own friends

____Group "railroaded"

____Group won over; did not relate pleasant manner to underlying autocratic attitude

____Group did not express own ideas

____Group low in participation and interest

____Stronger clique determined procedures

Laissez faire Atmosphere

____Leader passive
____Leader submissive
____Leader goalless
____Leader powerless
____Leader offers no suggestions, no summary
____Group uninterested

____Group shirks responsibility
____"Everyone for himself"
____Minority views not considered
____Group aggressive

Democratic Atmosphere

___Leaders elected from several candidates

___Leader permissive

___Leader seeks many participants

___Leader problem-centered

___Leader accepts decision of the group

___Group discussed responsibilities of leaders and

chose most competent leadership teams

___Group tolerant of other's views

___Group active; participation general

___Group worked toward solution

___Group used consensus devices

*Appendix E2.*_____

PERMISSIVE ATMOSPHERE — TEN COMMANDMENTS

The statements below have been gathered together from various parts of the book. They might be reproduced and distributed under the heading "How to Generate a Permissive Atmosphere." They will provoke discussion.

1. Let's not talk about people being *below* or *under* us.
2. Rather than saying someone works *under* or *for* us, let's speak of them as working with us.
3. Let us think of spreading information *out* rather than *down*.
4. Let us credit others when they have a new idea.
5. Let's not grab off more than our share of the conversation. If someone tries to stop you—stop!
6. Let's not applaud ourselves with such words as "obviously," or "It stands to reason."
7. Let's encourage rather than discourage differences. Unless we have differences we cannot learn anything new.
8. Let's not be too sure that "it won't work." Let's say, "I haven't been able to work it."
9. Let's not cover up error; everybody errs. Let's just not make the same error.
10. Let's not reserve courtesy for social occasions.

Appendix E3.————————————————

HOW TO WELD A CROWD INTO A TEAM

1. Build an adequate communications system.

    It must carry all kinds of information needed:
    a. Traditions, purposes, problems, and goals which effect the whole group.
    b. Procedures, and duties so that everyone will know the part he is to play.
    c. Responsibilities and authorities.
    d. Accountability and rewards.

2. The system of rewards and punishments must be adequate.

    It must provide members with the things they desire:
    a. Respect.
    b. Physical necessities equal to those enjoyed by associates.
    c. Control over own affairs.
    d. A clear picture of the forces at work and a knowledge of what happens and its causes.
    e. A chance to use the full range of abilities.
    f. The feeling that our actions and our principles are consistent.
    g. The feeling that we have a significant part in the activities or enterprises.

Appendix E4.————————————————

INTEGRATIVE vs. DISINTEGRATIVE BEHAVIOR — A GAME

Behavior either builds or destroys a group.

Disintegrative behavior	Integrative behavior
1. Rigidity	1. Flexibility
2. Wants his way	2. Wants merely to bring in his views

Disintegrative behavior	Integrative behavior
3. Wants to determine details	3. Suggests broadly
4. Refuses requests	4. Grants permission
5. Postpones	5. Expedites
6. Accepts no differences	6. Concedes differences
7. Blames and corrects	7. Approves
8. Warns, threatens	8. Extends invitation to participate
9. Attacks status of others	9. Protects status of others
10. Withdraws from activity	10. Participates
11. Insists he is right	11. Helps extend, enlarge, and define the problem
12. Unsympathetic	12. Sympathetic
13. Lectures	13. Discusses

These 26 terms might be reproduced each on a separate card (omit the numbers) and distribute to the members of a group as they assemble. The group should be instructed to assemble in two sub-groups according to the way the terms fit together to define a certain type of behavior. If the two sub-groups are correctly formed, the cards will be held as indicated by the two lists above. This should provide plenty of discussion. Each group should be asked to name itself. The following names would be acceptable:

Wreckers	Builders
Autocrats	Democrats
Warriors	Peacemakers

Appendix E5.

PRESERVING SMALL GROUP FUNCTIONS AND DEMOCRACY

If civilization is to succeed it must preserve the characteristics of the small group. Recent trends such as technical change, economic expansion, large scale organizations, and massive warfare have broken up social units without substituting anything in their places. Society has always been able to cohere at the level of the group or tribe; consequently, activities which contribute to group stability should be maintained.

The person-to-person election of officers and representatives is a method of chosing leaders characteristic of small groups. Trial by jury is a type of control maintained by small groups. The freedoms expressed in the Bill of Rights are small group expressions of privileges and responsibilities. Sharing of resources and benefits are methods adopted by small groups for distributing rewards. Education for all is a group method for advancement. Free speech is a small group method for finding concensus. Free press is the group way of expressing satisfactions and dissatisfactions.

Appendix E6.———————————

℞—HOW TO WRECK A GROUP

1. Never prepare in advance. Speak spontaneously—it keeps things on a superficial level.
2. Always take your responsibilities lightly. This reduces your anxiety and increases the frustration of the others.
3. Never try to understand the purposes of the group—this guarantees that you'll accomplish nothing.
4. Always do the lion's share of the talking. None of the others have good ideas anyway.
5. Never give credit, hog it all for yourself. The rest just love a braggart.
6. Always speak of your years of experience. This compensates for your lack of ability.
7. Never tell anyone how you do it else you may lose your prestige and position.
8. Always encourage the formation of cliques. The group can't last long when they begin to fight amongst themselves.

Appendix F1.————————————

EVALUATION SCORE CARD

The questions below may be used as the basis of an annual evaluative discussion of the group's activities. The questions may be read, a vote taken, and then the questions: "What?", "Why?", or "How" asked to stimulate greater insight into group behavior.

Score Card for An Effective Group

1. Does our group clearly understand its goals?
2. Has it agreed upon the relative importance of its various goals?
3. Has it agreed upon the means it can use to achieve its goals?
4. Can it mobilize energy behind group activities?
5. Can it coordinate the activities of different members?
6. Has it the resources it needs?
7. Can it find the resources it doesn't have?
8. Is it able to organize itself?
9. Has it an effective communication system?
10. Has it competent leadership?
11. Can it delegate authority and responsibility?
12. Does it participate in decision making?

An effective group hangs together—,it has cohesiveness. Indications of cohesiveness are found in the frequency of statements "we," and "our," in contrast to statements of "I," "me," "mine," and "they." Cohesiveness[1] is also indicated by the amount of pain and frustration the members will endure and in the way they defend the group and its members from attack.

————————

[1] See test for Cohesiveness. Libo, L., *Research Center for Group Dynamics,* University of Michigan, Ann Arbor, Mich., 1953.

Appendix F2.———————————

GROUP ORGANIZATION CHECK SHEET

This questionnaire aims to obtain the views of group members regarding the organization and functioning of our group. Below are questions which we hope you will answer.

Underneath each question is a line upon which you should check your answer. Check (+) at the left if your answer is "yes," "good," "like it," or "plus." Check (—) at the right if your answer is "no," "poor," "dislike it," or "minus." Check (o) in the middle if your answer is "some," "fair," "partly," or "zero." For example:

Yes Good Like it Plus		Some Fair Partly Zero	No Poor Dislike it Minus
_____	1. Is the group too big?	_____	_____
_____	2. Should it be reorganized into two groups?	_____	_____
_____	3. Should it seek new members?	_____	_____
_____	4. Should it divide into smaller groups at times?	_____	_____
_____	5. Does it use committees?	_____	_____
_____	6. Do committees act successfully?	_____	_____
_____	7. Does it call in experts to help?	_____	_____
_____	8. Does it fumble around?	_____	_____
_____	9. Do officers function properly?	_____	_____
_____	10. Were there disturbing noises?	_____	_____
_____	11. Was the meeting place comfortable?	_____	_____
_____	12. Did you say all you wanted to say?	_____	_____
_____	13. Does the group accomplish its goals?	_____	_____

Appendix F3.

INTER-GROUP RELATIONS CHECK SHEET

This questionnaire is an attempt to discover how group members feel about the group. Is it friendly? Is it stimulating? Does it know how to control its behavior? Answers to the questions below will help us improve group activities and relationships.

Underneath each question is a line upon which you should check your answer. Check (+) at the left if your answer is "yes," "good," "like it," or "plus." Check (—) at the right if your answer is "no," "poor," "dislike it," or "minus." Check (o) in the middle if your answer is "some," "fair," "partly," or "zero." For example:

Yes Good Like it Plus		Some Fair Partly Zero	No Poor Dislike it Minus
———	1. How friendly were the group members?	———	———
———	2. Was the leader autocratic?	———	———
———	3. Was there much conflict?	———	———
———	4. Were cliques formed?	———	———
———	5. Did the group act like a united group?	———	———
———	6. Was participation general?	———	———
———	7. Did some members act "upish"?	———	———
———	8. Do you like the members?	———	———
———	9. Did the members play needed roles?	———	———
———	10. Did the group waste time?	———	———
———	11. Were the members attentive?	———	———
———	12. Do you have much "at stake" in the group?	———	———

Appendix F4.

GROUP PROBLEM CHECK SHEET

Every group should try to discover how the members feel about its program. Are the problems of concern to you? Does it do business without delay? Answers to the questions below will help us make our program more satisfactory.

Underneath each question is a line upon which you should check your answer. Check at the left end if your answer is "yes," "good," "like," or "plus." Check at the right if your answer is "no," "poor," "dislike it," or "minus." Check in the middle if your answer is "some," "fair," "partly," or "zero." For example:

Yes Good Like it Plus		Some Fair Partly Zero	No Poor Dislike it Minus
____	1. Did you think the problem discussed was interesting?	_____	_____
____	2. Did you think it was useful?	_____	_____
____	3. Did you think it was urgent?	_____	_____
____	4. Did you think it was too difficult?	_____	_____
____	5. Did you clearly understand it?	_____	_____
____	6. Did group members have all the facts they needed?	_____	_____
____	7. Did the discussion advance step by step orderly?	_____	_____
____	8. Did you like the decisions reached?	_____	_____
____	9. How skillfully does the group conduct its business?	_____	_____
____	10. Were trivial problems discussed?	_____	_____

11. What was the group trying to do today? (Write answer)
12. What are the group's major objectives? (Write answer)

Appendix F5.——————————

A GOOD GROUP IS ——?

Below are four questions which may be useful in the annual evaluation meeting of your group. The questions may be duplicated and members asked to write in their answers. These should be summarized and used as the basis for a discussion.

This group will be a good group if it is:

This group will be a good group if it does:

Some members of this group have the following abilities and skills:

Some members of this group have the following short comings and weaknesses:

Appendix F6.——————————

PARTICIPATION ROLES

It is important to the success of a group that members participate differently. It is important to its welfare that members like or respect each other in some degree. Some persons may be very important but not necessarily well liked by every other member; but because you don't love him is no reason that you must hate him. In this questionnaire, we are trying to discover the differences in participation or degree of liking in your group.

Names of Group Members (Alphabetic Order)	A	B	C	D	
					In Col. A write 1, 2, 3, 4, 5, after the names of those who "talked the most." Include yourself.
					In Col. B write 1, 2, 3, 4, 5, after the names of those who "contribute the best ideas." Include yourself.
					In Col. C write 1, 2, 3, 4, 5, after the names of those who "did the most to guide the discussion." Include yourself.
					In Col. D write 1, 2, 3, for those whom you "personally like the best." Then write x, y, z, for those you personally like the least." Then write O after names of those whom you feel neutral toward. If possible use at least 1 number and 1 letter.
					If you like everyone in the group give each a number.

Now answer these four questions.

1. Consider the person you marked No. 1 in Col. B. Do you agree with the ideas he presented? Yes___ No___

2. Consider the person you marked No. 1 in Col C. Do you agree with what he did? Yes___ No___

3. Did the group come to any conclusions?

4. Do you agree with the conclusions it reached?

Index

A

Action, 26, 28, 30, 31, 32, 46, 49, 143
Actors, 30, 32, 38
Acquainted, 156
Adorno, T. W., 22
A. E. (George W. Russell), 75
Affectivity, 33, 41, 44
Aggressor, 22, 63, 166
Allocation, 30, 46
America's Resources, 108
Analogies, 122
Anarchy, 13, 49, 55, 58
Anderson, H. H., 16
Anderson, W. A., 86
Answers, two or more, 112
Arguments, 118
   if-then, 118
   some-all, 118
   either-or, 118
Atmosphere, 12, 139
   autocratic, 12, 177
   democratic, 12
   laissez faire, 12
   permissive, 225
   questionnaire, 224
Atomic Energy Commission, 1, 11
Atoms, 54
Audience
   report panel, 191
Authority, 49, 51, 114
   appeals to, 121
Autocracy, 15, 16, 219

B

Bach, Kurt, 98
Bakke, E. Wight, 16, 160
Balanced economy, 109
Bales, Robert F., 98, 163
Beliefs, 17
Benne, Kenneth D., 49
Benttey, Arthur F., 31
Berelson, Bernard R., 94
Bertowitz, Leonard, 152
Best liked, 22, 152, 153
Bigelow, Julian, 78
Bill of rights, 61, 106
Blamer, 23, 166
Blocker, 23, 166, 179
Board members
   errors, 223
   functions, 222
Bradford, Leland P., 178, 188

Brainstorming, 154
"Bright idea" stage, 154
Bryce, J., 84
Butler, John, 172
Buzz Session, 141, 190
   report card, 159, 160

C

Cantor, Nathaniel, 172
Carter, Launor F., 163
Caste, 13, 49, 52
Catchy phrases, 123
Cathectic orientation, 39, 40, 77
Cattell, Raymond B., 39, 133, 150
Censor, 23, 166
Central States Employees Club, 156
Chairman, 140
   duties, 154
   skills, 154, 156
Change, 89, 110, 120, 128, 130, 132
Change-agent, 105, 131
Chevrolet's battle plan, 14
Christian era, 50
Citizen characteristics, 83, 107
Classification
   schemes, 115
Clinic, 189
Coch, Lester, 134
Codes, 165
   agenda, 165
   person, 165
   problem, 165
   role, 163, 165, 166
Cognitive, 39, 40
Cohesion, 46
Cole, Natalie Robinson, 185
Combination of persons, 17, 138
Committee
   Atomic, 11
   failure, 10
   inventory of abilities, 10
   size, 214
Communication, 92, 158, 160
   expressive, 159, 176
   horizontal, 93
   instrumental, 159, 176
   mass, 95, 131
   two-way, 159
   vertical, 93
Communism, 48
Community, 49, 51, 67, 87
Competencies, 180
Competition, 46, 48, 201

235